AF564587

NEW DIMENSIONS IN HINDU LAW OF DIVORCE

NEW DIMENSIONS IN HINDU LAW OF DIVORCE

DR. KONALA MALATHI REDDY

Foreword by :

PROF. R. JAGAN MOHAN RAO
Former Principal and Dean of
Dr. Ambedkar Law College
Andhra University

REGAL PUBLICATIONS
New Delhi - 110 027

NEW DIMENSIONS IN HINDU LAW OF DIVORCE

ISBN 978-81-8484-268-5

Typeset by
RAHUL COMPOSERS
New Highway Apartments, Lakshmi Niwas
760, Pocket-D, Lok Nayak Puram, New Delhi - 110 041

Printed in India at
MAYUR ENTERPRISES
WZ Plot No. 3, Gujjar Market, Tihar Village, New Delhi - 110 018

Published by
REGAL PUBLICATIONS
F-159, Rajouri Garden, New Delhi - 110 027
Phone : 45546396, 25435369
E-mail : regalbookspub@yahoo.com, regaldeepbooks@yahoo.com

Dedicated to

my beloved father

SHRI K. PANDURANGA REDDY (Late)
Retd., Executive Engineer (R&B)

Contents

PROF. R. JAGAN MOHAN RAO
Former Principal and Dean of
Dr. Ambedkar Law College
Andhra University

Foreword

I take pleasure in writing this foreword to the proposed publication of "New Dimensions in Hindu Law of Divorce". Interestingly Mrs. Malathi has chosen the modern trend of Divorce Law affecting the stability of Hindu Marriage as the subject of her doctoral work.

Marriage is the result of the beastly act of sex which has been idealized by great Hindu sages as a sacred act meant for enjoying the marital bliss of the spouses for a long life of association of conjugal society and to ensure stability of marriage. *Sastric* Law of Marriage ensures stability of marriage. When this writer of this foreword met Dr. J.D.M. Derett, a great authority on Hindu Law living in London during the period of Common Wealth Academic Staff Fellowship in Cambridge University in the year 1978-79, Prof. Derett made an observation that Hindus are not wise enough in borrowing the Western concept of divorce in the statutory law. Under the influence of western culture and civilization, whereas in *Dharmic Law* of *Dharma Sastras* the Hindu couples are under the sacred obligation to live together for ever despite mutual bickering. The concept of Hindu marriage, for that matter, any kind of marriage, is said to be based on the tenets of mutual love, affection and understanding of both the parties which provide the foundation for the super structure of successful conjugal life.

On the contrary the modern Hindu society under the influence of modernization and industrialization Hindu couples live together willingly or unwillingly and they are compelled by circumstances to live due to religious and customary practices. More so because of the practice of arranged marriages which are said to be good for the welfare and well being of the spouses and hence the traditional indissoluble union of couples has now become the union of convenience which can be broken at the pleasure of either spouse by proving any one the grounds for divorce under the Hindu Marriage Act 1955 as amended to-date by the Hindu Marriage Laws Amendment Act 1976. Further, the increasing population of educated and earning spouses in the urban areas has become source blight but not a boon for the couples. An earning wife is treated as broiler chicken meant for serving her husband and her parents in law. However, there may be some sections of female spouses who regard it as their duty to provide necessary protection to their dependent in laws, whether parents in law, husband's dependant brothers and unmarried sisters.

In the modern Hindu society the western concept of nuclear family has come to stay in urban areas. Modern couples prefer to opt for nuclear family living for enjoying privacy and materialistic life. The old concept of joint family system based on the ideal of "all for each and each for all" has now become the thing of the past replaced by nuclear family system consisting of husband, wife and children. However some sections of Hindu males and females having human values accept the responsibility of maintaining their unemployed brothers and unmarried sisters apart from their old parents. The Central and State governments have also enacted a law for the protection of parents and the duty of sons to maintain dependent parents is mandatory in this Law.

The Hindu law budding scholar Dr. K. Malathi has done well in this work under the dejury guidance of Prof. Lalithkumar Deb of Berhampur University. Dr. K. Malathi deserves encomiums from the legal fraternity for the hard work she has put in for a period of three years. I am sure that this book will be useful to law students, scholars and teachers.

PROF. R. JAGAN MOHAN RAO

Prologue

Hindu Law is of great importance since majority of people in India are governed by Hindu Law and the rest are minorities such as Muslims and Christians. Marriage is the nucleus of family and family is the unit of the society. Hindu family plays a significant role since ancient society. Society provides the foundation for the scaffolding or superstructure of Hindu society. *Sastric* law recognizes Hindu Joint family consisting family members under the tutelage of the eldest male member such as the grand father or the eldest male member *Jesta Putra* who is the *Karta* of the family next to father or grand father consisting of lineal ascendants and descendants related by coparcener system in which females are treated as secondary members of the Joint family. When once a girl is married she becomes a *binna Gotra* belonging to husband's family. It is the son who continues the family name and saves the father from '*Punnama Naraka*'. Hence, the recognition of eight kinds of sons such as *Aurasa, Dattaka,* son purchased etc., Constitution of India provides equal protection to all religions in India in which Hindus constitute the majority and the others such as Muslims and Christians are minorities. Unlike the Western society which is homogeneous in nature, Hindu society is heterogeneous and hence Hindu society is divided by caste, creed, culture and language. As the author of this book is living in modern Hindu society, she has chosen to deal with 'Divorce, its new dimensions' in the modern Hindu society since divorce is unknown under *Sastric* Law.

This is done with a purpose since modern Hindu couples, willy-nilly, are forced to live together because of their elders' pressure and because of religious and caste restrictions. Hindu Marriage is governed by Hindu religion and *Sastric* law ensures stability of marriage and divorce or dissolution of marriage is unknown to the *Sastric* law. The interesting phrase "Bone with bone, flesh with flesh", indicates indissoluble nature of marriage. Most of the marriages are arranged and are considered to be stable marriages. But the choice of boy and girl is not considered as our society is male dominated society in which women are mostly dependant on men. And hence female spouses are forced by circumstances to like with their male partners willingly or unwillingly. The Western concept of 'Divorce' which may be granted by proving any of the grounds in Section 13 of the Hindu Marriage Act 1955 as amended to-date provided great relief to the unwilling Hindu spouses living together without love and affection. Divorce has now become much easier with the introduction of the new grounds such as 'mutual consent' and 'irretrievable breakdown of marriage'. The modern trend of easy divorce may shake the very foundations of Hindu society. Hence the author has chosen divorce as the subject of her book. Divorce, though affects the stability of marriage, provided succor to the needy spouse allowing them to get separated from their authoritarian life partners.

I express my gratitude to Dr. N.S. Jagannadha Rao, Dr. Bhagirathi Pangrahi, Dr. B.P. Panda, and Shri N. Naresh Kumar and Shri Prof. R. Jagan Mohan Rao for their valuable suggestions and cooperation in finishing this work.

I owe my gratitude to my husband Shri K. Prasad Reddy and mother Smt. K. Vanajakshi who have been a source of inspiration for undertaking this work.

I express my gratitude to my grand parents Shri K. Saheb Reddy (Late) and Smt. K. Satyavathi (Late) for their support during their life time.

DR. KONALA MALATHI REDDY

Abbreviations

AC	Appeal Cases
Agni. P	Agni Purana
AIR	All India Reporter
Aitbra	Aitareya-Brahmana
ALJ	Allahabad Law Journal
All	Allahabad
All ER	All England Reporter
ALT	Andhra Law Times
AP	Andhra Pradesh
Apa. Dh. S	Apastamba Dharma Sutra
ApasDS	Apastamba Dharma-sutra
Assm	Assam
AsvaGS	Asvalayana Grhya-sutra
AV	Atharvaveda
Bau. Dh. S	Baudhayana Dharma Sutra
BaudhDS	Baudhayana Dharma Sutra
Bhav. P	Bhavisya Purana
BHCR	Bombay High Court Reports
BLR	Bombay Law Reporter
Bom	Bombay
Bra. P	Brhma purana
Brh	Brhaspati
CA	Court of Appeal
Cal	Calcutta
CLR	Calcutta Law Reporter

CrLJ	Criminal Law Journal
CrLT	Criminal Law Times
Cut	Cuttack
CWN	Calcutta Weekly News
Del	Delhi
DMC	Divorce and Marriage Cases
EP	East Punjab
Fam	Family
FB	Full Bench
FC	Federal Court
FLC	Family Law Cases
Gau	Gauhati
Gau. Dh. S	Gautama Dharma Sutra
GouDS	Gautoma Dharma-sutra
Guj	Gujarat
HD	History of Dharmasastra by P.V.Kane
HLR	Hindu Law Reporter
HP	Himachal Pradesh
IA	English Law Reports, Indian Appeals
IA	The Indian Antiquary, Bombay
ICLO	Islamic and Comparative Law Quarterly
ILR	Indian Law Reporter
JandK	Jammu and Kashmir
JfamL	Journal of Family Law
JILI	Journal of the Indian Law Institute
Kant	Karnataka
KautArth	Kautilya Arthsastra
Ker	Kerala
KLT	Kerala Law Times
Ky	Koutilya
Lah	Lahore
LQR	Law Quarterly Review
M	Madras Series of Indian Law Reports
Mad	Madras
Mani	Manipur
Manu	Manu-smrti
Mark. P	Markandeya Purana
MarrLJ	Marriage Law Journal
Mat. P	Matsya Purana

MatLR	Matrimonial Law Reporter
MB	Madhya Bharat
Mbh.	Mahabharata
Mbh. San. P	Mahabarata Santi parvan
Mbh. Adi. P	Mahabharata Adi Parvan
Mbh. Anu. P	Mahabharata Anusasana Parvan
MIA	Moore's Indian Appeals
Mit. Yajn	Mitaksara on Yajnavalkya
MLJ	Madras Law Journal
MP	Madhya Pradesh
Mys	Mysore
Nag	Nagpur
Nar	Narada-Smrti
Ori	Orissa
P	English Law Reports, Probate Division
PandD	English Law Reports, Probate and Divorce Division
Pandh	Punjab and Haryana
Pad. P	Padma Purana
ParaGS	Parasara Grhya-sutra
Pat	Patna
PC	Privy Council
Pesh	Peshawar
PR	Punjab Record
Raj	Rajasthan
Ran	Rangoon
Rg/Rig	Rigveda
RV	Rgveda
Satbra	Satapath Brahmana
Sau	Saurashtra
SBE	Sacred Books of the East
SC	Supreme Court
SCC	Supreme Court Cases
SCJ	Supreme Court Journal
SCLR	Supreme Court Law Reporter
TaiS	Taittirya Samhita
TLL	Tagore Law Lectures of Calcutta University
TLR	Talune Law Review
Trav and Co	Travancore and Cochin

Va. P	Vayu Purana
VaikhaDS	Vaikhanasa Dhar-sutra
Vas	Vasistha-smrti
Vas. Dh. S	Vasistha Dharma Sutra
Vis	Visnu-smrti
Vis. Dh. S.	Vishnu Dharma Sutra
Vis.P	Vishu Purana
Vyasa	Vedavyasa-smrti
WLR	Weekly Law Reporter
WN	Weekly News
WR	Weekly Reporter
Yaj	Yajnavalkya-smrti
YV	Yajurveda

CHAPTER

1

Introduction

Marriage being a complex phenomenon cannot be explained by one single principle as remarked by Vina Gradoff, in Historical Jurisprudence. Marriage has not been defined in any statute or personal laws. It is known to be a process or even signifying the assumption of roles of husband and wife in accordance with the jural tenets prevalent in the society. Hence the law is that there is a presumption in favour of marriage and against concubinage when a man and woman have co-habited continuously for long period. The circumstances or evidence which would weaken or destroy the presumption must necessarily depend upon the facts of each case. There is no hard and fast rule can be laid down in regard to the matter. Therefore marriage is the nucleus of the institution of family, which is the basic unit of any society Western or Eastern hemisphere, if the nuclear family is the unit of Western Society, joint family is the endemic feature of the Hindu Society. Marriage amongst Hindus is a sacred and sacrosanct institution according to Dharma Sastras of Hindu Society in which Hindu Marriage is an indissoluble union, which cannot be broken even by the death of the spouses. And hence dissolution of marriage or divorce is unknown to ancient Hindu Society in which the biological instinct of sex act has been idealised by the sages as a sacred act.

In view of the sacred nature and its indissoluble character Divorce, except by caste custom is not known to ancient Hindu Society. However, divorce granted by caste elders has been endemic since ancient times to modern Hindu Society. Modern Hindu Law under the influence of Westernisation contains divorce as a matrimonial relief to either of the Hindu spouses or both at the instance of the other on any one of the grounds stated in the statutory law namely the Hindu Marriage Act 1955 as amended, which enunciates easy divorce for a Hindu spouse.

Hindu marriage has undergone quite a number of changes in recent times. Marriage may be solemnized through customary rites and ceremonies or by performing *Sapatapadi* i.e. taking seven steps around the sacred fire or through a simple process of registration. After passing the Hindu Marriage Act 1955, the parties to marriage have the right to claim their conjugal rights or seek judicial separation based on certain conditions. The Act also defines when the marriages are *void abnitio* and *voidable*.

Until Hindu Marriage Act passed in 1955, divorce was almost unknown in Hindu marriage. However, in many Hindu communities, particularly of lower social strata, divorce prevailed as a custom. Prior to Hindu Marriage Act some special statutes were passed in some of the States and provided for dissolution of marriage though ordinarily a Hindu marriage wasG indissoluble. When the Hindu Marriage Bill was being considered, the divorce aspect received a place in the Hindu Marriage Act. As the Hindu society does not favour divorce and, further, divorce creates many social problems, judicial separation was given prominence under Section 10 to offer the excited and estranged couple cooling off period and an opportunity to liquidate their differences. By 1976 amendments to the Hindu Marriage Act 1955 provides additional grounds of desertion, mutual consent, 'cruelty', impotency etc., have been incorporated to seek divorce.

An attempt to examine new dimenstions in the existing

Hindu Law of marriage and divorce has been made in this book with a view to strike a balance between the Sastric Law and Statutory Law. The former ensures the stability of the institution of Hindu marriage and latter provides for easy divorce adversely affecting the stability of marriage envisaged under Sastric Hindu Law. Modern Hindu Society requires neither a stable marriage without matrimonial relief directing the Hindu wife to cling to her husband at all times and under any circumstances, nor easy divorce throwing Hindu spouses, female spouse in particular without any socio-economic security. Man continues to dominate in the modern society also with few exceptions here and there in the urban society in which women are educated and employed claiming their individuality and independent personality. Hence they cannot tolerate male domination and chauvinism. It is only in the rural areas women, because of illiteracy, are subject to cruelty and harassment in the hands of their life partners as well as their parents.

CHAPTER

Sastric Marriage and Statutory Marriage

2.0 SASTRIC MARRIAGE

To understand the nature and concept of Hindu Marriage, the knowledge of marriage institution in ancient India is mandatory.

From the beginning of civilization, ways and means have been devised to discipline the sexual urge of human beings and marriage is the most potent and universally recognized institution devised to attain the goals. It is the very foundation of civil society and no part of the laws and institution of a Country can be of more vital importance to its subjects than those, which regulate the marriage. It is an ancient institution and around it, has grown up deep and powerful sentiments and traditions. It is an institution founded on the laws of nature. In all civilized Countries of the World, marriage has always been regarded as an institution in the maintenance of which, the society is deeply interested as much as it is the foundation of family and of the Society, without which there would neither be civilization nor progress. It has been regarded by all religions as basis of civilized society of sound morals and of domestic affection. It is the basis upon which the framework of civilized Society is built. In every civilized Society, people are deeply interested in the maintenance of institution of marriage as it is the foundation of family as well as of Society. It is an union of man and woman for love, respect, assistance and looking after each other, to live in harmony, to engage in procreation, to care for the children and to strive jointly for the welfare of family and for the building up of a new Society.

Marriage is a bond between a man and a woman recognized by law. Further 'marriage' means an act, ceremony or process, which brings about the legal relationship of husband and wife. Some systems regard it as a sacrament, some as a contract and some as a status imposed by the laws of the Country as in the English law, though in many systems it is a combination of any two, or all. In every society the State lays down certain rules regulating the competency of persons to enter into the relation, the mode of its solemnization, the incidents that flow from it after its completion and the grounds on which and the method by which, the rights and obligations, that it gives rise to between wife and husband.

In all the systems of law, marriage as an institution constitutes the cementing force in the Society. From the prehistoric period when social and State formations originated down to the age of modern industrial man, societal changes had registered changes in marriage concepts and rituals since marriage is the only institution to legalize man and woman relationship based on sex and property rights. It is thought to be an association for life, inculcating a sense of duties and rights in full partnership in this World and in the World beyond. This social institution is the best gift conferred upon society by social engineers. It's utility to bring about a settled life in an organized Society cannot be gainsaid.

The genesis of marriage among the Vedic Indians among other ancient peoples of the World is a subject of studies for the Socio-anthropologists. It shows that Promiscuous hereto-sexual relationship which prevailed in the primitive Society gradually moulded in patterns of sanctified sexual relationship with emergence of legal sanctions. Thus it is presumed that free sex relationship developed into legalized sex relationship with formations of Kinships, Society and the State with its attendant government to enforce discipline and regimentation. Emergence of marriage as a Socio-religious institution synchronized with the State and Society formations the World over.

The institution of marriage is multifaceted institution having Socio-legal and religious aspects. No part of the life of a community is likely to mirror the entirety of its Society and culture as perhaps in marriage. Birth, death and marriage are considered in Hindu Society as pre-destined. According to Hindus it is regarded as a permanent life-long, sacred union and an essential *Samskara* of Hindus. According to Hindu texts, marriage is a union not only of this birth, but for all births to come, in other words immortal, interminable and eternal. Again to a Hindu, marriage is not a social contract and it is a religious rite. A Brahman ought to marry because it is one of the sacraments of his life without which he is not complete, is not competent to perform any of the duties of *grihastha*. He also ought to marry because a son born of such marriage will save him and his ancestors from falling into the hell of *Puta*. Thus marriage is a religious obligation, for it enables a Brahman to fulfil his duties thoroughly.

2.1 GENESIS OF THE INSTITUTION OF MARRIAGE

The institution of marriage probably evolved by mankind over the ages, validated by individual needs and social utility sanctified by scriptural approval and fortified by a manifold norms and injunctions.

Regarding the origin of the institution of marriage it may be said that the social condition of primitive man was one, in which no such institution existed. Perhaps the earliest form of such an institution was communal marriages where all the man and woman in a small community were regarded as equally married to one another. But in reality these communal marriages were no marriages at all and were only another name of promiscuous intercourse. How the institution of marriage was evolved out of such promiscuity and why its assumed so many different forms is a matter more for the concern of sociologist than an academic lawyer. However, the early Indian conditions for the origin of the institution of marriage among Hindus were quite different from those found in the later age of civilizations. The origin of marriage between Aryan in India as among other ancient people is a matter for the science of anthropology. But it can be said that in the *Rigveda* there is no indication of the evolution of marriage through human agency. No doubt the Vedas, however, contain much that alludes to positive law, still then the basic principles of marriage are found in the Vedas or revealed texts, which are reputed to have been divinely inspired. Thus *Rigveda,* which is recognized as the most ancient religious scripture has recognized the institution of marriage. Since the period of the *Rigveda,* marriage was a well established institution and the Vedic Aryans had lofty concepts for a marriage relationship to have a well-knit Society when they began to settle down in the five river valleys and the cultivation expansion had brought affluence and solidarity in the Social formation. In the *Mahabharata* it has been mentioned that *Pandu,* father of the five great *Pandavas* informs his wife that free sex of men and women like cattle, continued till *Swetaketu,* son of the sage *Uddalaka* and the first man, introduced the institution of marriage.

2.2 SASTRIC CONCEPT OF MARRIAGE

Marriage among the Vedic Aryans in India, as among some other ancient peoples of the World like the Romans and the Greeks held a significant position in the State, Society and in the legal system. Hindus have, perhaps, from the very beginning of their civilization, regarded marriage as a sacrament, as a tie which once tied cannot be untied. The Hindu notion of sacramental marriage differs from the Christian in as much as the Hindus regard their marriage not merely a sacrosanct and inviolable union, but also an eternal union—a Union which subsists not merely during this life but for all lives to come. Marriage is an essential *Samskar* for all

Hindus. Every Hindu is enjoined to marry, to enter the *Grihasta-Ashrama*. According to the Vedas marriage is a union of "bones with bones, flesh with flesh and skin with skin, the husband and wife become as if they were one person."[1] Manu declared that to be mothers were women created to be practised by man together with his wife. He only is a perfect man who consists of his wife, himself and his offspring.[2] Thus, Hindus conceived their marriage as a sacramental union, as a holy union and not as a contract. For a Hindu, marriage is mandatory so that he can discharge his debit to his ancestor—the debt of begetting offspring. Marriage is also obligatory because without a wife a man cannot perform his religious and spiritual duties. Marriage is a holy union between a man and a woman for begetting a Son necessary for salvation and of religious duties. It is not considered to dissolve even after the death of any one of the partners. Since the begetting of male progeny brought merit not only in this world but the other also, marriage was considered universally important and made into a religious obligation. Marriage as a sacrament for Hindus implies three things:

(i) Marriage is a union primarily meant for the performance of religious and spiritual duties
(ii) That it is a permanent union which once tied cannot be untied i.e. it cannot be dissolved; and
(iii) It is an eternal union, which continues even in the next World.

Marriage under the traditional Hindu law is a Sacrament, a religious rather than a secular institution. From the Vedic period, the sacredness of the marriage tie was repeatedly reaffirmed. It is the last of the ten sacraments or purifying ceremonies for the Hindus, which are necessary for removing the taint of seed and womb and for complete generation. The *Grihya Sutras* generally begin with it, because marriage ceremony constitutes origin and focal point of all domestic sacrifices. Thus in the ancient texts the sacredness of the matrimony was repeatedly declared.

1. Shyama Charan Sarkar, "Vyavastha Chandrika", Vol. II, 480.
2. Manu Smriti, IX. 96.

Marriage marked the second stage in a Women's life. It is the only *Samskara* prescribed for Women as well as for the *Sudras*. It is obligatory to all except those who wish to adopt the life of perpetual celibacy or who renounced the world as a monk.

Apastamba, Manu and Kautilya have voiced a permanent character of Hindu marriage. *Apastamba* emphatically declares that no kind of separation between the husband and wife is possible, since in marriage they have to perform religious acts jointly.[3] Manu declares that a wife is not to be released from her husband until death.[4] *Kautilya* also remarks that the marriage solemnized according to the righteous forms cannot be dissolved.[5] Thus one cannot doubt that in the patriarchal Society of *Rigveda* the most important characteristics of a Hindu marriage were that it used to be a permanent and inviolable union. Hindus considered their marriage as a sacrament; the sacramental knot once tied could never be untied. Death could break it, and even then knot was not untied. This idea of Hindus about the marriage continued to be so in the entire Hindu period and even in our contemporary world many Hindus regard their marriage as a sacrament.

2.3 PURPOSE OF MARRIAGE

According to the *Smritis* and *Nibandhas, Dharmasampatti, Praja* (progeny and the consequent freedom from falling into hell) and *Rati* (sexual and other pleasures) are the principal purposes of marriage.[6] To be mothers were women created and to be fathers' men, therefore, the Vedas ordain that men together with his wife must practise Dharma.[7] Manu considers marriage as a social institution for the regulation of proper relations between the sexes.[8] The *Brahma Purana* also states that one should observe one's Dharma by marriage, as without

3. Apa, Dh. S. II.6.13. 16-17.
4. Manu smr, IX, 101.
5. Kaut, A.S., III. 3.
6. Manu. Smr. IX. 28.
7. *Ibid.*, IX 96.
8. Br. P., 228. 24-28.

marriage, there is no progeny and without progeny, one goes to hell. Thus according to the above *Puranas* also *Dharmasampathi*, Praja and Rati are the three main purposes of marriage, called their *Darmasangraha*.[9] Besides, the woman is half of the man and therefore in order to attain completion also, a man should marry.[10] Summing up, Hindu thinkers regarded dharma as the first and to highest aim of marriage and procreation as the second best.

2.4 MARRIAGEABLE AGE

The discussion of the purpose of marriage leads us to a study of their age at the time of marriage. At what age should men and women marry? This indeed, is a complex question. Early marriage is a part of the ancient Indian culture and heritage. In many Societies where early marriage is prevalent, it is with a view that lower the economic level the more important it is that parent be soon release, from the botheration of childcare so that they may devote their energies to more dependent youngsters. However, among the Brahmins of India religious prescription is more important than economic or biological factors.

In the ancient Hindu Law, no age limit was prescribed for a valid marriage, though it was possible to infer some limits from the other conditions prescribed. Marriage under the ancient Hindu Law was not a contract. It, therefore, could not be invalidated on the ground that the girl was given away when she was a minor. As ordained by the then Social Legislators the child marriage was a means of promoting the chastity of the young girls. Mention may be made of some references that indicate indirectly certain age limits of the bride and the bridegroom for marriage.

In the *Rigveda* the girls enjoyed the right of selection of their own husband.[11] There is mention of even some girls married very late and stayed away for long in their parents' home, known as *"Ambujas"*. The marriage ceremonies also

9. *Ibid*., 228. 24-29.
10. Br.P. 120. 61-62.
11. Rv. X 27.12.

support the post-puberty marriages because immediately after the ceremony it was followed by consummation of marriage. Some of the verses in the marriage of the *Rigveda* show that married girls could not have been child wives but must have been grown.[12] Thus in Vedic times when brides were married at a mature age, they had a more or less effective voice in the selection of their partners in life. Again during the *Rigvedic* period, positive evidence of the existence of the practice of pre-puberty marriage is not available[13] although some verses in the *Rigveda* indicated that girls were married before they attained puberty. Coming to the various prescriptions of the *Grhhya* Sutras, it may be found that the older *Grhya* Sutras allowing the practice of Vedic period described the consummation of marriage and it evidently imply that the bride was of matured age but the later *Grhya* Sutras and some of the Dharma Sutras, however, lay down the rule that the bride should be *'nagnika'*.[14] Further *Apastamba*[15] forbids marriage with a girl reaching the age of puberty. It is logical to conclude that in his time girls were married before puberty. According to *Brahma Purana* the marriage of a bridegroom younger than his bride is not proper and illustrates the point with the story of Sage *Vriddha Gautama*.[16] It further states that a young maiden for an old man is as beneficial as nectar.[17] But *Vishnu Purana*[18] went a step further and states that the age of the bridegroom should be three times that of the bride. Manu *Smriti* laid it down that a Virgin should wait for three years after attaining the age of puberty for a proper husband being arranged for her by her parents, failing such arranged husband, she could choose a husband for herself.[19] Manu further informs that a man aged

12. *Ibid.*, x. 85. 26-27, 46.
13. M.A. Indira, 'The Status of Women in Ancient India', Banaras, 1955, pp. 41-42.
14. The term 'nagnika' means a girl who wears no cloth, plays with grains or sand and does not cover her nakedness for the shame in the presence i.e. in other words, is not yet grown up.
15. Apa. Gr. S, I. 3.11.
16. Br. P, 107.31.
17. *Ibid.*, 107.47.
18. Vis. P, III. 10,16.
19. Manu. Smr, IX. 90 and 91.

thirty years should marry a girl of twelve years or a man of twenty four to a girl of eight. *Smrities* of Yajnavalkya, Vishnu and Narada are believed to enjoin marriages of girls at a tender age.[20] In the epic post-puberty marriage of Kunti, Damayanti, Draupadi and Uttara were held. As examined by Altekar from the evidence of the epics and the Buddhist literature remarks that the bride in cultured families used to be about sixteen at the time of her marriage.[21] Attention is, however, sometimes drawn to the Aranya Khanda passage of the Ramayana[22] referring to Sita's age as six when she was married. It is argued that instances of child marriage among the Kshatriyas are not lacking. P.V. Kane[23] and A.S. Altekar,[24] however, consider the passage as a later interpolation as the Bala Khanda of the same work clearly states that Sita and her sisters enjoyed in private love dalliance with their respective husbands immediately after marriage. Medhatithi agrees with the view of the epics of the preceding age and says that a girl should be given away in marriage when she is eight or six years old.[25] Jimutavahana in his Dayabhaga also quotes with approval the injunction of Vishnu and says that calamity would be fell on the family if a girl is married after puberty. He further quotes Manu that the prescribed age is twelve years for a girl to be married to a man of thirty, and eight years for one to be espoused to a man aged twenty-four years. P.V. Kane observes that the rule that Brahman girls were to be married between eight to ten years became general from about sixth and seventh centuries and continued down to modern times.[26] The fact that girls of a very tender age were generally given away in marriage is also corroborated by the statement of Albiruni who states that no Brahman was allowed to marry a girl above twelve years of age.[27]

20. Yajn. Smr, I 52, 64; Vishnu, XXIV. 38-39 and Narada, XII 20-22.
21. A.S. Altekar, PWHC, Benaras, 1956, p. 52.
22. Ram, III. 47, 10-11.
23. P.V. Kane, H.D., Vol. II, Part. I, BORI 1941, p. 445.
24. Medh. On Manu. Smr. IX. 88.
25. *Ibid.*
26. P.V. Kane, *loc. cit.*, p. 445.
27. E.C. Sachau, 'Albiruni's India', Vol. II, Delhi, 1964, p. 131

Passing to the marriageable age of the bridegroom, Manu says that a twice born, allowed by the elders, after taking ceremonious bath which marks the end of his studentship, should marry a bride who belongs to the same Caste and who possesses signs of good Omens. Thus, Manu insists that the groom must have completed his studies of the Vedas. This naturally meant that the bridegroom should be a major. As mentioned earlier according to him for a young man between the age group of twenty four and thirty was considered proper age for getting married. P.V. Kane[28] has remarked that, as there was no rule regarding who should arrange the marriage of groom, made it evident that minor males did not marry. Moreover, the groom has to receive the Kanyadana and this also seems to suggest that he should be a major. However, there is no positive stipulation, in the Smriti literature that he should be major.

In the Vedic period child marriage is not referred to and girls were given away at a fairly mature age. This rule continued till the time of the Grhyasutras. But from the Dharmasutras and later Smritis the opinions are found slowly growing in favour of an early marriage of girls and gradually the marriage of a girl before puberty became the general rule. Of course there are few exceptions in the above rule in the case of a Kshatriya. The prevalence of Swayamvara in the Kshatriya royal families shows that the girls were mature enough to choose their partners. As such the marriageable age of girls vary from childhood to maturity. Thus the true position of marriage age under the classical law of India has not been free from difficulties. In most of the cases Hindu scholars have expressed conflicting opinions. According to one section, age of marriage coincides with age of puberty and girls should not remain unmarried after attaining that age. The age of puberty too is not uniformly set. It ranges from eight to fifteen years, according to different findings; some think that even a pre-puberty marriage is at least permissible. The other section holds an opinion that none of the rules and precedents relating to age of marriage found in the classical legal and theological literature are of a binding nature. Again the marriageable age

28. P.V. Kane, *loc. cit.*, p. 502.

was prescribed more in terms of the maximum than the minimum, pre-puberty being more emphasized in the case of girls than in the case of boys. What ever may be the age-rules of the classical law relating to marriage have now no more than antiquarian value.

2.5 FATHER'S DUTY FOR EARLY MARRIAGE OF HIS DAUGHTER

Most of the Hindu religious scriptures preach pre-pubertal marriage for females. Keeping a daughter unmarried beyond the age of puberty tantamount to committing a sin on the part of the father. Parents therefore consider the marriage of their daughters as one of their major responsibilities and hence play an important role in the ceremony which is traditionally religious. Therefore, it was a religious duty imposed by Hindu Sastras upon the father or other guardian of a damsel that she should be disposed off in marriage at a tender age before the signs of puberty made their appearance. The reason of the rule prevailing in India appeared to be threefold, viz., firstly, marriage was contracted from the sense of religious duty and not from a desire of sexual pleasure, secondly, by marriage a girl became not only a partner in life of her husband, but a member of the joint family to which her husband belonged and, therefore, being admitted into the family at tender age with her mind and character which yet unformed, and placed amidst the association of peculiarities of the family of her husband, she became assimilated to it, upon which she was, as it were engrafted in the same way as a member born in it, and thirdly , the anxiety felt by the Hindu religion for securing the chastity of woman, which was the foundation of happiness of home, of the people of family and of relationship which are so prominent in Hindu society.

2.6 QUALIFICATIONS OF THE BRIDEGROOM AND THE BRIDE

The Brahma purana states that the qualities to be sought in the bridegroom are wealth, learning, youth, good family, fame, good nature and support of others. The Smriti-Chandrika as quoted by Yama also joins hands with the above statement and informs that one should seek for seven qualities in the bridegroom viz., good family, good character, body appearance, fame learning, wealth, support of relatives and friends. Katyayana states that persons with the following defects were to be avoided as bridegrooms: the lunatic, the guilty of grave sins, the leprous, the impotent, one belonging to the same gotra, one bereft of eye sight or hearing, an epileptic adding that these defects are to be avoided among brides also.

A study of Sutras and Smritis reveals that the rules for the selection of the bride were far more elaborate than those for selecting a groom, though; in some respects they are the same. The Asvalayana Grihya Sutra states that one should marry a girl who is endowed with intelligence, health, beauty, and good character.[29] The Brahma Purana describes the good qualities viz., beauty, youth, and devoted service of the parents in-law as worthy qualities in a bride.[30] This Purana further informs that a bride coming from a noble family is the greatest helpmate in a husband's life.[31] The Manava Grihya. Sutra[32] and Manu[33] state that the girl to be chosen must not be brother less. Because in ancient times when a man had no son, the daughter possessed the status of a son, i.e., she herself became Putrika. She was married on the condition that the son born of her would be her father's son and would offer pindas as a son to his maternal grand father. The result was that the son of such a woman would not offer pindas to his own father and would not continue the line of his father. In medieval times this prohibition against marrying a brother less girl came to be gradually ignored and as P.V. Kane sarcastically remarks in modern times the pendulum has swung the other way, a brother less girl being a coveted prize if her father is rich.[34] Again as regards the defects to be avoided in brides, Narada states that when the bride suffer from long standing or

29. ASV. Gr. S, 1.5-3 vide also Ap.Gr.S, 111.20.
30. Br. P, 111.51.
31. *Ibid.*, 167.25.
32. Manu. Gr.S, 1.7.8.
33. Manu. Smr, III.11.
34. P.V. Kane, *loc. cit.*, pp. 435-36.

disgusting diseases, when they are devoid of a limb or have already had a relationship with another man, when they are wicked or have their minds set or another, they should not be selected.[35]

2.7 LIMITATIONS OF MARRIAGE-RELATIONSHIP

Among the Hindus there are some rules or restrictions concerning marriage. The most common are the laws of endogamy which permit marriage only within the tribe and the laws of exogamy which requires marriage outside the tribe or class. The bar of exogamy is not peculiar to a Hindu but it is prevalent in other parts of the world too since it is prevalent in the barbarous tribes and in half-civilized world. In anthropological literature, hypergamy, or marrying up is a practice by which social estimation of a family is raised if its girls are married into a class of higher social status than its own. Members of the superior group may take daughters from the lower groups on payment, usually of a substantial bridegroom price, but do not give their daughters to them. But now a days the inter-varna marriage is no longer an approved custom and in most parts of India it has been discontinued.

2.8 CASTE CONSIDERATION IN MARRIAGE

In each sub-caste of Brahmans there are further sub-divisions often hierarchical classes, which from a number of endogamous unit or circles. This has led to hypergamous and hypogamous marriages. The custom of inter-Varna marriage was current in ancient India and both anuloma (hypergamous) and pratiloma (hypogamous) unions were permissible in the Vedic times. There is no text of Hindu law prohibiting an inter-marriage of persons belonging to the different sub-divisions of the same caste. Of course, all the lawgivers have condemned pratiloma marriage, but the anuloma marriage has been recommended for the first three varnas. According to the scriptures a girl should be married in her own varna, failing which she may marry one in any of the higher varna. As the

35. Narada Stripumsayaya, 36.

scripture writers lay down that marriage among persons of the same varna is preferable, while the 'anuloma' is regarded as of a hina (inferior) rank than a marriage between the persons of the same varna where as the 'Pratiloma' is looked down upon with positive disfavour and the issues of such union are equivalent to a chandala (The fifth varna). Though both the forms were allowed when there is a partition among sons of a man by wives of different varnas the share of those wives of an inferior Varna is invariably much less. Further, more of several wives being the Brahman Varna, the one first married enjoys the precedence, if they are of different varnas, the Brahmin wife is considered as dharmapatni and eldest in rank. She was only allowed to sit by her husband at the religious ceremonies.

Since Vedic times the literature speaks of inter caste marriages. As such inter-caste marriage was prevalent in the Vedic society. Aitreya Brahmana[36] shows that the son of a Brahmana and Sudra wife might yet be a Brahmana and that Brahmans could marry the daughters of members of the warrior class.[37] The Satpath Brahmana narrates a marriage of Cyavana, a Bhargava, with Sukanya, the daughter of king Saryata.[38] Apastamba[39] says that one should marry a girl of the same caste, who was not given before to another and marriage with whom is in accordance with the scriptures and by violating these rules sin is incurred. Manu says that among the twice born, a girl of the same caste is commendable for wifehood. But for those who are given to lust, girls from other castes can also be had in order.[40] Thus Manu calls inter-caste marriages as lustful and prescribed it for a person who could not restrain his passion. Again Manu further informs that the "Pratiloma" marriages were regarded very inferior, and the offsprings born were considered to be Varna-sankara (mixed Caste). But while dealing with the topic marriage the account of rejoining of the mixed castes as given by Manu and other lawgivers, shows that there were many of them that sprung

36. Ait. Br.II.19.
37. James Hastings (ed), ERE Vol. VIII, New York, 1967, p. 451.
38. Sat. Br. 4.1.5.
39. Apa, Dh.S, II.6.13, 1 and 3.
40. Manu, Smr, III.12 and X.12.

from sexual connection between inferior man and superior woman. Vasishta speaks that for a Brahmin a Sudra wife is allowable as being mentioned by one 'acharya' (authority), but he himself condemns it distinctly. Yajnavalkya described them altogether.[41] Therefore, lawgivers like Apastamba condemn inter-caste marriage, but Manu, Vasishta and Yagnavalkya etc. though permit the anuloma marriage, still then, they considered Pratiloma marriage as reprehensible. The Mitakshara deals with inter caste marriage in the Achara Khanda. Medhatithi says that in time of difficulty or in the event of not finding a girl of one's own caste, a girl of two other castes may be married by the Brahmana but not to a Sudra girl. Again many of the medieval digests and writers like the Smriti Chandrika quote verses from Brahma Purana on matters forbidden in the Kali age among which inter caste marriages are included. But these passages are not found in the present edition.

Hiuentsang states that the members of a caste marry within their own caste enclave.[42] Anuloma marriages which were regarded valid later on getting rare. Ibo Khurdaba testifies that inter caste marriages were getting more and more unpopular.[43] Albiruni also proves the paucity of such anuloma marriages. He remarks that every man may marry a woman of his own caste or one of the castes below but nobody is allowed to marry a woman superior to his own.[44] Al Idrisi, no doubt, takes a different view. According to him a Kshatriya could marry a Brahmana girl, but the Brahmana did not want to take up Kshatriya girls as their wives.[45] Albiruni's statement should however, be regarded as correct, for he had better knowledge among the foreign travellers about the Hindu Customs.

All smrtikaras recognised inter caste marriage as lawful but at the same time they condemned them in unequivocal language. Again they also ordain to perform necessary

41. Yajn. Smr. I.56.
42. T. Watters, On Yuan Chwang's Travels in India, Vol. I, Delhi, 1961, p.168.
43. J. Dowson and H.M. Elliot, Hist. India, Vol. I, p. 16.
44. E.C. Sachau, *loc. cit.*, pp. 155-56.
45. J. Dowson and H.M. Elloit, Hist. India, Vol. I, p. 16.

religious rites only in the marriages of same varna, however when a man was married to a woman of an inferior varna he took her by a ceremony different from that which was used when he married a woman of his own varna.

In the long-run gradually mixed marriages began to disappear and a stage was reached when pratiloma marriages were forbidden altogether. The issues of such unions were declared to be illegitimate. The anuloma marriages also ceased to be regarded as good and in course of time became altogether obsolete. Therefore, the various commentators and Digest writer denounced such marriages and declared them to be prohibited in the Kaliyuga. These married couples are to be ex-communicated from the caste enclave and excluded from inheritance of their relations.[46] While between themselves the relationship of husband and wife and parent and child are held legitimate and there might be reciprocal inheritable right among themselves.

Even in the medieval times Kulin Brahamans of Bengal owing to old conventions maintained hypergamy rule during their marriage. The Bengali Brahmins are divided into four classes. (1) Kulins, (2) The Siddha-Srotriyas, (3) the Sadhya-Srotriyas, and (4) the Kastha-Srotriyas. Ballal Sen the founder of Kulinism, used nine virtues as the criteria of ranking the Brahmans. The Brahmans who possessed all the nine virtues were called Kulins. Those Brahmans who possessed eight virtues were called Siddha-Srotriyas, the persons with seven virtues were placed in the category of Sadhya-Srotriyas, and the remaining ones were called Kastha-Srotriyas.

The custom of hapergamy also prevalent among the Brahmans of Bengal and they have the groups Kulin, Siddha-Srotriya, Sadhya-Srotriya and Kashta-Srotriya. The rule was that a man of the Kulin class could marry a woman of his own class or the two higher Srotriya classes; a Siddha-Srotriya could marry in his own group or in the Sadhya group; but the Sadhya and Kashta-Srotriyas might take wives only within the limits of their own classes. Conversely, the woman of the Sadhya-Srotriya class could marry in their own class or the two classes above them; Siddha-Srotriya women in their own class

46. Dayabhaga, XI. 2, 9.

or the Kulin class; while women at one end of the scale, and Kashta women at the other were restricted in their choice of husbands to the Kulin and Kashta groups. But *now-a-days* the above principle is no longer an approved custom and in most part of the Bengal it has been discontinued.

2.9 SAGOTRA, SAPINDA AND SAPRAVARA

The marriage between spouses who are related by blood is discouraged. The reason being that the off-springs born out of such union are often degenerated and have little appreciation for morality. Consequently they fall an easy prey to sex indulgence. It is for this reason that most of the personal laws forbid the marriage between those who are related by blood and are within the prohibited degrees of relationship. The qualification and disqualification for becoming parties to marriage is either absolute or relative according as it renders a party altogether incompetent to marry or only incompetent to marry a particular person. Gotra, Sapinda and Pravara were taken into consideration when a marriage between a boy and a girl was arranged. The parties must not be Sagotras, Sapindas or Sapravara. As the joint family system is the normal condition of the Hindu Society, the Sastrakaras prohibit marriage between larger numbers of relations then by other system of law. Therefore, there might not be the shadow of a doubt about the illicit relations among young boys and girls. Persons are said to be the same gotra when they can trace their origion of the same guru (sage). According to the Scriptures, no marriage can take place if the contracting parties have even one of the pravara rishis in common. The sapinda relationship has been discussed at length in all the books of traditional Hindu law or the Dharmasastras, for it is considered not only for determining the eligibility for marriage but also for the purpose of inheritance and purificatory rites on birth, death etc. If a Sagotra Marriage has taken place by an oversight the husband has to undergo some expiatory rites and according to some authorities, he should treat his wife like a mother. Again as a rule the adopted son drops out his gotra, i.e., the gotra of his natural father, on passing to the gotra of the adopter; but for purposes of marriage he cannot marry in his original and acquired gotras.

Rajbali Pandey informs that prohibition of marriage with the pravara was first found in the Grihyasutras but there is no prohibition of Sagotra marriage. Apastamba, Baudhyana and Parasara all avoid pravara but not gotra.[47] Few juridical authorities also disapprove of marriage with a bride whose pravara is the same as that of the bridegroom.[48] Manu does not mention pravara while Gautama and Vasistha have not mentioned Gotra at all. Almost all the Smrtis declare that the marriages within the same Gotra are ipso facto invalid. Such marriages could not be legalized nor the children born of such wedlock are legal.[49] Opinion is divided regarding the meaning of the word "Sapinda' between two schools represented by Mitakhara and the other Dayabhaga. However both are agreed that a Sapinda girl cannot be married, Mitakshara stated that Sapindas are persons who have in them the particles of the body of the same ancestor, while according to Jimutavahana, the author of Dayabhaga, Sapindas are the persons connected by the offering of a funeral cake at the Sradha. Thus according to Dayabhaga, Sapinda relationship is based on religious efficacy. This school of law excludes among Sapindas the mother's father and other relatives on the mother's line and thus considers only the agnates or the Sagotras. However, most medieval writers on this subject have accepted the theory of the Mitakshara on extending Sapinda relationship to the blood relations on father's as well as on mother's line. Mitakhsara lays down that Sapindas descending from a common ancestor traced on the father's side not beyond the seventh degree or the mother's side not beyond the fifth degree both the ancestor and the person in question being counted as one degree, cannot marry. Mitakhsara further says that the qualification that the bride should be non-sapinda applies to all castes, as the Sapinda relationship exists everywhere. However the qualification that she should not belong to the same gotha and

47. Rajbati Pandey, H.S., Delhi, 1976, p. 175.
48. Gau, Dh. S, I.4.2; Vis. Dha S, XXIV. 9.
49. Manu Smr, III.5; V. 60; Yajn, Smr, I.52-53 vide also Nar. Smr, XII. 7.

pravara applies only to the regenerated castes. Although the Kshatriyas and the Vaisyas have no gotras of their own, and therefore, no pravaras, yet as they have gotras and pravaras derived from their ancient preceptors, the rule is applied to them.

Though Hiuentsang says that a man should marry a girl of his caste, he observed that relations whether by the father's or by the mother's side do not inter-marry.[50] This statement seem to refer to the prohibition of one's marriage with one's fathers or mother's relation. Albiruni also mentions that according to Hindu marriage law a stranger was always better for marriage than a relative. The more distant the relationship of a woman with the family of her husband, the better. It was prohibited to marry female relatives if both were of direct descending line such as a granddaughter or a great granddaughter, and of direct ascending line such as a mother, grandmother and great grandmother. It is also forbidden to marry a collateral relation such as a sister, a niece, a maternal or Paternal aunt and their daughters except in case the couple of relations who want to marry each other are removed from each other by five consecutive generations.[51]

It has been commonly propounded that to abide by the rule of Sapinda exogamy one must take a wife who is related to him through a common ancestor upto the seventh generation in the father's line and the fifth generation on the mother's line. Irawati Karve has illustrated the method of counting the generation, and is of the opinion that the rigidity of the Sapinda rule for the father's or the mother's line vary in different regions, at different times and for different castes.

2.10 GUARDIANSHIP IN MARRIAGE

Sine the Vedic times the importance of the father has given him the position as the head of the family. The children act according to the commands of the father. His responsibility did not end with bringing them into the world. It was his duty to see that his children got all the Samskaras. But it was

50. T. Watters, *loc. cit.*, p. 168.
51. E.C. Sachau, *loc. cit.*, pp. 155-58.

considered to be the major duty of the father to get his daughter and son married. A father who did not discharge all his responsibilities including marriages of his children during his lifetime suffered in hell. Again in ancient days marriage involved the idea of the transfer of dominion over the damsel from the father to the husband. It appears to have owed its origin to the Patria-potestas or the father's dominion and unlimited power over the child. A daughter was an item of property belonging to her father who could therefore transfer her by sale, gift or other alienation, like any other property. Only in the case of Swayamvara form of marriage a girl may become a party to the matrimonial contract but this is an exceptional case. The bride was not in one sense, a real party to the marriage which was a transaction between the bridegroom and her guardian in which she was the subject of the gift. In ancient centuries the girls were absolutely dependent on their parents and guardians by whom the contract of marriage was to be made, and their consent or non-consent was not taken into consideration at all. In Hindu marriage as a rule marriages were negotiated, settled and solemnized through the parents of the spouses, as guardians in the marriage.

As regards the competence of a person to give a girl in marriage Yajnavalkya says that father, father's father, brother, a paternal male relative (i.e Sapindas, Sagotras, etc.) or the mother may be the giver of the bride, provided the giver would be of sound mind.[52] Narada also says that in the default of a father a brother, grandfather, maternal uncle or mother or an agnate or cognate should act.[53]

2.11 FORMS OF MARRIAGE

Throughout the world, man has been adopting various modes of selecting a woman as his wife, the modes depending upon the stage of social, mental and intellectual development that he has attained. For procuring a wife ancient Hindu law also recognizes eight distinct forms of marriage such as

52. Yajn. Smr, I.63.
53. Nar. Smr, XII. 20-22.

Brahma, Daiva, Arsha, Prajapatya, Asura, Gandharva, Rakshasa and Paisacha. J.D. Mayne refers to as many as eight forms of marriage which are typical of different Hindu sects. Hindu Sastrakaras have divided the above marriages into two groups for the purpose of distinguishing those that are dharma (approved) on account of those having no improper motive on the part of any person concerned in them and they are, therefore, declared to be religious, from those that are condemned on some ground or other and are, therefore, adharma (disapproved) and pronounced to be irreligious. Although the Hindu Sastrakaras have referred to this eight forms of marriage to be adopted by the ancient Hindus but as part of their systematizing process they referred to these forms because they noticed as facts that existed all around. Among the very approved forms of marriage there is a difference in merit and excellence. Brahma, Daiva, Arsha and Prajapatya are approved forms of marriage and Asura, Gandharva, Rakshasa and Paisacha are disapproved forms of marriage. Manu believes that a son born of the approved forms of marriage is hand-some, spiritually inclined, rich, famous and righteous whereas a son born of the disapproved forms of marriage is a liar, Cruel and deficient of the Vadas and religion. The principal difference between the approved and the disapproved forms of marriages is to be found in the matter of succession to Stridhana (woman's property). In the former case, the husband's and in the latter the parent's family is preferred. An equally cautious opinion has been voiced by L. Sternbach he also opines that a marriage contracted according to one of the orthodox forms of marriage (Brahma, Daiva, Arsha and Prajapatya) entailed different legal consequences than a marriage contracted according to unorthodox forms.[54]

Of these the first four, being approved marriages, are proper for the Brahmans. Thus the Brahmanas were not adapted to the Asura, Rakshasa or Paisacha forms of marriage. Asura was perhaps resorted to by the wealthy grooms who were not considered eligible for marriage because of some deficiency. The Rakshasa form of marriage suited well to the

54. L. Sternbach, Juridical Studies in Ancient Indian Law, Part I, Delhi, 1965, p. 347.

Kshatriyas since they had captured and brought many beautiful maidens during the wars. As such all these forms of marriage were practised by different people belonging to the different strata of society. But mention may be made here that unlike Manu, Yajnavalkya does not say which forms are allowable for which classes. While studying the various forms of marriage as stated by the Sastrakaras, several questions come to the mind. First were all the different kinds of marriage prevalent at the same time equally among the peoples of the different castes? Second was it a fact that one from of marriage was succeeded by another? If this question is answered in the affirmative, then which form of marriage came first and which later? Or were the different forms of marriage current at the same time? Thus to answer the above complicated questions, the present scholar is now going to examine some of the theories on the topic of the evolution of different forms of marriage as propounded by various scholars. According to one of those theories advocated by J.D. Mayne the earliest form of marriage was by capture and therefore according to him Rakshasa, the Paisacha and the Gandharva forms of marriage, which are all variants of marriage by capture come first. Then he further continues that the capture was replaced by sale which was ultimately supplemented by gift on the part of the father like Brahma, Daiva and Arhsa.[55] Sharply contradictory to this account of the evolution of different forms of marriage, there is the theory by G.C.Sastri.[56] To Sastri Asura form of marriage came first and this was replaced by the Brahma, Daiva and the Arhasa forms. The disapproved forms of marriages also existed side by side with different approved forms. L. Sterbach believes that although the development of the forms of the lack of sources the impression can be reached that the development of the forms of marriage quoted above cannot be proved owing to the lack of sources the impression can be reached that the development of the forms of marriage, from marriage by capture (Rakshasa, Paisacha) to marriage by

---

55. J.D. Mayne, 'A Treatise on Hindu Law and Usages', Madras 1900, pp. 80-83.
56. G.C. Sastri, 'A Treatise on Hindu Law', Chap. III, Calcutta, 1910, p. 85.

purchase (Asura) and the marriage by sham purchase (Arsha), further to marriage-based in the choice of a husband by the father of the girl independently of her consent (Brahma, Daiva and Prajapatya) and lastly to marriage by free consent of the bride and the bridegroom (Gandharva and ordinary Swayamvara) are likely to have occurred in ancient India.[57]

Therefore, from the times of Grihyasutras, Dharmasutras and Smrtis the ancient Indian law recognized the above eight forms of marriage.

Manu says that the eight forms are not final and that other forms may have evolved through inter-mixture of Characteristics of few or more of them.[58] The disapproved forms of marriage prescribed by the early Hindu lawyers existed in pre-Vedic times, which were legalized only by the performance of marriage ceremonies.

The principal difference between the legal effect of a marriage in an approved form and that of a marriage in an unapproved form lay in the order of succession to the Stridhana (Women's property) of the wife in each case. But the Gandharva was regarded to be an approved form of marriage for purposes of succession to Stridhana.[59] Therefore, the only real basis of the classification of these forms of marriage into approved and unapproved could be that the first four were approved because a marriage in either of those forms rested in the authority and approval of the bride's father, and the last four were not approved because a marriage in none of them had the approval of the bride's father. This was the reason given in Kautilya's Arthasastra for regarding the first four as Dharma-Vivaha. In the Asura form, although the approval of the father must be there if he be the person who accepted the consideration as Sulka (fees), but the marriage did not rest in his approval, if rested in the payment of consideration paid by the bridegroom for the bride. However, it is not necessary for our present purposes to delve into the question why the first four forms were approved, and why the last four forms though permitted, were not approved. The eight forms of marriage

57. L. Strernbach, *loc. cit.*, p. 423.
58. Manu. Smr. III. 26.
59. J.D. Mayne, 11th edn. S.94, pp. 130-31.

really resolve themselves into three modes of obtaining a Wife, namely, by gift, sale or mutual desire, and the three forms now extinct, the Brahma, the Asura and the Gandharva. Thus all but above three, have long since become obsolete. No doubt these three forms survived to day but the Courts presumed every marriage to be in Brahma form, which was regarded as the approved form, unless the contrary was proved.

2.12 THE SWAYAMVARA FORM OF MARRIAGE

Apart from the above eight forms of marriage there were other forms of marriage mentioned in the Scriptures. It may not be possible to enumerate all the conceivable forms of marriage, but as a matter of fact in the present study some paragraphs about the Swayamvara form of marriage may be mentioned. The custom of the bride selecting her own husband from among a number of Suitors is commonly known as Swayamvara marriage. In this form of marriage the father of the girl invites a large number of qualified grooms and the girl is given the permission to select her life partner from among the invited persons. The act of choice might be preceded by a trial of strength on the part of the Suitors, the victor being rewarded with the hand of the maiden or it might be an unconditional choice of the bride. This system of marriage indirectly proves that the bride is mature enough at the time of her marriage. Swayamvara is an institution which seems to have been widely prevalent in ancient India, from the earliest time of the Rigvada, It is also found in Indian literature and epigraphic evidences. Aitarya Brahmana[60] narrates the legends of the marriage of Prajapati's daughter in this form of marriage. In the epics there are many illustrations of the Swayamvara form of marriage. But the Swayamvara of the epics is not mentioned in the Smritis which, however, recognize the Gandharva form of marriage. Therefore, the Smrtis do not recognize a form of marriage which plays a great part in the puranas. This is the reason why Swayamvara is not included in the usual list of the eight forms. The marriage of Sita in the Ramayana and Draupadi in the Mahabharata are both

60. Ait. Br, IV. 17.I.

celebrated in this form of marriage. Besides this Savitri, Damayanti and Rukmini also married in this form. In the medieval history of India also the most famous Swayamvara was that of the princess Sanjukta daughter of Jayachandra, the Gahadavala King of Kanauja where she had thrown the garland round the neck of Prithiviraja's statute. Probably this institution was mainly prevalent among the Kshatriyas.

It has also been ordained that if father or the guardian of the maiden fail to find a suitable groom, the girl after her first menstruation, is entitled to find her own husband. Again the ancient lawgivers opine that the girl should wait for three months[61] or three years[62] after reaching puberty. Thereby the texts are Conflicting and contradictory. Only in these particular circumstances the girl was allowed to choose her own mate. In this connection P.V. Kane also has drawn attention to a passage of the mahabharata.[63] Swayamvara was allowed only if the father or the guardian failed to arrange his daughter's marriage. This particular prescription might have paved the way for the development of the Swayamvara form of marriage in ancient India. Later on when early marriages came in vogue, Swayamvara naturally died away.

2.13 HOW THE MARRIAGES ARE SETTLED?

Generally selection of the spouse is made at individual level. The parents take the initiative, and either personally or with the help of Wooers, negotiate the marriage of their children. According to the practice prevalent in ancient India the bridegroom was a more passive agent in marriage, what to speak of bride's position. In the early Vedic times girls could choose their life partners.[64] But in the later period, when early marriage had come into vogue, the Custom of Self-choice naturally receded to the background. Thus the Brahma Purana definitely disapproves of girl's choosing her own husband. Of course, the ancient Indian literature is replete with instances of

61. Gau. Dh.S, XV. 3.20 and Vis. Dh.S, XXIV. 40.
62. Bau. Dh.S, IV. I. 14; Vas. Dh.S, XVII. 67-68, Manu. Smr. IX 90.
63. Mbh. XIII. 44.16.
64. Rv, X 27.12; Av II.36.

boys and girls falling in love. But the society in general approved the father's right to arrange a suitable bridegroom for the daughter and to give her away in marriage to a husband of his choice. To Alberuni the parents arranged the marriage of their sons.[65] The same thing must have been true in the case of the girl. Only Vatsyayana says that a young man could under special occasions apply himself to win the girl of his choice by Courtship or even by trickery and Violence.

As stated earlier, among the Hindus their parents arrange marriage of boys and girls. It was the boy's father to whom a proposal for marriage was made. But very often the proposal was mooted by the boy's marriage negotiator popularly known as 'Varakas" or "Ghatakas", who while praising the girls beauty and her family side all they could in favour of such a match. They pretend to know everything about the Vamsavali (genelogy) of the bride and bridegroom of their locality. Generally in the higher Castes Purohita and among the lower Caste people, Rajakas do the work of matchmakers. They travel up and down the Country looking for bridegrooms for girls and brides for boys. In other cases elder persons of the family negotiate marriage. Even in some of the Grihyasutras mentions occur of negotiators who were sent for finally settling the marriage. As in the Hindu Sastras have always had an exaggerated idea of the influence of planets on the destiny of individuals a marriage is believed not to lead to success if the horoscopes of the boy and girls are unmatched? Thus once the negotiations begin the horoscopes of the boys and girls are consulted. Sometimes many otherwise promising marriages are prevented by astrologers because of the incompatibility of horoscopes. Astrology which came to the front in later times now forms an integral part of the authorities governing marriage. The astrological comparisons in Gana, Rasi and Lagna are set-aside sometimes by many persons without practical inconvenience and with perfect impunity. The comparisons are made chiefly with reference to the stars ruling at time of birth of the parties to the changes of Planets, to the comparison of the twelve signs of the Zodiac and to the parties names.

---

65. E.C. Sachau, *loc. cit.*, Vol II. p. 155.

Marriage is preceded by a Contract called Vagdana (betrothal) made in more or less solemn forms by the guardians of the parties. During this time the father of the bridegroom with a few nearer relatives, friends and a priest congregate in the bride's house. It is called Magni and Sagai in India. Marriage is a completed transaction, the betrothal is only a contract and is revocable. Thus some of the Sastrakaras held that a girl betrothed to a man, who dies before the actual marriage process is completed, could afterwards be married to another. Manu ordains that if after the engagement a man finds that the proposed bride is blemished, diseased or deflowered and has been given by the parents with fraud[66] he is at liberty to renounce her. As such according to Hindu law a betrothal is not to be treated as an actual and complete marriage. It is a promise to give a girl in marriage. Hence, a specific performance of a betrothal cannot be enforced. Damages however may be awarded against the father for breach by him of the contract of betrothal[67] under the Specific Relief Act a Contract of betrothal cannot be specifically enforced.

2.14 AUSPICIOUS TIME FOR MARRIAGE

The Scriptures have enjoined that marriage must be Solemnized during an auspicious time. The Grahyasutras give detailed rules regarding the proper seasons for marriage. According to it the season usually performed for performing the marriage ceremony is Sisra. The Hindu month of Vaisakha is also considered the most auspicious in this connection. Again it is not enough to know the auspicious month; the lucky day and lucky hour must be ascertained. This is usually done by astrologer after consulting the stars of the proposed bride and bridegrooms.

A first point to be noted is that time of marriage is not referred to before the Grihyasutras. Bharadvaja and Gobhila Grihyasutras mention only an auspicious day for marriage during the northern course of the Sun but do not make any

66. Manu. Smr IX. 72.
67. Mulji Thakersey *v.* Gomti, 1887, 11. Bom. 112.

reference to the Stars, whereas Parasara[68] remarks that it should be performed under one of the three stars of which 'Uttara' is the best. It further says that it should be performed under the Mrugasira and Rohini. Apastamba[69] also opines that all seasons are fit for marriage with the exception of the two moths of Sisira season and the last month of the summer.

As marriage is a very important event in human life it is necessary that it must be performed on an auspicious day. Thus the proper time of marriage is that the marriage should be performed during the northern Course of the Sun, increasing moon and on an auspicious day. But mention may be made here that none of them prescribe that the principal rite of marriage should be performed at night.

2.15 MARRIAGE RITES AND RITUALS

Among all people, savage as well as civilized, legal marriage is usually accompanied by some form of ceremony which expresses the sanction of the group to the union, though in a few people it is apparently purely social. All the texts concerning the ceremonies and rituals connected with marriage refer to the bride as being given away by the father as her guardian in the family who invites the bridegroom. In all Hindu marriages the status of husband and wife is brought about by the performance of the marriage rites and rituals. Without it the relationship between a man and woman will be only that of Concubinage. In regard to Hindu marriages the Vedic rites and various customary rituals are absolutely necessary. The same rites and rituals may be observed by the Sudra whether with or without mantras. In order to constitute a valid marriage, no ceremony was necessary. If any ceremony was Customary and recognized by the Caste as essential, it was obligatory to perform the same. The religious ceremony is required for all forms of marriage. The different forms of marriage such as Gandharva, Rakshasa, Paisacha where consummation may have taken place before, even then the

68. Par. Gr. S I. 4.5.7.
69. Apa. Dh. S. 1.2.12.13.

marriage ceremony must be performed to legitimise and sanctify the marriages. If such ceremonies are not performed then the girl so seduced or forcibly taken away may be given away in marriage to another as she is to be considered as a maiden.

Further initiation into the life of a householder or married life, laws of social stratification, nature of Kinship, transition in the life of the bride and the bridegroom, and their role and relationship with the members of the family, restrain in social behaviour, and public approval of marriage are very reflected at various stages in the marriage ceremony. The necessary ceremonies according to the works on rites and rituals are the formal gift and acceptance accompanied by religious ceremonies consisting of the recitation of the Vedic texts and the performance of the nuptial homa and Saptapadi etc. Even after the passing of Hindu Marriage Act of 1955 marriage ceremonies do not change or amend the pre-Act law on the point, but declare it. The main purpose served by this definition of Hindu marriage is to emphasize that not withstanding the changes brought about by the Act in the conditions are essential for, and the rites and obligation arising from a marriage in the Hindu form, its essential character, namely, that it is sacramental, remain unchanged. The Sanctity of the marriage tie is further illustrated by the numerous rites which are held essential in the wedding ceremony. But mention may be made here that every Ceremony contains now a sign indicative of the man's desire to acquire the woman in marriage and her willingness to be acquired by him. Today in modern time the Orthodox segment of the Hindus are tenacious of their wedding ceremonies though reforming sects have launched several attempts to eliminate superstitious elements form the system. The rites and rituals also clearly indicate that matrimony is a holy bond and not a contract. Manu appears to lay down that the essential rites and rituals for creating the status of marital relationship of the husband is the gift of the damsel by the father or other person having authority on his behalf, the religious ceremonies being performed for procuring good fortune to the bride. Vasistha says that if a damsel has been abducted by force and not been wedded with Sacred Mantras she may lawfully be given to another man, she is even like a maiden.[70] Narada also remarks that the mantras for marriages are considered to be essential to make a girl into a wife and the seventh step taken along with the girl is the Culmination of that Ceremony.

The Hindu Ceremony of marriage properly so called has only one form as laid down by the Dharmashastras. There are certain recognized customary variations of it but that does not establish the existence of so many kinds or forms of Hindu marriage. The Asvalayana Grihyasutra, while laying down the common form of marriage rites also said that the customs of different Countries and villages should be observed at Weddings. It prescribed the marriage rites of the Rigvedins.[71] The Apastamba Grihyasutra laid down the marriage rites of the Yajurvedins.[72] But G.D. Benerjee in his exposition[73] gives the marriage rites of the Samavedins. However all these rites are more or less similar. Generally rites and rituals have three main objectives. First, it gives opportunity to the relations of the parties for social inter relationships. Second, it gives publicity to the solemnization of marriage. Third it strengthens the marital tie. As such there are three parts, viz preliminary, essential and the subsequent in the observance of the marriage rites and rituals but the essential rites are Panigrahana, Vivahahoma, Agni Pradakshina and Saptapadi. But relying on a passage from J.D.Mayne to the effect that the performance of the Homa, the Panigrahana or taking hold of the bride's hand and going round the fire with Vedic Mantras, the treading on the stone, and the seven steps or Saptapadi, these are the more important rites. The marriage becomes complete and irrevocable on the completion of Saptapadi or ceremony of seven steps.[74] The marriage rituals prescribed by the Sutrakaras are very lengthy, clumsy, much more complex and have Sacerdotal order. Even the minute details did not escape the

70. Vas. Dh. S, XVII. 73.
71. Asv. Gr. S, 1.7.3-22.
72. Apa. Gr. S, IV, V, VI, VIII.
73. G.D. Benerjee, The Hindu law of Marriage and Stridhan, TLL, 5th edn. Calcutta, 1896, pp. 101-07.
74. J.D. Mayne, A Treatise on Hindu Law, Usage, 11th edn. Madras, 1900 Sec. 120, p. 161.

attention of the Brahmanas. The comparative study of the Vedic rituals and that of the Grihyasutras shows that the essential elements of the marriage ceremony of the Grihyasutras go back to the Vedic period. According to the Grihyasutra the number of religious ceremonies to be performed at the time of marriage are indeed too many. Again they differed from one to the other. It is submitted that as different Grhyasutras were composed at different times and places many regional Customs grow up side by side and they had to be incorporated in the extinct ritual literature, but in course of time many old rites were replaced by new ones.

All the Sutrakaras mention the essential and central parts of the rites and rituals although they differ with regard to the order in which they should be performed. Thus there is a great dispute in the ancient texts in this connection. It was probably due to the fact that every Vedic family had its own Sutras containing local and tribal Customary Variants.

The marriage Ceremonies can be broadly divided into three groups such as mystical, religious and symbolical. There are certain rites in Grihyasutras which are mainly religious and Symbolical. According to the same work marriage Ceremony is supposed to be open to danger at every stage, which can only be got rid of by mantra. Thus in the Grhyasutra, with the Vedic rites and rituals the mystic rituals of the prehistoric and tribal customs and of the Tantra system got mixed up. It is believed, that if one performs a ritual according to the prescribed guidelines, the evil spirits which are especially susceptible to the newly wed bride could be averted by seeking the favour of beneficient spirits which could be invoked by appropriate mantras.

It may be concluded that there is no agreement among the Sutrakaras, the direction to abide by Caste customs and usages are generally followed. Thus the Vedic rites and rituals of marriage differed in different localities in so far as they are followed in customary rituals. Thus Asvalayana,[75] Apastamba[76] and Parasara[77] Grihyasutras expressly say that the customs of

75. ASV. Gr S, 1.7.1.
76. Apa. Gr.S, 1.2.15.
77. Par. Gr.S, 1.8.11.

gramavacana (the village customs) are to get precedence at the wedding ceremony. This is also called as Janapadadharma, Kulachara, lokachara or Striachara. It is logical to conclude that the remainder is customary, and these are again supplemented by many more.

In the ancient times and even now among certain Orthodox families the marriage was not consummated on the Wedding night, but on the fourth or sometimes the tenth night, by which time the evil eyes would be removed form the bride's Soul. Thus at any time during the marriage a special rite called Garbhadhana (fertilization of the ovary) Ceremony could be performed in order to secure the progeny. The Hindu Sastrakaras enjoin the early marriage of female, they do at the same time, condemn in strongest terms, the premature consummation of the same. Among a certain class of Hindus, after the marriage of a girl and on the first appearance of her menses, a religious ceremony is performed which, in ordinary parlance, is called "Second marriage", but otherwise known as Garbhadahn. After this ceremony actual consummation of the marriage takes place, as usually Hindu girls are married before they attain puberty. This "Second marriage" before co-habitation is not required by the general Hindu law. In Assam this ceremony is known as Santibiah or Panchibiah. It is said there that if a girl cohabits with her husband without this ceremony, she is defiled and both she and her husband are out casted.

2.16 REVOCATION OF MARRIAGES

As regards marriages among the three higher Castes, rejection of a bride, before the Ceremony of Panigrahana (Clasping of the hands) is valid, but among the Sudraas, before consummation. Kautilya, the lawgiver of the Maurya period of the Indian history opines that even in the case of couple that has gone through the ceremony of clasping of hands, rejection of bride is valid on discovery of a defect connected with Sex.[78]

78. Kaut. AS, III. 15.12.

But under no circumstances with revocation of marriage be valid, when they have begotten children.[79]

2.17 MODERN CONCEPT OF HINDU MARRIAGE

The Institution of marriage has undergone a sea change; The earlier Dharmik concept of sacred nature has been transformed into a consensual union which can be broken at the instance of either party on the basis of some ground or the other. It is one of the essential samsakaras of every man or women's life, which drastically changes the status of both parties. Womanhood is described as fortunate phenomenon. When once married, she places the role of the queen of the house and takes care of the development of the personality of her children and her husband. While Hindu scriptures speak very high about the religious sanctity of marriage, the modern law speaks about the secular aspects of the marriage. Speaking about the importance of the marriage Sir John Hanner observed[80] in *Durhan* vs. *Durhan* that marriage is a contract, which is very simple one, which does not require any paraphernalia. Again another jurist called Lord Penzence[81] stated that it is the voluntary union of one man and one woman for a long life of companionship to the exclusion of all others. A great authority of the Hindu Law[82] J.D.M. Derrett opines that Hindu Marriage is both status and also a contract. It is a contract in the sense a man and woman promise to live together till the time of their death. Marriage is also a status because when once married man or woman attains a new status of becoming husband and wife. From sociological point of view 'marriage is a prolonged relationship between male and female which can be broken by either of them when once they think that they are not suited to each other.

79. *Ibid.*, III, 15.13.
80. (1885) 2 p. 130.
81. Hide *v.* Hide (1866) 1 p. 130.
82. JDM Derrett, Introduction to Modern Hindu Law, Bombay 1963, p. 136.

2.18 HINDU MARRIAGE—A SACRAMENT OR CONTRACT

A Hindu male could take any number of wives, though very few Hindus practiced polygamy. The Hindu Marriage Act 1955 has abolished polygamy and introduced strict monogamy for all Hindus Divorce also has been recognized However, religious ceremony is still necessary for most marriages. The question now is whether the Hindu Marriage becomes a contract?

The Hindu marriage Act does not lay down that a marriage without the consent of the parties is void, though it does not lay down that if consent of a party to marriage obtained by fraud or force, the marriage is voidable. Similarly when one of the parties to marriage is of unsound mind, the marriage is voidable. It is laid down that bride should not be less than 18 years and bridegroom not less than 21 years in age. But marriage performed under those ages is valid. It is well-established rule of law of contracts that a contract for want of capacity is void. It is evident from the provisions of the Hindu Marriage Act that consensual element is a valid marriage has not been emphasized rather a marriage without consent is a valid marriage. Non-age does not render the marriage void and voidable. So does insanity. A combined reading of section 5, 11 and 12 of the Hindu Marriage Act (1955) leaves no doubt that consent is not an essential aspect of Hindu Marriage.

It is argued that when two persons under go the ceremony of marriage consent may be implied. It is submitted, it may be so; or it may not be so; it would depend upon the facts and circumstances of each case. Suppose a spouse to a marriage is able to show that despite the fact that he under went the ceremonies of marriage he did not in any manner consent to the marriage, can declaration of nullity be obtained? It is submitted that no such declaration can be obtained. For instance a girl shows that she underwent the ceremony of marriage in deference to the sentiments of her ailing and orthodox father, while she has no intention to marry, can her marriage be declared to be null and void? In our opinion no such declaration can be obtained, such a marriage is not voidable either.

On the other hand, the marriage has no longer remained an indissoluble and eternal union. Widow marriages are allowed. Divorce is also permitted. It may still be called a holy or sacramental union, in the sense that a sacramental ceremony is necessary. Thus, one may say that Hindu Marriage has neither become a contract nor has remained a sacramental union, it has semblance of both. However, various scholars tried to give varying thought to it and put forth their views through a social angle and where as the pure Indian thought reflected in the scriptures depicts a concept deeply religious rooted on which the super structure of a well regulated society is raised.

Sir John Hanner in Durham *v.* Durham

> Observed that the contract of marriage is a very simple one, which does not require a high degree of intelligence to comprehend.[83]

Lord Peryzence Observed:

> "To conceive that marriage as understood in christiandom, may this purpose be defined has the voluntary union for life of one man and one woman to the exclusion of all others.[84]

However Vina Grandoff, contrary to Sir John Hanner, kept the matter in suspense when he remarked that marriage, being a complex, phenomenon, cannot be explained by one single principle, idea or notion, as it represents a synthesis of several principles, ideas and notions and one cannot draw from it a perfectly logical set of rules.[85] Thus he had kept the options open to define marriage as on looks at it from the angle he views it. So different shades of opinion can develop but the fulcrum point shall remain intact.

---

83. (1885) 2 p. D.80.
84. Hyde *v.* Hyde 1886 I.P.D. 130.
85. Vina Gradoff, Historical Jurisprudence, Vol. I, pp. 163-66.

Market Puxon does not define marriage but dwells units' concept as an amalgam of tradition, religion, superstitions, instinct and reason which concerns us.[86]

Similarly, Lord Jowitt puts it in an oscillating way that what marriage means to different people will depend upon their upbringing their outlook and their religious beliefs.[87]

So marriage can be defined in various ways, such as religious or spiritual angle it is a samskara. Materialistically, It is a contract but not confined or cabined into the four walls of a Contract Act From matrimonial point of view it is a relation on which the foundation of a regulated society is based. It is a status which directly flows out of it or it is a social institution in which the interest of the society is paramount.

So the scholars, out of various facts of marriage choose one out of them, as their viewpoint. According to J.D.M. Derett marriage is a status fulfilling a contract marriage is a contract[88] by which a man and a woman undertake to live together until one of them dies. Sociologists view it from a different angle. Westermarck holds the view that marriage is more or less a durable connect in between male and female lasting beyond the mere act of propagation or the birth of off springs.

But the sociologist at another place says that in the ordinary sense of the term, marriage is a social institution which may be defined as a relation of one or more men to one or more women that is recognized by custom or laws and involves certain rights and duties both in the case of parties entering the union and in case of the children born out of it. According to him marriage is also an economic institution which may in various ways affects the proprietary right of the parties.

Even the judicial opinion seems to favour the sacramental concepts of Hindu Marriage and its indissolubility which is the essential corollary of the sacramental concept of marriage. It is a permanent stable union. Wife regarding husband as god and

---

86. Margaret Puxon, The family and the law, p. 15.
87. Weatherly *v.* Weatherly 1947 A.C.628.
88. J.D.M. Derrett, Introduction to Modern Hindu Law, Bombay 1963, p. 136.

wife verily the half of the husband ordained to discharge religious duties, is nothing but samaskara. Judicial view gives it full recognition.

2.19 MARRIAGE UNDER STATUTORY LAW

Essential Conditions of Hindu Marriage :

The Hindu Marriage Act, 1955 is an Act to amend and codify the law relating to marriage among Hindus. In this section 5 deals with the conditions of a Hindu Marriage.

Section 5

A Marriage may be solemnized between two Hindus if the following conditions are fulfilled.

1. Neither party has a spouse living at the time of the marriage.
2. At the time of the marriage, neither party.
   - A. is incapable of giving a valid consent, to it in consequence of unsoundness; or
   - B. though capable of giving a valid consent, has been suffering from mental disorder of such a kind or to such an extent as to be unfit for marriage and the procreation of children; or
   - C. has been subject to re-current attacks of insanity or epilepsy.[89]
3. The bridegroom has completed the age of twenty-one years[90] and the bride the age of eighteen years at the time of marriage.
4. The parties are not within the degrees of prohibited relationship unless the custom or usage governing each of them permits of a marriage between the two.
5. The parties are not sapindas of each of other, unless the custom or usage governing each of them permits of a marriage between the two.

---

89. Substituted by Act 68 of 1976 Section 2 for clause (II).
90. As amended by the Child Marriage Restraint (amendment) Act 2 of 1978 substituting for the words 18 and 15 the words 21 and 18.

2.20 TYPE OF MARRIAGE

2.20.1 Valid Marriages

Any marriage solemnized under this Act as valid marriage which may be performed in accordance with *shastric* rites and ceremonies or in accordance with the customary ceremonies prevalent in the community to which bride or bridegroom belongs and fulfils the following conditions specified under Section 5 of the Act:

1. Neither party should have a spouse living at the time of marriage. The spouse does not include a divorced husband/wife.
2. At the time of marriage, the parties should be capable of giving a valid consent to the marriage. A person who is of a sound mind shall be considered to be a person capable to give a valid consent. Neither party, though capable of giving a valid consent should be suffering from mental disorder of such a kind or to such an extent as to be unfit for marriage and procreation of children.
3. Neither party should be suffering from recurrent attacks of insanity or epilepsy to such an extent as to be unfit for marriage and procreation of children.
4. The bridegroom should have attained the age of 21 years and the bride should have attained the age of 18 years at the time of marriage.
5. The parties should not be within the degrees of prohibited relationships, unless the customs or usage, permits such a marriage.
6. The parties should not be sapindas of each other, unless the customs or usage permits such a marriage.

2.20.2 Void Marriages

Section II : Void Marriages

Any marriage solemnized after the commencement of this Act shall be null and void and may on a petition presented by either party thereto against the other party be so declared by a decree of nullity if it contravenes and one of the conditions specified in clauses (I), (iv) and (v) of section 5.

Section II corresponds to section 24 of the Special marriage Act-1954, section-18 of the Indian Divorce Act 1869, and section 30 of the Parse Marriage and Divorce Act 1936.

This section II is not applicable to marriages solemnized before the commencement of this Act. Under this section Husband or Wife has to present a petition, if the marriage between them is to be declared null and void or if a dispute arises between the parties and others regarding the validity of marriage. It does not confine the right to the aggrieved party alone.

Through section II gives a right to the parties to file a petition for declaring the marriage a nullity, the filing of petition is not a condition precedent for putting an end to the marriage. (*Kamla Devi* vs. *Atma Ram*)[91]

Section 5 prescribes six conditions for valid marriage; section II renders marriage solemnized in contravention of conditions (I), (IV) and (V) of section 5 only void.

Section 5

(I) Either party has a spouse at the time of marriage

(IV) The parties were with in the degrees of prohibited relationship unless accepted by their custom.

(V) The parties were 'sapindas' except when their custom permitted such marriage

Section 5(I)

Before 1955 Hindu Law permitted polygamy for men, but after the Hindu Marriage Act came into force no Hindu can re-marry except widows, widowers and divorcees. Not only the second marriage before dissolution of first marriage, is null and void but also an offence punishable under section 494 and section 495 of Indian penal code.

91. 1980 HLR 398.

Section 494

Marrying again during Life Time of Husband or Wife

Whoever, having a husband or wife living marries in any case in which such marriage is void by reason of its taking place during the life of such husband or wife, shall be punished with imprisonment of either description for a term which may extend to seven years and shall also be liable to fine.

Exception

This section does not extend to any person whose marriage with such husband or wife has been declared void by a court of competent jurisdiction.

Nor to any person who contracts a marriage during the life of a former husband or wife, if such husband or wife, at the time of the subsequent marriage shall have been continually absent from such person for the space of seven years and shall not have been heard of by such person as being alive within that time provided the person contracting such subsequent marriage shall before such marriage takes place, informs the person with whom such marriage is contracted of the real state of facts so far as the same are within his or her knowledge.

Section 495

Section 495 of Indian Penal code provides that "whoever commits the offence defined in the section 494, having concealed from the person with whom the subsequent marriage is contracted the fact of the former marriage, shall be punished with imprisonment of either description for a term which may extend to ten years and shall also be liable to fine.

A Petition under section 11 for annulment of second marriage can be brought only either by husband or by wife (sheelwa *vs.* Ram Nandani).[92]

The second wife whose marriage is void under this section will not get maintenance under section 125 of Cr. P.C. (Naurang Singh *vs.* Sapla Devi)[93]

---

92. AIR 1981 All 42.
93. AIR 1968 All 412.

Section 5(IV) and Section 5(V)

"The parties are not with in the degrees of prohibited relationship and sapindas of each other unless the custom or usages governing each of them permits of a marriage between the two".

When the parties are with in the prohibited relationship and sapindas of each other, then the marriage will become void. Section 3(f) and section 3(g) deals about the definition of "Sapinda Relationship" and "Degrees of prohibited relationship".

Section 3(f)

1. "Sapinda Relationship" with ref to any person extends as far as the third generation (inclusive) in the line of ascent through the mother, and the fifth (inclusive) in the line of ascent through the father, the line being traced upwards in each case from the person concerned, who is to be counted as the first generation.
2. Two persons are said to be "Sapindas" of each other if one is lineal ascendant of the other with in limits of sapinda relationship, or if they have a common lineal ascendant who is within the limits of sapinda relationship with reference to each of them.

Section 3(g) : "Degrees of Prohibited Relationship"

Two persons are said to be within the "degrees of prohibited relationship".

1. If one is lineal ascendant of the other; or
2. If one was the wife or husband of a lineal ascendant or descendant of the other, or
3. If one was the wife of the brother or of the father's or mother's brother, or of the grand father's or grandmother's brother of the other, or
4. If the two are brother and sister, uncle and niece, aunt and nephew or children of brother and sister or of two brothers or of two sisters.

Explanation

For the purpose of clause (f) and (g) relationship includes:

1. Relationship by half or uterine-blood as well as by full-blood;
2. Illegitimate blood relationship as well as legitimate;
3. Relationship by adoption as well as by blood; and all terms of relationship in those clauses shall be construed accordingly.

Expressions "full-blood", "half-blood" and "uterine-blood" are also defined in section-3.

Two persons are said to be related to each other by full blood when they are descended from a common ancestor by the same wife, and by half blood when they are descended from a common ancestor but by different wives. Two persons are said to be related to each other by uterine-blood when they are descended from a common ancestor but by different husbands.

If a person marries his sister's daughter, the marriage is null and void and such wife is no better than a concubine. (Meenakshi vs Nammalwar)[94]

When a spouse of first marriage wants to get second marriage by other party, declared null and void, he should file suit under section 9 of the code of civil procedure-1908 read with section 42 of specific Relief Act-1963.

According to section 11 and section 17 of Hindu Marriage Act-1955 there is remedy in case of husband married another lady. In common law she has right to file a suit for declaration that the marriage of her husband with second wife is illegal and void. (Birendera Kumar Singh *v.* Kamala Devi)[95]

The marriage solemnized under special marriage Act is void not only on the ground of violation of monogamy and marriage with in degrees of prohibited relationship but also on the ground of impotency, insanity and minority. (Section 24 of special Marriage Act-1954)

---

94. AIR 1970 Mad. 402 at 406.
95. AIR 1995 All 243.

2.20.3 Voidable Marriages

Section 12

1. Any marriage solemnized whether before or after the commencement of this Act, shall be void able and may be annulled by a decree of nullity on any of the following grounds namely
   - (a) that the marriage has not been consummated owing to the impotency of the respondent; or)[96]
   - (b) that the marriage is in contravention of the condition specified in clause (ii) of section; or
   - (c.) that the consent of the petitioner or where the consent of the gurdian in marriage of the petitioner (was required under section 5, as it stood immediately before the commencement of the child marriage restraint (amendment) Act 1978 (2 of 1978)[97] the consent of such guardian was obtained by force (or by fraud as to the nature of the ceremony or as to any material fact or circumstances concerning the respondent).[98]
   - (d) that the respondent was, at the time of the marriage pregnant by some person other than the petitioner.
2. Not with standing any thing contained in sub-section (1) no petition for annulling a marriage
   - (a) On the ground specified in clause (c) of sub-section (1) shall be entertained if :
     - (i) the petition is presented more than one year after the force has ceased to operate or, as the case may be the fraud had been discovered; or
     - (ii) the petitioner has, with his or her full consent lived with the other party to the marriage as husband of wife after the force

96. Caluse (a) of subs by Act No. 68 of 1976, Sec. 6.
97. Subs by No. 2 of 1978, the schedule, for the words "is required under Section 5".
98. Subs by Act No. 68 of 1976, Section 6 for words "for fraud".

had ceased to operate or, as the case may be, the fraud had been discovered.

(b) On the ground specified in clause (d) of sub-section (i) shall be entertained unless the court is satisfied

(i) that the petitioner was at the time of the marriage ignorant of the facts alleged.

(ii) that proceedings have been instituted in the case of a marriage solemnized before the commencement of this Act within one year of such commencement and in the case of marriage solemnized after such commencement within one year from the date of the marriage; and

(iii) that marital intercourse with the consent of the petitioner has not taken place since the discovery by the petitioner of the existence of (the said ground)[99]

The voidable marriage remains valid until declared void. In the case of voidable marriage, an aggrieved party is entitled to get the marriage declared void or to accept the marriage as valid.

A voidable marriage is one that will be regarded by everyone as a valid subsisting marriage until a decree annulling it has been pronounced by a court of competent jurisdiction.[100]

In English Law the form of decree was the same as in case of void marriage. Pronouncing the marriage "to have been and to be absolutely null and void to all intends and purposes in the law whatsoever'. This led to great deal of confusion and conflict. This confusion has been now avoided by Nullity of Marriage Act, 1971.

In this Act section 5 lays down 'A decree on nullity granted after the commencement of this Act on the ground that a marriage is voidable shall operate to annual the marriage only as respects any time after the decree has been made

99. Subs by Act No. 68 of 1976 Section 6 for the words "the ground for a decree".

100. Laxshamma *v.* Thayamma, AIR 1974 AP.

absolute, and the marriage shall notwithstanding the decree, be treated as if it has existed upto that time.

A voidable marriage is a perfectly valid marriage so long as it is not avoided. A voidable marriage can be avoided only on the petition of one of the parties to the marriage. If one of the parties does not petition for annulment of marriage, the marriage will remain valid. If one of the parties dies before the marriage is annulled, no one can challenge the marriage. The marriage will remain valid forever.

The voidable marriage confers a status of husband and wife on the parties. The children are legitimate children. All mutual rights and obligation of the marriage arise from it. After the annulment of the voidable marriage the children are treated as legitimate children.

2.21 GROUNDS OF VOIDABLE MARRIAGE

Under Hindu Law the Marriage is Voidable on the following grounds:

1. Failure of the respondent to consummate the marriage on account of impotency.
2. Capacity of the respondent to give a valid consent in consequence of unsound mind, or though capable of giving valid consent respondent was suffering from mental disorder of such kind or to such extent as to unfit for marriage and procreation of children or respondent was subject to recurrent attacks of insanity or epilepsy.
3. Respondent's pregnancy at the time of marriage of which the petitioner was not the cause and of which petitioner was ignorant at the time of marriage, and the petition is brought with in one year of the solemnization of marriage, and further that the petitioner has had no marital intercourse with the respondent after the knowledge of respondent's pregnancy.Petitioner's consent was obtained by force or fraud as to the nature of ceremony or as to any material fact or circumstances, concerning the

respondent, provided that the petitioner did not live with the respondent as husband or wife after the discovery of fraud or cessation of force, and provided further that the petition was presented with in one year of the discovery of fraud or cessation of force.

2.22.1 Impotency

Impotency in matrimonial cases means incapacity to consummate the marriage. It means incapacity to perform conjugal intercourse with the spouse.

A party is impotent if his or her mental or physical condition makes consummation of the marriage a physical by impossibility.[101]

The word impotency has not been defined in Hindu Marriage Act but it has been made ground for getting the marriage annulled if the same is not consummated owing to the impotence of the respondent-spouse.

In order to consummate marriage a normal sexual intercourse must take place,[102] but the degree of sexual satisfaction obtained by the parties from each other is not relevant.[103]

Where complete coitus is established the discharge of semen in wife's body is not necessary condition consummation,[104] nor the removal of the wife's Uterus by a operation offers the potency.[105]

2.22.2 Unsound Mind

According to section 5(ii) at the time of marriage none of the parties should be incapable of giving a valid consent to it in consequence of unsoundness of mind, not if capable has been suffering from mental disorder of such a kind or to such an extent to be unfit for marriage and procreation or children.

Meaning there by that the person suffering from insanity, epilepsy or unsoundness of mind cannot give valid consent for

---

101. Yuvraj Digvijay Singh *v.* Patap Kumari, AIR 1976 SC 137.
102. G. Venkateswar Rao *v.* G. Naga Mani, AIR 1962 AP 151.
103. Rafinder Kaur *v.* Man Mohan Singh, AIR 1972 P and H 142.
104. Moina Khosla *v.* Amardeep Khosla, AIR 1986 Del. 399.
105. Smar Som *v.* Sadhna Sam, AIR 1975 Cal 413.

marriage. In other words consent of both the parties is also a condition for valid Hindu Marriage.[106]

When the consent obtained by force or fraud then the marriage can be annulled by section 12. The words 'force' and 'fraud' have not been defined in this Act. For the purpose of section 12 force means threat of violence, physical juxtaposition or other kind of injury (including mental) to party giving consent or his near one and it should be present at the time of marriage.[107]

To constitute fraud there should be deliberate concealment of material fact or same perfection of facts, material facts which are false to the knowledge of person protecting or getting protected for the purposes of obtaining consent.

1. Concealment for factum of annulment of first marriage at the time of second marriage.[108]
2. Non-disclosure that party-getting marriage to petitioner in partially disabled because of polio in childhood.[109]
3. Threat to commit murder or to commit suicide.[110]
4. Impersonation at the time of selection for marriage. It means person shown was different than person actually married to the petitioner.[111]

Examples in which ground of fraud cannot be to be sufficient for the purpose of annulment :

1. Respondent allegedly, suffering from heart disease from childhood.[112]

---

106. K.Bala *v.* Bhairo, AIR 1982 All 242.
107. Ananth Nath *v.* Lajjabati, AIR 1959 Cal 778.
108. Kiran Bala *v.* Bhairo Prasad, AIR 1982 All 242.
109. Balbir Kaur *v.* Maghar Singh, AIR 1984 PandH 417.
110. Purabi *v.* Basudeb Mukherjee, AIR 1969 Cal 293.
111. Raja Ram *v.* Deepa Bai, AIR 1974 MP 52.
112. Sarala bai *v.* Kamal Singh, AIR 1991 MP 358.

2. Concealment of fact that the respondent was suffering from tuberculosis.[113]

Section 12(2) makes clear that if after discovery of alleged fraud, petitioner still have had sexual intercourse freely, the petition of annulment shall not be entertained, condemnation after disclosure of fraud disentitled the party the relief of getting marriage annulled under this section.[114]

Where petition under the section is not maintainable in view of sub-section (2) or it and by amendment, it was sought to be converted into one under section 13 of the Act, the plaint cannot be reflected[115]

2.22.3 Pregnancy of the Respondent at the Time of Marriage

The ground for annulment of marriage is not available if the pregnancy at the time of marriage was from the petitioner himself. Other conditions required are that :

1. The petitioner was ignorant of that fact at the time of marriage.
2. Marital intercourse with consent of petitioner did not take place after the discovery of such pregnancy.

If the petition is brought after the above period no relief of annulment of marriage can be granted.[116]

Similarly. Where the husband had the knowledge of such pregnancy at the time of marriage or he had sexual intercourse with his wife after the discovery of the above fact, the marriage cannot be annulled.[117] The burden of proof as to the pregnancy lies upon the husband only.[118]

---

113. Anath Nath *v.* Laffabai, AIR 1959 1994 MP 18.
114. Mohinder Kau *v.* Bikar Singh, AIR 1979 HIR 751.
115. Mecra Asthana *v.* Rajendra Nath, AIR 1994 MP.
116. Sarala Bai *v.* Kamal Singh, AIR 1991 MP 358.
117. C.S. Rangobhattar *v.* C. Choodamani, AIR 1992 AP 103.
118. Nand Kishore *v.* Munni Bai, AIR 1979 MP 45.

CHAPTER

3

Divorce under Sastric Law

3.0 DIVORCE IN SASTRIC LAW

The term "divorce" is of Latin origin. It comes from the word "*Divortium*" which means 'to turn aside', 'to separate from'. The word 'divorce' is known throughout the world and its concept is found in every language and religion. The term divorce refers to the disruption of marriage relationship. It is the final tragic document of marital bond. It is the dissolution of a valid and subsisting marriage. It is the antithesis of marriage, divorce, since it disintegrates the family unity, is, of course, a social evil in itself, but it is a necessary evil. It is better to wreck the unity of family than to wreck the future happiness of the parties by binding them to a companionship that has became odious. Membership of a family founded on antagonism can bring little profit even to the children.

Divorce or dissolution of marriage or termination of marital tie is recognized as an important matrimonial remedy in almost all the legal systems in the World. The institution of divorce exists from time immemorial in various forms in various ages throughout the World. Among all the nations of antiquity the power of divorce was regarded as a natural corollary to the marital right. Originally this power was exclusively vested in the husband, and the wife was under no circumstances entitled to claim a divorce. Later on the progress of civilization and the advancement of ideas led to a partial amelioration in the condition of women. They too acquired a qualified right of divorce, which they were never backward in exercising freely until the facility with which marriages were contracted and dissolved. Divorce is an escape valve from the marriage relation where marriage cracks occur. Divorce as an institution has been allowed in most countries for certain causes. It has never been intended to produce an alternative to the monogamous family, but merely to mitigate hardships where, for special reasons, the continuance of a marriage seems to be intolerable. Divorce has always been appreciated and condemned alternately as a remedy for matrimonial ills. The law on the subject has been extraordinarily different in different ages and places. From the legal point, divorce may be regarded as a technique developed in society in collaboration with law in which the mismatched or the fallen out spouse finds a legal release or relief granted by the Courts.[1] Marriage, traditionally regarded as a life long family bond is now crumbling fast. Divorce is sometimes described as a social innovation and an escape valve for the inevitable tensions of marriage.

Divorce is something alien or foreign to Hindu viewpoint. Hindus considered marriage as a sacrament which is regarded as unbreakable throughout the life. Normally a spouse should not be allowed to dissolve his or her marriage. But this rule cannot be absolute. Divorce was though unknown to the Hindu textual law but custom and usage recognized it in certain communities. According to Hindu Law marriage also creates indissoluble ties between the husband and wife. As such divorce is not common among Hindus. Divorce was unknown to the *Sastric Law* and to the Hindu Society for about two thousand years. Absence of divorce was the general rule and acceptance of it was due to custom and exception. Therefore in

1. R. Jagan Mohan Rao, "Indissolubility of Marriage & Easy Divorce" in Law towards Stable Marriages, P. Diwan & Virendra Kumar (ed.), Delhi, 1984, p. 167.

ancient Hindu law divorce was out of question, still then, divorce under custom was available easily. Among several castes and tribes of Hindus, divorce by mutual consent, divorce on such grounds, such as adultery, abandonment or apostasy was available and practically no formalities were required it indissoluble has been eroded gradually and thorough legislations the right of divorce has been introduced in all legal system in India.

Divorce is not tolerated by the ancient juridical textbooks and has not the sanction of the Priest. The idea of indissolubility of relationship between the husband and the wife has led to the fiction of identity of the two. J.D.M. Derrett believes that, in ancient Hindu law divorce was unthinkable.[2] The right of divorce where it exists is valid only by virtue of custom, since the customary divorce has always been approved and held valid under Hindu law.[3] The doctrine of *'Tyaga'* was also prevalent in the Hindu Society. *'Tyaga'*, as distinguished from *'Moksha'*, was not an unfamiliar form of divorce. *'Tyaga'*, is a technical term denoting separation from conjugal intercourse as opposed to *'Moksha'* the technical divorce. Thus in case of *'Tyaga'*, she remained a legal wife according to *Sastrakaras*, though given up by the husband. In *Mitakshara School* the word *Tyaga* means depriving the wife of her right of co-habitation and association in religious affairs but should not be understood in the sense of expulsion from the house.[4] As such *Tyaga* is not pure divorce in the true sense of the word and differ from the term *Moksha* whose meaning is unclear. K.P.Jayswal opines that *Tyaga* is a technical term denoting separation from conjugal intercourse while *Moksha* is technical divorce.[5] In the *Atharvaveda*[6] there is a word *"Parivrkta"* which

---

2. J.D.M. Derrett, "The Death of a Marriage Law, New Delhi, 1978, p. 4.
3. Rajkumari Agrawal, "Matrimonial Remedies under Hindu Law", Bombay, 1974, p. 67.
4. Mit. on Yajn. I. 72.
5. K.P. Jayswal, "Development of Law in Manu and Yajnavalkya, TLL, Calcutta, 1930, p. 230.
6. AV, VII. 113. 2.

means the neglected wife.[7] The *Atharvaveda*[8] also enjoins a woman to remarry probably in the lifetime of her husband which suggests the existence of such practices. M.A. Indira remarks that in the Vedic age they had absolutely no knowledge of the possibility of nuptial relation even being suspended or ended. N. Sengupta also opines that the general philosophy behind the Vedic marriage do not leave any scope for divorce. In the Vedic literature there is no reference to divorce and there is not much evidence in the Post-Vedic literature. In a different page again Sengupta remarks that in the Veda there is no evidence of divorce.[9] P.V. Kane upholds the same view.[10] But it is difficult to believe that divorce was non-existent in the Vedic age.

Apastamba states that no one should obtain another wife if the first one is righteous, dutiful and has offspring. He further emphatically declares[11] that no kind of separation between husband and wife is possible since in marriage they have to perform religious acts jointly. In the Mahabharata[12] the concept of 'Union for life' of husband and wife has been furnished. Thereby according to Mahabharata there is no divorce. Brihaspati also corroborates the same view.[13] According to Manu the wife is not released from her marital obligations even if she is sold or repudiated.[14]

Some of the earlier writers allowed divorce under certain well-defined circumstances. Manu does not approve of dissolution of marriage in any conditions. He declared, "Let mutual fidelity continue till death, this in brief may be understood to be the highest dharma of husband and wife. The

7. A.B. Keith and A.A. Macdonell, Vedic Index, pp. 496-97; Usha Apte, "The Sacrament of Marriage in Hindu Society from Vedic period to Dharmasastras, Delhi, 1978, p. 25.
8. AV, IX 27.8.
9. N. Sengupta, "Evolution of Hindu Marriage", Bombay, 1965, pp. 142.24
10. P.V. Kane, HD, Vol. II. Part I, 1974, p. 619.
11. Apa. Dh.S, II. 5.11.12. 109. *Ibid.*, II. 6.13, 16.17.
12. Mbh. Adi. p. 74.40 & Mbh. Santi. p. 114.60.
13. Brah. Smr; XXVI. 92.
14. Manu. Smr, IX. 46 & 101.

duty of a wife continues even after her death. She can never have a second husband." But on the other hand we find some texts in Narada and Parashar codes of law, which permit divorce to wife in certain conditions of life. According to Narada, there are five conditions as under by which a woman could renounce her husband and choose another:

(1) Husband lost and unheard of for a period of seven years;
(2) Husband is dead;
(3) Husband renounced the world;
(4) Husband became impotent;
(5) Husband is ex-communicated.

In Arthasastra, Kautilya declared that marriage might be dissolved by mutual consent in the case of unapproved forms of marriage. According to him a wife could repudiate her marriage under the following conditions:

(a) Husband's misconduct with the wife,
(b) Husband's prolonged absence,
(c) Husband's banishment,
(d) Husband becoming dangerous to the wife's life,
(e) Husband ex-communicated,
(f) Husband having become impotent.

Majority of ancient jurists expressed their disapproval of the divorce. It was only in unapproved forms of marriage that they favoured divorce, that too in extreme cases of distress.

There is one Smriti text which has been the source of great controversy. The School of Narada speaks about divorce. According to the comment of Narada on a passage of Manu there is a rule that a marriage as well as betrothal should be dissolved on the discovery of a blemish. In that case the bride shall be enjoined to another man by her relatives or in their absence, she shall go to live with another man. Narada[15] states that when husband and wife leave one another from mutual dislike it is a sin and marriage performed in accordance with

15. Nar. Smr. XII. 29, XII. 12 & 90.

the customs of the first four kinds cannot be dissolved. As Narada was not in favour of an unapproved marriage, he indirectly supports divorce rule for it. In *Kautilya's Arthasastra* we are in a better position to understand the precise connotation of divorce, since for the first time Kautilya possibly recognizes the necessity of divorce. Kautilya informs that a man or a woman hating his or her marriage partner could not dissolve his or her marriage against the partner. But from mutual enmity divorce may be obtained which is known as "*Parasparamdevesanmoksah*". If a man apprehends danger from his wife and desires divorce from her it is according to him is "*Moksamichchhet*". In that case he shall return what ever is obtained from her as dowry on the occasion of her marriage. In the case of woman under apprehension of danger from her husband she must forfeit her claims to property.[16] Kautilya also suggests that though marriage performed in an approved form such as Brahma, Daiva, Arsha and Prajapatya cannot be dissolved but a marriage performed in an unapproved form such as Asura, Gandharva, Rakshasa and Paisacha can be dissolved by mutual consent. Thus mutual hatred or dislike is accepted as a ground for divorce. Truly speaking Kautilya is the only lawgiver who goes a step further and permits divorce but only in disapproved forms of marriage and on the apprehensions of danger. As such Kautilya goes beyond abandonment as prescribed by all other *Sastrakaras* and allowed divorce, of course, only on certain restrictions and in exceptional circumstances. It may be submitted that Kautilya does not lend his unqualified support to the practice. He is cautious in approving it which he certainly treats as a necessary evil. Again Kautilya being progressive in outlook of the later period treats the husband and wife almost on an equal footing in this respect. Ram Sharan Sharma finds in Kautilya that among the three higher varnas, rejection of the bride before the rite of *Panigrahana* is valid but among the Sudras this is valid before the time of cohabitation.[17] Thus inspite of the conception that a Hindu marriage is a sacrament, divorce of a kind was also recognized by the early writers.

---

16. Kautilya AS, III. 3. 15-18.
17. *Ibid.*, III. 3.155, III. 3.15.

Albiruni remarks that the Hindu husband and wife can only be separated by death, as they have no divorce.[18] On the other hand, in the early centuries in the Buddhist circles wives were allowed divorce by becoming nuns and even in later centuries becoming a temple dancing girl was a method of putting an end to one's marriage.[19]

It is evident that the institution of divorce was unknown to the ancient Hindu juridical texts, excepting very few. It also seems that during the Smriti period in some very exceptional cases wife or husband were allowed to give up each other. But the law became more rigid in the post-Smriti period, and the marriage came to be established firmly as an indissoluble union. Marriage is not a temporary association to be dissolved at the fancy of the parties to them.

3.1 DIVORCE BY CASTE CUSTOM

In some of the areas of India there is a custom among the Hindus under which they were allowed to divorce their wives. J.D.Mayne opines that although divorce was not generally allowed in Hindu law it is recognized customarily in certain castes of the Hindu Community.[20] P. Diwan also agrees with him.[21] J.D.M. Derrett opines that since customary divorce is allowed, it requires quasi-judicial validity.[22] According to M.A.Quareshi customary divorce is very common in Assam for a husband and wife to agree to a divorce by a duly executed deed.[23]

Contrary to the general notion regarding the indissolubility of Hindu Marriages, customary forms of divorce, recognized both socially and judicially, have been

18. E.C. Sachua, *loc. cit.* p. 154.
19. J.D.M. Derrett, *loc. cit.*, p. 59.
20. J.D. Mayne, "Hindu Law and Usages, 11th ed. 1953, pp. 174-76. S. Jaffer Hussain, "Marriage Break down and Divorce Law Reform in Contemporary Society", New Delhi, 1983, p. 150.
21. Paras Diwan, "Family Law", New Delhi, 1983, p. 32.
22. Paras Diwan, "Family Law", New Delhi, 1983, p. 32.
23. M.A. Qureshi, Marriage and Matrimonial Remedies, Delhi, 1978, p. 32.

widely practised among the lower castes of people in the various states. As the ancient Hindu jurists were farsighted and reasonable enough to realize there might be, would not be possible for one and all. Consequently, the law was based on two-tier system, one for intellectual or cultural elite and the other for the less sensitive or ill informed. Accordingly customary Hindu law approved the divorce to some Hindus. Among the low caste Hindus it is neither infrequent nor unlawful to divorce a husband and marry another.

There is also a clear semblance in views that customary divorce was prevalent and recognized. How it was recognized by the General Hindu Law and under what conditions and constraints it was acceptable judicially. Divorce for castes previously unfamiliar with it by custom has been a shock and has temporarily upset the balance of some groups of society, especially when they visualize it in conjunction with the dubious increase of "love-marriages." Marriage performed correctly according to the shaṣtra is still a samskara, and judicial divorce cannot end that aspect of marriage. It merely terminates (subject to orders relating to alimony, matrimonial property and the custody of children) the secular rights of one spouse against the other, and frees each to enter into another union.

A custom may be briefly described or defined as a continuing course of conduct which by the acquiescence, or expressed approval (though not in a statutory form) of the community observing it, has come to be regarded as fixing a rule or norm of conduct for the members of the community. Custom grows by conduct, from practices adopted for the convenience of society and the individual. Their roots go down deep into the soil of national ideas and institutions. So what prevails amongst a set of people, as the result of their consensus of opinion and approval is custom.[23a]

A custom is a particular rule which has existed either actually or presumptively from time immemorial, and has obtained the force of law in a particular locality although contrary or not consistent with the general common law of the

23a. P.S. Atchuthen Pillai, Jurisprudence and Legal Theory, pp. 104-5.

realm.[23b] However, all customs are purely local and confined to particular places. There cannot be a custom in one place to do something in another. The land in a particular place and the inhabitants in respect thereof may be charged by custom, for matters within the place, but custom will not apply to matters out of it.[23c]

In black's Law Dictionary by Henry Campbell Black 5th edn., it is stated that a usage or practice of the people, which, by common adoption and acquiescence, and by long and unvarying habit, has become compulsory, and has acquired the force of law with respect to the place or subject-matter to which it relates. It results from a long series of actions constantly repeated, which have, by such repetition and by uninterrupted acquiescence, acquired the force of a tacit and common consent.[23d]

'Custom' and 'usage' are two different concepts. They are not synonymous terms though they are often used interchangeably. Strictly speaking there is a clear distinction between the two. 'Usage' represents the twilight stage of custom-custom begins where usage ends.[23e]

If there is specific prohibition in the sacred laws about a particular aspect of a usage or custom, then how far its legality will be acceptable judicially or otherwise. K.L. Sarkar is of the opinion that it is enough if it is not positively condemned by the Smrtis[23f] the judicial pronouncements, will add more clarity to it.

1. Collector of Madura *v.* Moottoo Ramalinga,[23g] The judicial committee of the Privy Council said, under the Hindu system of Law, clear proof of usage would outweigh the written text of law.

23b. Halsbury's Law of England by Lord Simonds, 3rd edn.

23c. R.v. Ecclesfield (Inhabitants) [1818] IB & Ald 348 per Lord Ellenborough C.J. at p. 360.

23d. Taken from Louisville & N.R.Co. *v.* Reverman 243 Ky 702.

23e. Mayne's Hindu Law and Usage, 13th edn., p. 457.

23f. K.L. Sarkar, Mimamsa, 247-8.

23g. [1868] 12 MIA 397, 436.

2. Neelkisto Deb *v.* Beerchunder.[23h] That a custom may be in derogation of Smriti law and where proved to exist may supersede that law.
3. Hurpurshad *v.* Sheo Dyal[23i] A custom is a rule which, in a particular family or in a particular district, has from long usage obtained the force of law. It must be ancient, certain and reasonable and being in derogation of the general rules of law must be construed strictly.
4. Parbati *v.* Jagdish[23j] the tenacity of family custom even under the strain of migration has been repeatedly recognized in the Kali Prashad *v.* Amund Roy.[23k] That though local and family custom, if proved to exist, will supersede the general law, the general law will in other respects govern the relation of the parties outside that custom.
5. Mookka Kone *v.* Ammakutti Ammal.[23l] In this case their Lordships discussed threadbare every aspect of custom and said that in order to give effect to a custom which is set-up and which is at variance with the ordinary Hindu Law, it should be ancient, invariable, continuous, notorious, not expressly forbidden by the legislature and not opposed to morality or public policy and as regards instances in support of the custom they should be established by clear and unambiguous evidence and must be conclusive what is ordinarily understood as Hindu Law is not the Customary Law of the country like the common Law of England. The Supreme Court in Gokalchand *v.* Parvin Kumar,[23m] A custom in order to be binding, must derive its force from the fact that by long usage it has obtained the force of law, but the English Rule that "a custom in order that it may be

23h. [1868] 12 MIA 523, 542.
23i. [1875] 3 IA 259, 285
23j. [1902] 29 IA 82.
23k. [1887] 15 IA 18.
23l. AIR 1928 Mad 299 (FB); AIR 1915 PC 30.
23m. AIR 1952 SC 231

> legal and binding, must have been used so long that the memory of man runneth not to the contrary", should not be strictly applied to Indian conditions. All that is necessary to prove is that the usage has been acted upon in practice for such a long period and with such invariability as to show that it has, by common consent, been submitted to as the established rule of a particular locality.

Section 29(2) of Hindu Marriage Act, 1955 Postulates

Nothing contained in this Act shall be deemed to affect any right recognized by custom or conferred by any special enactment to obtain the dissolution of a Hindu marriage, whether solemnized before or after the commencement of this Act.

This section has to be read with section 3 (a) of the said Act:

> The expressions 'custom' and 'usage' signify any rule which, having been continuously and uniformly observed for a long time, has obtained the force of law among Hindu in any local area, tribe, community, group of family:
>
> Provided that the rule is certain and not unreasonable or opposed to public policy: Provided further that in the case of rule applicable only to a family it has not been discontinued by the family.

These stipulations are to be further read with Article 13(3)(a) of the Constitution of India:

> 'Law' includes any ordinance, order, byelaw, rule, regulation, notification, custom or usage having the force of law in the territory of India.

The cases where the parties to the marriage sought customary divorce and when challenged, how they were viewed by the judiciary:

1. Khemkor *v.* Umiashankar.[23n] In this case the question was whether a Sompura brahmana woman who has contracted a marriage with a man of that caste, during the lifetime of her husband and without his consent, is entitled to maintenance
   Held that among Sompura brahmana natras or remarriages are allowed among them but with the consent of the first husband but since consent was lacking, it was held that the second marriage in not valid as per custom of her caste, relying upon 2 BHCR 124.
2. Sundor *v.* Nihala[23o] Held that it was found that by the custom of jats of Sialkot a woman who has received a written divorce from her husband was free to contract a second marriage.
3. Kudomee Dossee *v.* Joteeram Kolita.[23p] It is a case where a Hindu husband sued his wife for restitution of conjugal rights and the defendant pleaded divorce. It was held that though the Hindu Law does not contemplate divorce, still in those districts where it is recognized as an established custom, it would have the force of law. There can be no doubt that the Hindu Law has been affected in particular districts by particular usages and these usages have hitherto been respected unless clearly repugnant to the Principles of Hindu Law. Referring to Sham Churu's Vayuastha Darpana, p. 387, where it is said that reason and justice are more to be regarded than mere texts and that wherever a good custom exists, it has the force of law.
4. In [1870] 7 BHCR 133 also the question arose about natra marriage and it was held that a custom which authorizes a woman to contract a natra marriage without a divorce, on payment of a certain sum to the caste to which she belongs is an immoral custom and one which shall not be judicially recognized.

23n. [1873] BHCR 381.

23o. [1889] 84 PR 1889. See also Jasan v. Nihala [1884] 78 PR 1884.

23p. [1877] ILR 3 Cal. 305.

5. Sankaralingam Chetti *v.* Subban Chetti and Another.[23q] The question in issue is whether there has been a valid and legal divorce between plaintiff and second defendant and the only point argued is that whether the caste custom is valid as it was contended that it is immoral and that the courts will not recognize it .It was held that divorce in this form is consistent with the 'original' custom of the potters and if this be so, the custom is sufficiently ancient and it is not immoral since it does not ignore marriage as a legal institution but provides a special mode by which it may be dissolved.
6. Keshav Hargovan *v.* Bai Gandi.[23r] In this case the Court held that a custom by which the marriage tie can be dissolved by either husband or wife, against the wish of the divorced party and for no reason but out of mere caprice, the sole condition being the payment of a sum of money fixed by the caste, is opposed to public policy and is also repugnant to Hindu Law and, therefore, cannot be judicially recognized. In this case the custom pleaded was not recognized by the Court.
7. Bai Ganga *v.* Emperor.[23s] It was a case under section 495 of IPC. The Court held that Courts do not recognize the authority of a caste to dissolve a marriage or to declare it void or give permission to a married woman to remarry.
8. Basant Singh and Another *v.* Bhagwan Singh and Another.[23t] Held that according to the customary law of the Sialkot district among Hindus, divorces must be in writing and in the absence of such writing the oral relinquishment by a Jat of his wife would not be sufficient under the custom binding on his tribe.

23q. [1894] 17 ILR Mad. 479.

23r. AIR 1916 Bom 97.

23s. AIR 1915 Bom 197. See also (1875-7) 1 Bom. 347 Reg *v.* Shambhu Raghu, Jukni *v.* Queen Empress [1892] 19 Cal 627, Reg *v.* Karsan Goja [1864-66] 2 BHCR, Narayanan Bharti *v.* Laving Bharti [1877-78] 2 Bom 140, Uji *v.* Hathi Lalu [1870] 7 BHCR 133.

23t. AIR 1933 Lah 755.

9. Jina Magan Pakhali *v.* Bai Jethi.[23u] In this case the custom was pleaded. It was a case for restitution of conjugal rights wherein the plea of customary divorce was taken to resist the case. It was held that custom of divorce in Pakhali community does exist and if the consent of the husband has been given it would not be against the spirit of Hindu Law.

   In this case reliance was also placed, besides the judicial precedents, on treatises that divorce is not contemplated by the Hindu Law but it is not repugnant to its principles, and if there be a well established custom in its support, it may override the general provisions of that law.[23v] Also that in the lowest classes divorce is attainable between a husband and wife provided it is allowed by the custom of the caste.[23w]

10. In Thangammal *v.* Gengayammal and others[23x] the validity of custom was challenged. It was held that there is no invalidity in a custom by which married couple being unable to live together, by consent seek divorce and are divorced by the parties, approaching the headman and other relations, paying certain amount and taking away the tali from round the neck of the wife and giving it back to the husband. It is only where the divorce is Effected against the wish of the wife that the custom permitting the divorce may be illegal.

    In Mayne's Hindu Law, para 37, p. 50, 13th edn., November 1991, it is said that it was doubted whether a custom authorizing her to marry again during the lifetime of her husband and with her consent, would have been valid.[23y]

23u. AIR 1941 Bom 298.

23v. Tagore Law Lectures 1908, Customs and Customary Laws in British India.

23w. Sir William Strange, Treatise on Hindu Law.

23x. AIR 1945 Mad 308.

23y. Khemkar *v.* Umiashankar [1873] 10 BHC 381; In re. Gedula Narayana AIR 1932 Mad 561.

Kodu and another *v.* Lola and another.[23z] It was a case of dispute about property wherein the custom of marriage and divorce was pleaded. Held that the presumption under Hindu Law is that marriage should be deemed to be in an approved form and that a pat marriage in curi form is no exception but herein it does not and cannot by any stretch of reasoning, support the contention that Mt. Sita's curi marriage with Lola was in an unapproved form. Evidence clearly shows that the remarriage and earlier divorce were as per approved custom and valid.

11. Pujam Liklai Singh Bhabando Singh v. Moiranthem Maipak Singh and another.[23aa] It was a case for declaration for entitlement to the properties specified in the plaint wherein the question of divorce by custom was raised. It was held that according to the report of the customs prevailing in Manipur, divorce or khainaba is permissible amongst the Hindus of Manipur and it can be from husband's side or from the wife's side. There is no condition attached and it can be done at pleasure. It is done even at a slight pretext. Gandharva form of marriage is also recognized in Manipur. The union of a man with a divorced woman is also recognized as a local valid marriage. It is also held that the performance of ceremony of laukatpa is not a condition for a marriage to be legal and valid.
12. Shivalingiah *v.* Chawdamma.[23ab] The case was regarding legitimacy of the appellant where marriage as per custom was pleaded. The Court held that separation by mutual consent and dissolution of the marital tie so as to enable the woman to remarry. Another man in what is called kuidike form and have the full status of a wife, are proved to be Possible in the community to which the parties belong and the

23z. AIR 1948 Nagpur 141.

23aa. AIR 1956 Manipur 18

23ab. AIR 1956 Mysore 17.

Court also relied upon the evidence adduced regarding the doctrine of factum valet.

13. Mt. Savitri Devi *v.* Naukhi ram.[23ac] In this case the lower Court granted divorce on the basis of custom wherein no custom was pleaded. The Court held that it is nobody's case that the marriage had been or was to be dissolved in accordance with custom and in the second place it is not the function of the Court constituted under the Hindu Marriage Act, 1955 to grant a decree of divorce or a declaration of divorce on the basis of custom.
14. Rapeti Bulli Tatayya *v.* Rapeti Nookaraju.[23ad] In this case the Court held that Hindu Law does not permit divorce. if a plaintiff relies upon customary divorce, he must allege and prove incidents of that custom. The mere writing of a letter cannot dissolve a legal marriage unless it is established that the customary method of divorce of that particular community could be achieved by the mere writing of a letter.
15. Nallathangal *v.* Nainan Ambalam.[23ae] The case was under section 488 of CrPc, 1898 wherein the point of divorce by custom was agitated. The Court held that though Hindu Law does not recognize divorce between husband and wife, nevertheless the custom in certain communities may permit a valid divorce by means of a caste, Panchayat or similar tribunal. Even after passing of the Hindu Marriage Act, 1955, customary rights of divorce were saved and such divorces continue to have the force of law among the communities where the custom prevailed.
16. Kishenlal *v.* Mst. Prabhu.[23af] It was a case of customary divorce and the Court held that Courts do not recognize the authority of the caste to dissolve a marriage or to give permission to a married woman to remarry. Therefore, a custom by which a caste

---

23ac. AIR 1958 HP 15.

23ad. AIR 1958 AP 611.

23ae. AIR 1960 Mad 179.

23af. AIR 1963 Raj 95.

panchayat can grant a divorce whenever it thinks fit irrespective of the mutual consent of the parties cannot be countenanced by Court of law as valid custom. It is incumbent on the plaintiff to state with precision and clarity what the custom is.

17. Sudhia Alial Gulabi *v.* Sankappa Raj.[23ag] In this case section 10 of the Madras Aliya Santhana Act was challenged as ultra vires of Art. 14 of the Constitution wherein the point of customary divorce was agitated. The Court held that a marriage that is purely contractual in character couldn't be said to be against public policy. Though it is not desirable that matrimonial ties should be broken at the caprice of one of the parties to the marriage and that neither the society nor the parties to the marriage will be benefited by yoking together two persons who pull in opposite directions there is no virtue in making a mockery of married life. Views on this question, as in most other questions differ. Often times those views are the products of customs, habits and environments. It is not proper to elevate those views to the position of absolute truth.
18. Premanbai *v.* Channoolal Punao.[23ah] It is a case wherein the validity of customary divorce was challenged. The Court held that divorce is unknown to Hindu Law and is a creature of custom amongst the communities in which it obtains. Where a custom permits a divorce between patvas with the mutual consent of the spouses, the age of discretion under the Mitaksara School of Hindu Law does not govern the case and a wife in a patva community can, at the age between 14 and 15 years, when she has attained sufficient maturity of understanding to comprehend the nature of the act she is doing, validly consents to her divorce from her husband in a caste Panchayat held for the purpose and a consent so given is binding on her according to the caste custom.

23ag. AIR 1963 Mys 245.
23ah. AIR 1963 MP 57.

19. Gurdit Singh *v.* Mst. Angrej Kaur and others.[23ai] In this case the point regarding customary divorce and the remarriage of the wife during the lifetime of the first husband was in issue. The Court held that a custom exists among the Hindu Jats of the Jalandhar district, which permits a valid divorce by a husband of his wife which dissolves the marriage. On the dissolution of such marriage, the divorced wife can enter into a valid marriage, with a second husband in the lifetime of the first husband. In this case the Supreme Court affirmed [1962] 64 Punjab LR 1179.
20. Mal Singh *v.* Ram Kaur.[23aj] Another case of the same nature came before the Punjab and Haryana High Court where it was held that there is a custom in tarkhan community of divorcing a woman by repudiation and the repudiated woman is free to remarry in the lifetime of her first husband.

A catena of cases have been cited above to show that custom is not cabined or confined within a particular locality but is prevalent throughout the country having force of law. The facts of Hindu life show that husbands are under the thumbs of their parents who have arranged their marriages, and often when they have not; wives are under the thumbs of their husbands or their own parents. Pleadings based on confessions or admissions, maneuvred or extorted from the female party are not unheard of. If divorce by consent were available, far too many marriages would be broken at the will of one party or of his relations. Cases are known where attempts have been made to get wives to agree to a divorce even in castes where customary divorces are not yet known! Parliament was wise in rejecting the idea and in limiting the grounds for divorce to matters generally regarded as impossible to mend.

Dr. Ganganath Jha said that the principle was canvassed that custom should be regarded as of equal authority to the Sruti itself, and still later on custom came to be regarded as

23ai. AIR 1968 SC 142.

23aj. P.V. Kane's History of Dharmasutra, chapters III and IV.

more authoritative than anything else and it was declared that the custom of a region (discard) should be given the first consideration and in every region custom alone should be observed.

But in spite of the supremacy of a custom, it clearly appears that law was based on two-tier system, one for the intellectuals or cultural elite and the other for the less sensitive or ill informed. Accordingly, Hindu Law approved the divorce which was applicable to non-caste Hindus, i.e., the lowest rung of the ladder in the socio-cultural hierarchy and perhaps this lowest rung of the ladder was in vast majority. Derrett while talking to Late Pt. Jawaharlal Nehru regarding divorce as antithesis to marriage got an answer that 80 per cent of the Hindus are already covered by the customary divorce.[23ak] But now the present trend is quite different, Custom has almost started giving way to statutory provisions.

Before the passing of the Hindu Marriage Act, 1955, divorce was not contemplated by the Hindu law, but it is not repugnant to the principles, and if there be a well-established custom in its support it may over-ride the general provisions of that law.[24] In the lowest classes a divorce is attainable between a husband and wife provided it is allowed by the custom of the caste. Further, among the lower classes of people, whether in Bombay, Bengal or in Southern India caste people allowed divorce. The grounds of divorce are generally habitual ill treatment, impotency, and the depraved habits of the husband. The divorce is usually affected by mutual consent, on payment of some compensation for marriage expenses incurred at the first marriage. Again Panchayat or Head of a Caste could determine marriage and grant divorce. But in some cases the Courts have declined to recognize the authority of the Panchayat in granting a divorce. Furthermore in several castes and sub-castes divorce under customs has prevailed from an early Hindu period. Since customs derogatory to sacred law are allowed to prevail[25] customary divorces have been recognized.[26]

23ak. Derett, The Death of a Marriage Law.

24. Kudomee Dasee *v.* Jotiram Kalita. 1878 ILR 3. Cal. 305.

25. Collector of Madura *v.* Mootoo Ramalinga, 1868 12 MIA 397.

26. G.D. Benerjee, *loc. cit.*, p. 242 ff.

Customary modes of divorce are easy. In some cases marriage can be dissolved by mutual consent. Very little formalities for dissolving marriage are needed. In most cases, it is purely a private act of the parties. In some communities some forum like Gram Panchayat or Family Council are recognized. Such has been the importance of customary divorces in Hindu law that even after reform and Codification of Hindu law of marriage, the customary divorce continues to be recognized.[27] But customary divorce has been the privilege of the lower Castes; only in a very few high Castes divorce by custom has been available. In a nutshell, customary divorce means a verdict or decree granted by Caste Council or tribunal orally to dissolve the marriage of the parties which have approached their caste elders or elders in the village in which they are living, who constitute a Caste Court or Tribunal. That is the easy way of breaking the marital tie at the will and pleasure of the parties to the marriage at whose instance both spouses dissolved their marriages, according to Prof. R.Jagan Mohan Rao in the State of Andhra Pradesh where this type of divorce by Caste custom is still very popular in some districts such as the districts of Visakhapatnam, Vizianagaram and Srikakulam. Further he adds that the significant feature of this method of obtaining divorce based on caste custom is that this is very cheap and easier than the judicial divorce which requires the observance of many formalities and highly litigious in nature and hence more expensive than customary divorce. The advantage with customary divorce is that, caste elders without any delay would speedily dispose off the cases of such divorce and it does not require any rigid formalities. Thus customary divorce is quicker and cheaper than judicial divorce.[28] Derrett who is of the same view that Customary Divorce is an informal affair and needs neither grounds nor quasi-judicial hearing.[29]

Therefore among Hindus in certain castes divorce by custom is allowed. The Courts have recognized customary divorce if the custom is a valid custom and the procedure followed for obtaining the customary divorce has been

27. The Hindu Marriage Act, 1955, Sec. 29 (2).
28. R. Jagan Mohan Rao, Supra. N. 98, p. 176.
29. J.D.M. Derrett, *loc. cit.*, pp. 122-23.

consistent with natural justice. Divorce is commonly practised among the Indian tribes and may be obtained by one of the parties refusing to continue to live in wedlock, by abandoning the spouse. The Khasis permit divorce for reasons of adultery, barrenness and compatibility of temperament, but the separation can take place only after mutual consent. In some cases, the party desiring the dissolution may have to pay compensation to the other party. There is no possibility of remarriage between two such people who have separated by divorce. The divorce has to be a Public Ceremony. The mother gets the custody of the children. Instances of divorce can be cited from other Indian tribes also. The Gand allow divorce freely on grounds of marital infidelity, carelessness in household work. Here either party can take the initiative in obtaining dissolution.

Referring to some of the Court cases in this connection it can be stated that there are some communities in which divorce was permitted by custom.[30] The Madras High Court held that there is nothing immoral in a custom allowing divorce by mutual consent.[31] Some of the customary forms of divorce recognized by the Courts are customs of divorce for the Lingayats of South Kanara,[32] Pat for Maratha[33] and Chader Andari for the Punjabi and the Jaths of Jullunder district.[34] In Pakhali Jiwa *v.* Bai Jethi[35] it was said that among Pakhali caste of Ahmedabad a custom of divorce with mutual consent of the spouses was not repugnant to law in general or Hindu law in particular.

A divorce by mutual consent was also recognized in Kerala.[36] In a Gujarati Kasara caste a wife can get a divorce from her husband on the ground of ill treatment.[37] Thus in a

30. Kudomee Dosee *v.* Joteeram Kolita. 1878, ILR 3 Cal. 305; Munda *v.* Timmaju Hensu 1. Mad. 380.
31. Sankaralingam *v.* Subba, 1894, ILR 17. Mad. 479.
32. Virasangappa *v.* Rudrappa, 1885. 8. Mad. 440.
33. Mani *v.* Zaboo 1926 AIR. Nag. 488
34. Gurdit Singh *v.* Mst. Angrez Kaur, 1968 AIR SC. 142.
35. 1941 AIR Bom. 535.
36. Vasappan *v.* Sarda 1958 Ker. 39 FB & Nangu *v.* Appi 1966 Ker. 4 FB.
37. Kasiram Kriparam *v.* Umbaram Hurreechanel. 1. Borrodaile. 387.

case[38] when Kasiram sued his father in-law complaining his refusal to send his wife 'Itcha' with her dower; it was alleged that ill-treatment compelled her to leave her husband. A decree was passed directing her to return and this was upheld in appeal. But on a petition of ill treatment, the Court of Appeal called up the Patels of the caste for opinion and the Court on the basis of prevailing custom pronounced a divorce. In another Gujarat case[39] one Kasee sued to get possession of his wife but the Court held that divorce pronounced by the caste was valid one. Thus customary divorce has always been approved and held valid under Hindu Law.[40] Besides customary divorce Hindu Law did not recognize divorce in any situation even if one of the spouses was guilty of infidelity,[41] desertion[42] or conversion to another religion,[43] the other spouse could not get a release from such a marriage by means of divorce. In some cases[44] the Court rejected to recognize the judgement of the Panchayat to grant tyagapatra or customary divorce without the consent of the husband. In an another case[45] the Bombay High Court appears to have gone a step further and ruled that "Courts of Law will not recognize the authority of a caste to declare a marriage void, or to give permission to a woman to remarry." In modern times there have been numerous cases where alleged customary divorces were negativated by the Courts[46] either on the ground that they have never took place of that the caste did not have such a custom.

38. *Ibid.*, 1. Born. 387.
39. *Ibid.*, 1. Born. 387.
40. J.D.M. Derrett, "Divorce by Caste Custom", 65 Bom. L.R. 161.
41. Subrraya *v.* Ramaswami, 1900, 23 Mad. 171.
42. Narain *v.* Trilok, 1907. 29. All. 4.
43. Gobradhana *v.* Jasadamoni, 1891, 18. Mad. 252.
44. Reg *v.* Sambhu Raghu, ILR 1. Bom. 352; Reg. *v.* Karsan Goja, 2 Bom 117; vide also Narayan Bharthi *v.* Laving Bharthi. ILR. 2. Bom. 140.
45. 1876 ILR. 1. Bom. 347.
46. Udaya *v.* Satya 1970, 36 CLT (Orissa) 1330; Rahunath *v.* Urmila 1973 AIR All 203; vide also Chinnaperumar *v.* Mariyayee. 1976, AIR Mad. 179.

In the case of Jina Magan *v.* Bausi Jethi[47] divorce by mutual consent between the husband and the wife among the lower castes was sanctioned by custom and it was held that there was nothing repugnant to the Hindu Law. On the basis of mutual consent of the parties as in the case of Pemabai *v.* Channoolal[48] the court recognized the divorce which was held in front of the Panchayat. In contrast a custom permitting divorce against the wish of either spouse is illegal.[49] Even a custom permitting divorce to one spouse against the wishes of the other is also void being against Public Policy and unreasonable.[50] Lastly, in the cases of Ramesh *v.* Mokheshwar[51] and Jagjit *v.* Mohinder[52] it was affirmed that unless he can prove that the Caste has a custom of divorce and that the custom was properly executed a married man subject to the custom couldn't claim to have been divorced by it. Disputes between a Hindu husband and a wife must be decided according to the principles of justice, equity and good conscience.

Denial of divorce, in ancient India was the most unfair and uncharitable attitude toward the fair sex. The belief of the ancient Hindu Clergymen in an absolute indissolubility of the marital tie, despite the textual references to the rule of Tyaga, might have been based on a misreading of the Holy Dharmasastra. For this reason, and for adopting the law to the demands of time, it could have been inevitable for the reformers of Hindu Law to open up the doors of divorce. As stated earlier that in the absence of a custom to the contrary, there can be no divorce between a Hindu husband and his wife who, by their marriage, had entered into a sacred and indissoluble union, and neither conversion nor degradation, nor loss of caste nor the violation of an agreement against polygamy, dissolve the marriage tie. Absence of divorce was the general rule and acceptance of it was only due to custom and exception.

47. 1941. ILR Bom. 535.
48. 1963. M.P.57
49. 1945 AIR Mad. 308.
50. Gurdit *v.* Angrej 1968 SC 142.
51. 1961 AIR Assam, 53.
52. 1968, 70 Punj. LR 838.

Later on the British Government in India realized the impact of divorce and introduced it in various forms. Jaffer Hussian also opines that the need for reform in Hindu Law of Marriage and Divorce was felt during the British regime.[53] Gradually with the impact of occidental notions some legislations were introduced in certain individual States.[54] But this too did not mean that the Hindu Law accepted divorce, as these instances were only exceptions. It is only in the year 1955 that divorce was introduced as a general matrimonial remedy in the Hindu Law. When the Hindu Marriage Act, 1955 was codified, the right to seek a divorce was given to all the Hindus governed by the Act. In this Act there are certain matrimonial offences which entitle the aggrieved spouse to file for a divorce available under the Act. These are cruelty, desertion, adultery, impotency or non-consummation of the marriage and bigamy, etc. Divorce Law for Hindus under Section 13 of Hindu Marriage Act, 1955 is to operate retrospectively. The only pre condition for Section 13 to be operative is that the marriage should be valid. Again the remedy of divorce can be claimed only by one of the parties to the marriage. A third party is given no authority to move for the dissolution of another person's marriage. Presently, the Hindu Marriage Act, 1955 provided grounds based on all the three theories of divorce viz., fault, consent and breakdown theories. In divorce by mutual consent, the problems relating to maintenance, custody of children etc., does not pose a serious problem since all these related matters are mutually sorted out by the parties themselves at the negotiation table. Moreover, generally divorce by mutual consent of the parties happens in the early years of marriage. Therefore most of these marriages remain childless. Recently the fault theory by which a marriage can be dissolved only if the spouse is guilty of what is called a matrimonial offence is under heavy attack. The important

53. S. Jaffer Hussian, *loc. cit.*, p. 150.
54. To illustrate: The Malabar Act in 1933; The Bomaby Divorce Act, 1947; The madras Hindu (Bigamous Prevention and Divorce) Act, 1949; The Saurashtra Hindu Divorce Act, 1950; vide also The Madhya Pradesh Divorce Act, 1955.

question for consideration now is whether a marriage should be dissolved only on proof of fault or whether it may be dissolved merely because it has broken down without the fault of either spouse. This controversy is reflected in many High Court decisions. The 71st Law Commission Report has advocated the adoption of the breakdown of marriage as a ground for dissolution of marriage, irrespective of whether any of the spouses is guilty of a fault. The Hindu Law Marriage Amendment Bill, 1981 seeks to add Section 13(c) to the Hindu Marriage Act is a compromise between these two Schools of Thought. One School advocates that divorce must follow on a breakdown of marriage. The other cautions that while breakdown may be a ground for divorce, the Court must have the discretion to consider the equalities of the case and it must have the power to refuse divorce, if equity and justice so required.

Divorce at best is a remedy for sick marriages that tend to become a menace for the children and each other. But Prof. R.Jaganmohan Rao raises a doubt that even today in the modern Hindu Society, despite the recognition of judiciary to obtain divorce from the Courts and majority of Hindus prefer to swallow the bitter pill of unhappy marriage, rather than initiating proceedings in the Courts of law to obtain divorce. This is mainly because the Hindu Society is still tradition and custom-bound and marriages are still mostly performed in the Sastric form with all social pomp and religious paraphernalia.[55]

Thus, the legislature and the judiciary have adorned the Hindu woman with matrimonial rights equal to that of man. But Hindu Society should be able to Swim along with the current of time and enable women to exercise their legal rights.

Divorce legally dissolves the marriage tie but it cannot erase the past. Because through divorce we may sever the legal link between the Spouses and yet, they might link to continue their relationship with their children, particularly if they are minor or young. This means, there must remain some connection between the spouses themselves even after divorce

55. R. Jaganmohan Rao, *loc. cit.*, pp. 170-71.

for the sake of their children. Again divorce not merely separates spouses but also separates children from their parents. As such it ends misery and brings misery. Therefore the future good divorce law's objective should be to buttress marriage and to dissolve it when dissolution is the only alternative.

It is submitted that divorce has to be granted in exceptionally hard cases where the spouses have reached a point of no return; again it should not be too easy as in the case of the Marriage Laws Amendment Act, 1976 nor too difficult as previously under the Hindu Marriage Act, 1955. Many times divorce serves as a legal insurance or safety valve in the legal sense for avoiding bad matrimonial risks by remarriage. Though divorce is doubtless a social evil, it seems a necessary evil in the light of the needs of the Society. Good morals and interests of the Society require that the precious institution of marriage should be carefully safeguarded and is severance has to be allowed only in the rarest of the rare cases. However, once the relationship between the husband and wife becomes unbearable and so strained that is incapable of any reconciliation then there can be no rationality in keeping the marriage un-dissolved. In the end, that divorce is necessary is now accepted on all hands. In modern times with the advancement of education and growth of understanding the social stigma of divorce is fast disappearing. It is no more odd to come across a divorce is fast disappearing. It is no more odd to come across a divorce even in middle-class society. It is not an antithesis of marriage. It is rather there to strengthen the institution of marriage. The present trend, therefore, is to consider divorce more favourably, calling it the mark of emancipation, specially, of the fair sex, a type of escape valve for the release of undesirable tension of Marriage.

From the above discussion it is clear that customary divorce or divorce granted by Caste elders in Village Panchayats was very popular in most of the States in India. However, this practice has come to be regarded as a sign of backwardness and so most of the people would prefer to approach Civil Courts for getting Judicial Divorce. In the State of Andhra Pradesh, customary divorce is on the decline in almost all the communities but in the District of Srikakulam amongst Koppula Velamas, Kinthala Kalingas, Thoorpu Kapus, Reddikas the practice of customary divorce is still prevalent. It is one of the essential criteria for declaring them as backward classes. In recent time even in these communities the incidence of customary divorce is not being practisSed due to urbanization and modernization.

CHAPTER

4

Statutory Divorce

4.0 DIVORCE UNDER MODERN HINDU LAW

Before we take up divorce under Statutory Law as covered by Hindu Marriage Act, 1955, it is but incumbent to deal with the historical perspective of matrimonial law and its evolution leading to the enactment of Hindu Marriage Act, 1955 and subsequent amendments thereto.

The Britishers came to India as traders. By employing all types of means both fair and file, they went on acquiring trading rights. Then by taking advantage of the rivalry between the States, they started siding one State against the other and extracting the self suited mileage which culminated in the Battle of Plassey (1757). In 1765 East India Company got the Diwani of Bengal and Orissa from Shah Alam, the Moghul Emperor. The year 1765 is the founding year of the territorial domination and sovereignty of the Company and the beginning of real territorial expansion and annexation and also the administration of Civil and Revenue cases. Various regulations were promulgated, particularly in the matter of personal laws which speak of exclusiveness.

Mr. Justice Field[1] said that the British Rule at the outset of its authority in this country recognized the rule as applicable to Hindus and Mohammedans.

(i) Regulation of 21st August, 1772 which laid down the exact scope of the application of the Hindu and Mohammedan Laws and the omission to provide for the cases which do not fall within the rule was supplied by the;

(ii) Regulation of the 5th July 1781 which directed that 'in all cases for which no specific directions are hereby given, the judges do act according to justice, equity and good conscience.

(iii) The latter part of the rule was reproduced in section 21 of the Regulation III of 1793 and re-enacted in section 15 of Regulation IV of 1793 which lay down: "that in suits regarding succession, inheritance, marriage and caste and all religious usages and institutions, the Mohammedan Law with regard to Hindus, are to be considered as the general rules by which the judges are to form their decisions."

(iv) To the two-fold rule so laid down, addition was soon after, made by Regulation VIII of 1795 which enacted that in cases in which the plaintiff shall be of a different regulated by the law of the religion of the latter excepting where Europeans or other persons, not being either Mohammedans or Hindus, shall be defendants, in which cases the law of the plaintiff is to be made the rule of the decision in all plaints and actions of a civil nature.

(v) The next important piece of legislation on the subject was Regulation VII of 1832, section 9 of which, while affirming the rules to which reference has already been made, added a new preposition as an injunction to the Courts administering justice under the East India Company.

---

1. Regulations of Bengal Code, pp. 169-71. Also see a Code Gentu Laws by NB Halhed.

So the history of Statutory Law in India, particularly in matters of marriage, divorce, and inheritance, etc., took birth and then almost it became a movement perhaps to deform the Hindu Law.

The important statutes are as under.

1. Caste Disabilities Removal Act, 1850.
2. Hindu Widows Remarriage Act, 1856.
3. Convert's Marriage Dissolution Act, 1866.
4. Hindu Disposition of Property Act, 1916.
5. Hindu Inheritance (Removal of Disabilities) Act, 1928.
6. Hindu Law of Inheritance (Removal of Disabilities) Act, 1929.
7. Hindu Gains of Learning Act, 1930.
8. Hindu Women's Right to Property Act, 1937.
9. Arya Marriage Validation Act, 1937.
10. Hindu Marriage Women's Right to Separate Residence and Maintenance Act, 1946.
11. Hindu Marriage Disabilities Removal Act, 1946.
12. Hindu Marriage Validity Act, 1949.

Coming events cast their shadow before. Another three Acts, i.e, Indian Divorce Act, 1869, Dissolution of Muslim Marriage Act, 1939 and Parsi Marriage and Divorce Act, 1936, do point out what is in store for Hindus. It is only a matter of time. So the Britishers along with their consolidated political supremacy started deforming the divine personal laws when it is said that between man and god, state has no business to be there.

However, taking cue from these statutes, Indian States at their own level showed initiative either at the instance of so-called liberals or due to extraordinary over zealousness of men in power and brought out legislations bringing in statutory divorce. In the Legislative Assembly of British India H.S. Gaur's Bill to introduce Divorce was rejected several times between 1928 and 1933.

However, Baroda, small State having a small Brahman population in proportion to its numbers of 'lower' castes governed by much less strict customs, the humane idea of allowing judicial divorce first came to fruition in the "Hindu Lagna Viccheda Nibandha" of 1931' repealed and replaced by sections 147-54 of the (Baroda) Hindu Nibandha (Hindu Act) 37 of 1937.[2]

4.1 THE HINDU NIBANDHA (HINDU ACT) 1937

Section 148 of the said Act made judicial dissolution of marriage available to those who were not covered by the customary divorce. Judicially divorce was on the following grounds of the respondent:

1. Disappearance for seven years or more;
2. Becoming a recluse;
3. Changing his/her religion by conversion;
4. Being guilty of cruelty so as to cause injury to (a) life, (b) limb, or (c) bodily or mental health so as to give rise to a reasonable apprehension of such danger;
5. Being guilty of desertion without reasonable cause for more than three years after cohabitation commenced.
6. Being addicted to intoxicants for more than three years and thus unable to fulfil marital obligations:
7. Committing adultery; or
8. Marrying a second time during the lifetime of the petitioner.

Moreover, the wife had additional grounds if her husband:

(i) Was impotent;
(ii) Habitually committed an unnatural offence, or
(iii) Refused to allow the wife to stay with him for more than three years without reasonable cause.

The husband on his part had additional grounds:

2. J.D.M. Derrett, 'The Death of a Marriage Law'.

1. If the wife was pregnant at the time of the marriage by a person other than himself, and the fact was unknown to him or, if he was a minor, to the guardian in marriage, or
2. Failed to stay with him for more than three years without reasonable cause.

Derrett observed that under the social conditions, all or most of these grounds amounted to a statutory relief for the wife against aberrations on the part of her husband.

Though this enactment, being a pioneer work attracted the attention of many and in particular allured, Mysore and being allured Mysore Act 10 of 1933 was legislated and many other States followed suit:

1. Bombay Hindu Divorce Act, 1947.
2. Madras Hindu (Bigamy & Divorce) Act, 1949.
3. Saurashtra Hindu Divorce Act, 1952.
4. Madhya Pradesh Divorce Act, 1955.

4.2 HINDU CODE BILL

But this historical perspective shall remain incomplete without the Hindu Code Bill which was passed by the Parliament, but could not get the assent of the President and lapsed. Section 30 deals with dissolution of marriage and grounds, whether it is solemnized before or after the commencement of the Code.

The grounds on which marriage can be dissolved:

1. Impotency of either party at the time of marriage and if it continues.
2. The husband keeping a concubine or the wife becoming a concubine of any other man.
3. If one of the parties changes his or her religion
4. If either party is of unsound mind and continuously under treatment for a period of five years.
5. If either party is suffering from a virulent form of leprosy.

Part II, chapter III deals with the restitution of conjugal rights and avoidance of marriage. Section 33 mentions the grounds for judicial separation and they are:

1. Desertion for at least two years.
2. If one party is so cruel that it is not safe for the other to live with him or her.
3. If the other party suffers from an incurable venereal disease and in a communicable form not contracted from the petitioner, for a period not less than one year immediately before the presentation of the petition.
4. If the other party is suffering from a virulent form of leprosy.
5. Has been habitually of unsound mind since the date of marriage.
6. Has committed adultery during the marriage.

Section 36 deals with dissolution of marriage and section 38 gives additional specific grounds for such dissolution. These provisions are somewhat similar to the provisions of the Corresponding Bombay Act XXIII of 1947. Sections 39 to 44 deal with the questions of procedure and jurisdiction in regard to the applications for judicial separation or dissolution.

This Code though could not become an Act, but still it was hailed by many celebrated authorities on Hindu Law like B.P. Gajendrabadkar.[3] He while supporting it has said that:

> "I do not for a moment suggest that the provisions for the divorce of a Hindu marriage which are included in the Hindu Code can claim to receive consistent and uniform support from the Hindu texts. I am only concerned to show that similar provisions are found in some texts."

Then he refers to Parasara, Devala and Narada and says that:

3. B.P. Gajenderagadkar, two lectures delivered by him before the Karnataka University, December 15, 1951.

"The point which I wish to make is that it is not correct to say that in permitting divorce, the Hindu Code makes an encroachment upon Hindu religion."

Shakuntala Rao Shashtri said:[4]

"It is heartening to see modern India attempting to re-establish the time honoured laws of this ancient country, which were, however, forgotten during these changing centuries.

Whatever the reaction may be, favourable or otherwise, the orthodox element in Hinduism became triumphant but the rebellious element in liberalism did not sleep over the matter. Realizing the irritated thinking of highly religious Hindus and even deep thinking patriots, towards the marriage part of the code, it was better thought to split the Hindu Code into four parts and bring them one by one. Not only that, real political manipulative game was played to test the patience of orthodoxism and thought it practicable to reform the Special Marriage Act and then using that as the thin end of the wedge, to proceed to amend the Hindu Law of marriage.[5]

So the Special Marriage Act, 43 of 1954 came into the statute book. In this garb, repealing and replacing the Act of the same name of 1872, the whole range of matrimonial remedies was introduced. So an advantage was taken of the fact that respectable Hindus may be few to get involved in it, while fashionable folk would find no difficulty in cross-communal marriages. So it encouraged the propounders of the reforms in Hinduism or to deform Hinudism and paved the way for introducing the Hindu Marriage Act, 1955."

4.3 HINDU MARRIAGE ACT, 1955

The object of the Act is to amend and codify the law relating to marriage among Hindus. Herein we are concerned

4. Shakuntla Rao Shastri, Women in the Sacred Laws.
5. Derrett, The Death of Marriage Law, p. 22.

with the provisions governing divorce for the purpose of this thesis. Section 13 deals with divorce.

1. Any marriage solemnized, whether before or after the commencement of this Act, may, on a petition presented by either the husband or the wife, be dissolved by a decree of divorce on the ground that the other party—
   (i) is living in adultery; or
   (ii) has ceased to be a Hindu by conversion to another religion; or
   (iii) has been incurably of unsound mind for a continuous period of not less than three years immediately preceding the presentation of the petition; or
   (iv) has, for a period of not less than three years preceding the presentation, been suffering from a virulent and incurable form of leprosy; or
   (v) has, for a period of not less than three years preceding the presentation, been suffering from a virulent and incurable form of Venereal disease; or
   (vi) has renounced the world by entering any religious order; or
   (vii) has not been heard of as being alive for a period of seven years or more by those persons who would naturally have heard of it, had that party been alive; or
   (viii) has not resumed co-habitation for a space of two years or upwards after the passing of a decree for judicial separation against the party; or
   (ix) has failed to comply with a decree for restitution of conjugal rights for a period of two years or upwards after the passing of the decree.
2. A wife may also present a petition for the dissolution of her marriage by decree of divorce on the ground:
   (i) in the case of any marriage solemnized before the commencement or that any other wife of the husband married before such commencement

was alive at the time of the solemnization of the marriage of the petitioner:

Provided that in either case the other wife is alive at the time of the presentation of the petition; or

(ii) that the husband has, since the solemnization of the marriage, been guilty of rape, sodomy or bestiality.

4.4 MARRIAGE LAWS (AMENDMENT) ACT 1964

In 1964, section 13(1) was modified by omitting the last two clauses, i.e, clause (viii) and (ix) and the said two omitted clauses were brought in section 13(1A) is significant as it indirectly brings in the theory of irretrievable breakdown of marriage, because two years period was in realty a period for change of mind to save the marriage.

Section 13(1A) Stipulates

Either party to a marriage, whether solemnized before or after the commencement of this Act, may also present a petition for the dissolution of marriage by a decree of divorce on the ground :

(i) has not resumed cohabitation for a space of two years or upwards after the passing of a decree for judicial separation against the party; or

(ii) has failed to comply with a decree for restitution of conjugal rights for a period of two years or upwards after the passing of the decree.

But this amendment did raise a judicial controversy as to mere expiry of the specified period of the decree of judicial separation or restitution of conjugal rights is sufficient to grant divorce or it is only a prerequisite for creation of a ground for applying for divorce and the divorce is to be granted or not depends upon the merits of a case and in such cases section 23(1)(a) has been invoked which reads as follows:

In any proceeding under this Act, whether defended or not, if the court is satisfied that—

(a) any of the grounds for granting relief exists and the petitioner [except in cases where the relief is sought by him on the ground specified in sub-clause (a), sub-clause (b),or sub-clause (c) of clause (ii) of section 5 is not in any way taking advantage of his or her own wrong or disability for the purpose of such relief, and—

When section 13(1A) was introduced by the Amendment Act of 1964, Section 23 was already there. So the question arises as to whether the Legislature knew fully well the implications of section 23 in regard to section 13 (1A) and kept section 23 untouched the Legislature failed to appreciate the implications of section 23 with regard to section13 (1A).

However, this point was repeatedly agitated before the higher Courts and the Apex Court.

In Laxmibai Laxmi Chand Shah *v.* Laxmichand Ravaji Shah,[6] the Court held that section 13(1a) is subject to section 23(1)(a) of the Act. It is open to the Court to consider whether provisions mentioned in sub-section (1) of section 23 are satisfied but the Court is under an obligation to consider that question. Section 23 is in the nature of an overriding provision.

In Ram Kali *v.* Gopal Khanna C.J[7] (as he then was) observed in different way that it would not be practical and realistic, indeed it would be unreasonable and inhuman to compel the parties to keep up the façade of marriage even though the rift between them is complete amd there are no prospects of their ever living together as husband and wife.

In Bimla Devi *v.* Singh Raj[8] the court held that the only reasonable way of construing the provision and giving effect to legislative intent is to say that section 23(1)(a) applies to cases

6. AIR 1968 Bom. 332.
7. AIR 1968 Bom. 332.
8. AIR 1977 P & H 167.

based on the concept of wrong or disability and not to section 13(1A) which is not based on that concept.

The supreme Court in Dharmendra *v.* Usha,[9] adapted a middle course that in order to be a wrong within the meaning of section 23(1)(a) the conduct alleged has to be something more than a mere disinclination to agree to an offer of Union, it must be misconduct serious enough to justify denial of relief to which the husband or wife is otherwise entitled. So the Supreme Court kept the question open and made it to depend upon the facts and circumstances of the case.

In Anil Jayanti Vyas *v.* Sudhaben,[10] the Court took the stand that mere non-compliance per se would not amount to taking advantage of his own wrong.

In N. Varalaxmi *v.* N.V. Hanumantha Rao[11]where the Court held that the fact that the wife's attempts at resumption of co-habitation has been thwarted by the husband would be immaterial. Volition of both parties is needed.

In Soundarammal *v.* Sundara Mahalinga Nadar,[12] the High Court referring to various rulings observed that in order to be a wrong within the meaning of section 23(1)(a), the conduct alleged has to be something more than a mere disinclination to agree to an offer of re-union. However, held that law can never give a helping hand to a wrongdoer.

Andhra Pradesh High Court in Akkama *v.* Jagannadham[13] has said that a marriage which has irretrievably broken down should not be allowed to continue and that a marriage buried in fact should also be buried in law.

The Supreme Court in Saroj Rani *v.* Sudershan[14] again took a stand that when the marriage has broken down and the parties can no longer live together as husband and wife, if such is the case, it is better to close the chapter.

The above-cited cases point out two things:

---

9. AIR 1977 SC 2218.
10. AIR 1978 Guj. 74.
11. AIR 1978 AP 6.
12. AIR 1980 Mad. 294.
13. AIR 1981 AP 269.
14. AIR 1984 SC 1562.

(i) It is of no use keeping the empty shell of marriage intact which in fact has completely dried up of its juice.

(ii) However, the wrongdoer should not be allowed to take advantage of wrongdoing.

In R. *v.* Jacrson[15] it is said that conjugal rights cannot be enforced by the act of either party and a husband cannot seize and detain his wife by force.

4.5 MARRIAGE LAWS (AMENDMENT) ACT, 1976

The Marriage Laws (Amendment) Act, 1976, provisions concerning divorce and as a result of which the provisions concerning divorce and other allied matters stand as below:

4.5.1 Section 13

(1) Any marriage solemnized, whether before or after. the commencement of this Act, may, on a petition presented by either the husband or the wife, be dissolved by a decree of divorce on the ground that the other party....[16]

- (i) has, after the solemnization of the marriage, had voluntary sexual intercourse with any person other than his or her spouse; or
- (ia) has, after the solemnization of marriage treated the petitioner with cruelty; or
- (ib) has deserted the petitioner for a continuous period of not less than two years immediately preceding the presentation of the petition; or
- (ii) [17]has been incurably of unsound mind, or has been suffering continuously or intermittently from mental disorder of such a kind and to such an extent that the petitioner cannot reasonably be expected to live with the respondent.

---

15. [1891] IQB 671.
16. Substituted by Act 68 of 1976, Section 7, for the former clause.
17. Substituted by Act 68 of 1976.

Explanation: In this clause:

(a) the expression 'mental disorder' means mental illness, arrested or incomplete development of mind, psychopathic disorder or any other disorder or disability of mind and includes schizophrenia;

(b) the expression 'psychopathic disorder' means a persistent disorder or disability of mind (whether or not including sub-normality of intelligence) which results in abnormally aggressive or seriously irresponsible conduct on the part of the other party, and whether or not it requires or is susceptible to medical treatment; or

(iv) [18]has been suffering from a virulent and incurable form of leprosy; or

(v) [19]has been suffering from venereal disease in a communicable form; or

(vi) has renounced the world by entering any religious order; or

(vii) [20]has not been heard of as being alive for a period of seven years or more by those persons who would naturally have heard of it, had that party been alive.

[21]Explanation:

In this sub-section, the expression 'desertion' means the desertion of the petitioner by the other party to the marriage without reasonable cause and without the consent of such party and includes the wilful neglect of the petitioner by the other party to the marriage and its grammatical variations and cognate expressions shall be construed accordingly.

18. Substituted by Act 68 of 1976.
19. *Ibid.*, certain words omitted by Sec. 7.
20. *Ibid.*, word 'or' is omitted.
21. Inserted by Sec. 7 of Act 68 of 1976.

(1A) [22]Either party to a marriage, whether solemnized before or after the commencement of this Act, may also present a petition for the dissolution of the marriage by a decree of divorce on the ground.

(i) [23]that there has been no resumption of co-habitation between the parties to the marriage for a period of one year or upwards after the passing of a decree for judicial separation in a proceeding to which they were parties; or

(ii) [24]that there has been no restitution of conjugal rights between the parties to the marriage for a period of one year or upwards after the passing of a decree for restitution of conjugal rights in a proceeding to which they were parties

(2) A wife may also present a petition for the dissolution of her marriage by a decree of divorce on the ground—

(i) in the case of any marriage solemnized before the commencement of this Act, that the husband had married again before such commencement or that any other wife of the husband married before such commencement was alive at the time of the solemnization of the marriage of the petitioner:

Provided that in either case the other wife is alive at the time of the presentation of the petition; or

(ii) [25]that the husband has, since the solemnization of the marriage, been guilty of rape, sodomy or bestiality; or

---

22. Inserted by Act 44 of 1964, Sec. 2.
23. Substituted by Act 68 of 1976, Sec. 7 for 'two years'.
24. Substituted by Act 68 of 1976, Sec. 7 for 'two years'.
25. Substituted by Act 68 of 1976, 'or' is added after bestiality.

(iii) [26]that in a suit under section 18 of Adoptions and Maintenance Act, 1956 (978 of 1956) or in a proceeding under section 125 of the Code of Criminal Procedure, 1973 (2 of 1974) or under the corresponding section 488 of the Code of Criminal Procedure, 1898 (95 of 2898), a decree or order, as the case may be, has been passed against the husband awarding maintenance to the wife notwithstanding that she was living apart and that since passing of such decree or order, cohabitation between the parties has not been resumed for one year or upwards; or

(iv) that her marriage (whether consummated or not) was solemnized before she attained the age of fifteen years and she has repudiated the marriage after attaining that age but before attaining the age of eighteen years.

Explanation:

This clause applies whether the marriage was solemnized before or after the commencement of the Marriage Laws (Amendment) Act, 1976 (68 of 1976).

4.5.2 Section 13A[27]

Alternate relief in divorce proceedings:

In any proceeding under this Act, a petition for dissolution of marriage by a decree of divorce, except in so far as the petition is founded on the grounds mentioned in clauses (ii), (vi) and (vii) of sub-section (1) of section 13,the court may, if it considers it just so to do having regard to the circumstances of the case, pass instead a decree for judicial separation.

4.5.3 Section 13B

Divorce by mutual consent:

26. Inserted by Act 68 of 1976.
27. Inserted by Act 68 of 1976.

(1) Subject to the provisions of this Act a petition for dissolution of marriage by a decree of divorce may be presented to the district Court by both the parties to a marriage together, whether such marriage was solemnized before or after the commencement of the Marriage Laws (Amendment) Act, 1976, on the ground that they had been living separately for a period of one year or more, that they have not been able to live together and that they have mutually agreed that the marriage should be dissolved.

(2) On the motion of both parties made not earlier than six months after the date of presentation of the petition referred to in sub-section (1) and not later than eighteen months after the said date, if the petition is not withdrawn in the meantime, the Court shall, on being satisfied, after hearing the parties and after making such enquiry as it thinks fit, that a marriage has been solemnized and that the averments in the petition are true, pass a decree of divorce declaring the marriage to be dissolved with effect from the date of the decree.

4.5.4 Section 14

By section 9 of Marriage Laws (Amendment) Act, 1976 changes were brought in section 14 of Hindu Marriage Act, 1955 by which the period of three years has been reduced to one year. So wherever in the section 'three years' was mentioned, it was substituted by 'one year', but under the provision, the Court is conferred a discretionary power to entertain the petition before one year if it finds on the allegations in the affidavit in support of the petition that prima facie there is exceptional hardship to the petitioner or exceptional depravity on the part of the respondent. This section 14 has a special bearing on the petition for divorce.

We have taken the historical perspective of divorce under Statutory Law. Hindu Marriage Laws (Amendment) Act, 1976 is a step forward to make the divorce easy and quick, though the social awakening has not reached that stage warranting such changes. It is perhaps a wrong notion that Western civilisation is superior to Indian civilisation and that we have to take inspiration from Western ideas where woman is considered a mere playmate. Without making much comment at this stage, it is worthwhile stating that we feel proud in forgetting our own exalted culture and civilization and to imitate that culture which it takes root in our country, we shall definitely be heading for creation of millions of broken houses, deserted wives and neglected children. Lord Evershed M.R.[28] Said,

> If men and women of a hundred years ago had been told that in the enlightened days of their great grandchildren, 30,000 marriages would be dissolved by the civil Courts in each year in the majority of cases upon the petition of the wife-they would, I do not doubt, have been greatly shocked. And if they have asked the natural question what becomes of the tens of thousands of innocent children of those marriages, they would have raised one of the most important and most perplexing problems that is now presented to us.

Greavson: himself observes as follows:

> For the present we may, perhaps, rejoice in the opportunities for easier divorce as one of the outstanding features of the past century. But we cannot forget that 'if the divorce as is no longer a disgrace, it remains a tragedy. Ten per cent is a high mortality rate for marriage. The victory of emancipation has its shadow of Greek tragedy. For emancipation, in so far as it connotes easy divorce, carries in its train disintegration of family as a unit of the society and so ultimate by the society itself.[29]

Since the concept of divorce in Hindu Law is a pure act of imitation, necessarily we have to glance through the global perspective firstly, and then to see as to how we have destroyed our own ethics and ethos of which we were always

---

28. In his foreword to RR Greavson and FR Grand's A Century of Family Law.
29. R.R. Greavson, A Century of Family Law, 1957, p. 412. It refers to Matrimonial Causes Act 1857 (English Law).

proud of and how we have defiled our own dharma which was the foundation of Hindu society. In support of this Prof. Derrett in his book on Death of Marriage Law remarked that the Hindu Marriage Act, and its Amendment Act, 1976 in particular destroyed Hindu Law of Marriage (the Dharmic Law).

4.6 ENGLISH LAW OF DIVORCE

The Anglo-Sexon Law before the Norman Conquest allowed divorce by mutual consent or on the ground of the wife's infidelity and recognized a right to remarry.[30]

Then came the Matrimonial Causes, Act, 1857 which made the first inroad in the ecclesiastical divorce law. A Royal Commission was appointed in 1850 to look into the question of reforms in the matrimonial law. The Commission recommended cruelty and desertion in addition to adultery as ground upon which divorce could be granted.

However, the purpose of the Act appears simply to take away the jurisdiction of the Ecclesiastical Courts over matrimonial matters and gave powers to the Secular Courts to dissolve the marriage. The ground for divorce was that the husband could obtain divorce on the ground of adultery coupled with incest, bigamy, cruelty or alternatively rape or an unnatural offence.[31] This distinction was already there prior to this Act and the Matrimonial Causes Act, 1857 retained this distinction.

This distinction was, however, removed by the Matrimonial Causes Act, 1923 by which this strange distinction between the inequity. This Act brought the husband and wife on an equal footing by permitting the latter to petition on the grounds of adultery alone.[32]

Then came the A.P. Herbert's Matrimonial Causes Act, 1937 by which further grounds were added for seeking divorce.

30. See 2 Holdsworth, A History of English Law 90 (4th edn. 1936), Pollock and Maitland, The History of English Law (Second edn. 1959) Kitchin, A History of Divorce, 171 (1912), Worsley Boden.
31. See Matrimonial Causes Act 1857, Sec. 27.
32. N.C. Gregor, Divorce in England, pp. 20-1 (Comments on the Dist[illegible], L.J. Blom—Cooper, A Century of Divorce (1958) 25.

Under the Act[33] Divorce or judicial separation could be obtained for cruelty or desertion without cause for three years or incurable insanity.

From that time onward various Royal Commissions were appointed to enquire into the law of matrimonial guilt and how insanity was added is not understood as insanity is not based on the principle of matrimonial guilt but was added as a ground for divorce. So the divorce law needed reforms. Thus, after 1939 the Matrimonial Causes (War Marriages) Act, 1944 gave the Court temporary jurisdiction to entertain petitions for divorce or nullity where the husband was, at the time of the marriage domiciled outside the United Kingdom and the wife was immediately before the marriage domiciled in England and the parties did not reside together in the country in which the husband was then domiciled. Then came the Law Reform (miscellaneous Provisions) Act, 1949 by which an extensive permanent enlargement of jurisdiction was effected. However, this Act was repealed and replaced by the Matrimonial Causes Act, 1950. It can be said that by a touch here and a twist there the law was altered and consolidated in the Matrimonial Causes Act, 1950. The law as further amended, repealed and finally consolidated in the Matrimonial Causes Act, 1965.

4.6.1 Matrimonial Causes Act, 1965

Matrimonial Causes Act, 1965 contained 46 sections. Schedule-I and Schedule II section 1dealt with grounds of divorce.

(1) Subject to the next following section, a petition for divorce may be presented to the High court (hereinafter in this Act referred to as 'the Court'):

(a) by the husband or the wife on the ground that the respondent—

(i) has since the celebration of the marriage committed adultery; or

(ii) has deserted the petitioner without cause for a period of at least three years immediately preceding the presentation of the petition; or

---

33. Matrimonial Causes Act, 1937, Sections 2 & 3.

(iii) has since the celebration of the marriage treated the petitioner with cruelty; or

(iv) is incurably of unsound mind and has been continuously under care and treatment for a period of at least five years immediately preceding the presentation of the petition.

(b) by the wife on the ground that her husband has since the celebration of the marriage been guilty of rape, sodomy or bestiality.

(2) It deals with clause (1)(a) (ii) of the Act and provides details concerning desertion;

(3) It deals with clause (1)(a)(iv) of the section and gives required details to satisfy the ground of insanity.

(4) It also deals with clause (1)(a)(iv), further to clause (3) above.

Matrimonial causes Act, 1965 is in 4 parts, i.e.,

Part I deals with Divorce, Nullity and other Matrimonial suits.
Part II deals with the Ancillary Relief.
Part III deals with Protection of Children.
Part IV deals with Miscellaneous and General Miscellaneous provisions.

Thus, this Act is comprehensive in nature. It is to be noted that except insanity, the law of divorce is based on the principle of matrimonial misconduct or popularly known as fault theory. Then there arose a general realization that the ground of matrimonial misconduct is not enough. There can be other causes for the spouses to part asunder due to emotional or psychological behaviour. Thus, it was felt to probe further into the matter and to this effect a group was appointed by the Archbishop of Canterbury in January 1964 and the report of the group was published in July 1966.[34] In this report it was observed:

34. Putting as under: A Divorce Law for Contemporary Society—The Report of a Group appointed by the Archibishop of Canterbury.

> Unsatisfactory as the law based on the matrimonial offence has proved in practice to be, it has yet to be shown that the substitution of some other basis would improve the situation. It is after all conceivable that the only alternative to the frying pan might turn out to be the fire in which case it would be safer to stick to the frying pan.[35]

So the group stuck to the frying pan as it was safer in their own estimation and recommended that breakdown of marriage should be the sole ground for divorce as it was by far the better alternative.

Meanwhile, the Law Commission which was also seized of the matter relating to matrimonial causes, also gave its report in November, 1966. Wherein the Law Commission endorsed the views of the Archbishop's Group that the law based on the concept of fault was unsatisfactory.

The Law Commission observed:

> It does not achieve the maximum possible fairness to all concerned, for a spouse may be branded as guilty in law though not the more blameworthy in fact. The insistence on guilt and innocence tends to embitter relationships, with particularly damaging results to the children, rather than to promote future harmony. Its principles are widely regarded as hypocritical.[36]

The Law Commission did not subscribe to the concept of 'breakdown with inquest' as propounded by the Archbishop's Group but instead suggested that a good divorce law should be able to achieve two objectives.[37]

1. To buttress, rather than to undermine, the stability of marriage; and
2. when regrettably, a marriage has irretrievably broken down, to enable the empty shell to be destroyed with

35. Para 46 of p. 33 of the Report (1966).
36. The Law Commission, Reform of the grounds of divorce; the field of choice para 28 at p. 16 (1966).
37. *Ibid.*, Para 15 at p. 10.

the maximum fairness and the minimum bitterness, distress and humiliation.

4.6.2 The Divorce Reforms Act, 1969

On the suggestion of the Law Commission the Divorce Reform Act was passed which got the Royal assent in October, 1969 and came into effect on January 1, 1971, wherein a single ground based on specific matrimonial offences, namely the irretrievable breakdown of marriage. Accordingly, the whole of section 1 of the Matrimonial Causes Act, 1965, setting out the grounds of divorce is replaced by para 1 of the schedule of the 1969 Act.

Such breakdown had to be established by a petitioner satisfying the Court of one or more of the following facts.[38]

Section 2 (1)

(a) That the respondent has committed adultery and the petitioner finds it intolerable to live with the respondent.

(b) That the respondent has behaved in such a way that the petitioner cannot reasonably be expected to live with the respondent.

(c) That the respondent has deserted the petitioner for a continuous period of at least two years immediately preceding the presentation of the petition.

(d) That the parties to the marriage have lived apart for a continuous period of at least two years immediately preceding the presentation of the petition and the respondent consents to a divorce being granted.

(e) The parties to the marriage have lived apart for a continuous period of at least five years immediately preceding the presentation of petition.

This substitution of a single ground for divorce-'irretrievable breakdown' of marriage on the fact that it marks a notable change in the English Law of divorce, without,

38. Divorce Reforms Act, 1969, Sec. 2 (i).

however, affecting the jurisdiction of the Court. Judges and practitioners will doubtless have to consider how far these facts which, during the Parliamentary Debates were styled 'guidelines', will come into play.[39]

These guidelines apart, the basic and the main question is still to be answered. 'Is the breakdown of marriage irretrievable'? So necessarily the Court had to keep in mind two things which are inherently present in the Act.

1. Balance of probabilities having regard to the evidence.
2. Possibility of reconciliation.

The various provisions of the Act though appear simple apparently but latently appear to be very difficult to comply with. This is perhaps, which appears manifest, candid, clear and comprehensive, the attempt to make divorce difficult and positively not easy, especially while pleading the matrimonial misconduct, as along with matrimonial misconduct, it is also to be shown as to how it is leading to the irretrievable breakdown of marriage.

For an example, in section 2(1)(a), two facts are to be proved:

1. The respondent has committed adultery.
2. It is intolerable to live with the respondent.

Not only that, it is a complex situation whether these two facts are independent in nature or linked with each other. In Goodrich *v.* Goodrich[40] it was held that the phrase 'has committed adultery and the phrase 'and the petitioner finds it intolerable to live with the respondent', were independent of each other. Between the two phrases the word 'and' is used. But in Roper *v.* Roper, Faulks J.,[41] took the stand that—

> I think common sense tells you that where the finding that has got to be made is that the respondent has committed

39. Latey on Divorce (15th edn.).
40. [1971] 2 All ER 1340.
41. (1971) 3 All ER 668.

adultery and the petitioner finds it intolerable to live with the respondent. It means, 'and in consequence' of the adultery the petitioner finds it intolerable to live with the respondent.

Text writers such as Raydon,[42] Tolstoy,[43] Bromley,[44] and Passingham,[45] subscribe to the view taken in Goodrich's case whereas Barton,[46] has advocated that there must be some link between adultery and intolerability. Rosenbaum,[47] says that to construe that there need be no link between adultery and intolerability, is to betray the intention of the drafter of the divorce Reform Act.

The legislative intention as manifest is:

1. That section 2(1)(a) and 2(1)(b) which speak of matrimonial misconduct, have been relegated to a very low position.
2. That section 2(1)(c) which is also a matrimonial misconduct has been qualified with the phrase 'continuous period of two years'. So it has to be read with section 3(5) of the Act. So here the case is of actual desertion (see para 37 at 16 in Passingham's the Divorce Reforms Act, 1969).
3. Section 2(1)(d) speaks of mutual consent but 'living apart' for a continuous period of two years is a prerequisite. 'Living apart' is again a complex phrase as to whether it means physical separation or not.[48] Whether intention 'never to return' is to be reckoned

42. Rayden on Divorce 205 [1972].
43. Tolstoy on divorce 54 (7th edn. 1971).
44. Bromley, Family Law 209 (4th edn., 1971).
45. Passingham, The Divorce Reform Act, 1969, 86 LQR 348 (1970).
46. Barton, Questions on the Divorce Reforms Act 1969, 86 LQR 348 (1970).
47. Rosenbaum, Divorce Reforms in England. The decline of the Matrimonial offence, 12 J Fam L 365 at 370 (1972-73).
48. See Santos *v.* Santos (1972) 2 All ER 246. Where it is said that "living apart" did not mean physical separatation.

or not. Or whether two years period is a mere formality.

4. Section 2(1)(e) poses again a complex situation that whether a 'continuous period of five years' is a blameless period or blemished period on the part of the petitioner because for centuries the hallmark of English Law of divorce had been that no one should be allowed to take advantage of his own wrong.
5. Then the ground of divorce has to be seen in the light of section 4 and section 5 of the Act which are the defences available. In Banik *v.* Banik,[49] though the case fell under section 2(1)(e), but the plea of the wife that she will not only have financial hardship and also being a Hindu she will be regarded as outcast and shall carry a social stigma. The Court agreed readily and set aside the decree nisi granted by the lower Court.

Even in Richards *v.* Richards[50] she filed a petition under section 2(1)(b) that her husband had become mentally ill, suffered from moodiness, taciturnity and insomnia and had behaved in such a way as to make her life intolerable. All was proved in evidence but still the Court did not grant decree of divorce as she failed to establish that thehusband behaved in such a way that she could not reasonably be expected to live with him. If we analytically look to the complex sub-grounds along with safeguards provided, this Act had not made divorce easy but rather difficult.

If we go through the various judicial decisions, we find two things:

1. Firstly, this Act is not to make divorce easy but it is an indirect vigorous attempt to save marriage. It has shown utmost respect for the canonical concept of marriage that it is indissoluble and it must be protected.
2. However, if the marriage is subjected to such strains

49. [1973] All ER 45.
50. [1972] 3 All ER 695.

> of misconduct or otherwise unbearable stresses, it is better to let it dissolve so that the stigma of bitterness and the element of undesirability is buried once for all. It is again a negative approach to save the institution of marriage. So the whole stress is on the marriage and not on divorce.

In Ash *v.* Ash,[51] Bagnall J., quoting the Law Commission's Reform of the grounds of divorce in section 2(1)(b) said:

> The objects of the 1969 legislation . . . are not, in my view simply to make divorce easier but . . . to buttress, rather than to undermine, the stability of marriage and when regrettably, a marriage has irretrievably broken down, to enable the empty shell to be destroyed with the maximum fairness, and the minimum bitterness, distress and humiliation.

In Santos *v.* Santos[52] it is said that it has sometimes been said that the object of the Act of 1969 is to make divorce easy, but that hardly seems correct when in some instances it has made it more difficult. . . . It is more appropriate to say that whilst in practice additional grounds for divorce are provided by the Act of 1969, yet it is designed to assist maintenance of marriages other than those reduced to a mere shell. Whilst sympathizing . . . with those Judges who have to take the undefended list, it is still the case that the Legislature intended the procedure before them to involve Judicial Care as opposed to rubber-stamping.

So in view of bars, defences, reconciliation, proof of breakdown, financial and other hardships, the Legislative intention is manifestly clear to make divorce 'a rare of rarest' concept and as such, such provisions are incorporated in the Act.

---

51. [1972] Fam 135 at 140.
52. [1972] 2 WLR 889, 901 CA, See also Huxford *v.* Huxford (1972) 1 WLR 210, 213, 214, Hollings J. giving leave to a wife to file an answer alleging admitted adultery.

4.6.3 Matrimonial Causes Act, 1973

This being so, the said Act has been replaced by the Matrimonial Causes Act, 1973 which is simply a replica of the Divorce Reforms Act, 1969 and stress on the stability of marriage is paramount. The possibility of reconciliation should be explored as more conducive to the happiness of spouses and their children than the forensic prosecution of matrimonial litigation and regarding 'wrong', in order to construe it as such, regard must be had to the circumstances of those involved, including children and to the balance which must be maintained between upholding the sanctity of marriage and the desirability of ending marriages which have become empty shells.[53]

4.7 PROPOSITIONS GIVEN BY HINDU LAW

Hindu Law[53a] has given three propositions regarding the concept of marriage which involves three distinct aspects.

1. Observance of certain formalities by the parties
2. Emergence of the status between them.
3. Possibility of the termination of that status under stated circumstances.

First of all we have to take the third aspect which comprehends the causes leading to the termination of status (generally known as dissolution of marriage. To dwell on the causes given under sections 13, 13(1A) and 13B, let us first take the origin of statutory law in India.

4.8 INDIAN DIVORCE ACT, 1869

The Indian divorce Act, 1869[54] was the first Act regarding divorce in India which applied only to cases where both of the

---

53. Talbot *v.* Talbot, The Times, Oct. 19, 1971, Dunn J. has said, see also Mathias *v.* Mathias, The Time, May 3, 1972 CA.

53a. Prof. B.N. Sampat, Hindu Marriage as a Samskara, A resolvable conundrum, Vol. 33, JILI, p. 319.

54. Under section 10, a husband can get his marriage dissolved if he can prove that his wife has, since the solemnization of the marriage, been guilty of adultery. At the same time a wife who wants to get

spouses converted into Christianity and one of them applied for divorce after it. However, this Act was a true replica of Matrimonial Causes Act, 1857.

4.9 PARSI MARRIAGE AND DIVORCE ACT, 1936

Parsi Marriage and Divorce Act, 1936 section 32 enumerated ten grounds for seeking divorce such as wilful refusal to consummate marriage, unsoundness of mind at the time of marriage, pregnancy by some other person at the time of marriage, adultery-fornication-bigamy-rape or unnatural offence, caused grievous hurt, has infected venereal disease or compelled to prostitution by the plaintiff, imprisonment for seven years or more for an offence under the Indian Penal Code, desertion for three years, sexual intercourse absent after an order was passed for judicial separation-maintenance, non-compliance for a period of one year of an order for restitution of conjugal rights, apostasy or conversion.

Other enactments concerning divorce which were enacted at State level.

1. Baroda Hindu Marriage Act, 1937.[55]

---

her marriage dissolved should necessarily prove that her husband has exchanged his profession of some other religion and gone through a form of marriage with another woman or has been guilty of incestuous adultery, or bigamy with adultery, or of marriage with another woman with adultery or rape, sodomy or bestiality, or of adultery coupled with such cruelty as without adultery would have entitled her to divorce a mensa et thoro or of adultery coupled with desertion, without reasonable excuse for two years or upwards.

55. Grounds of divorce were: Disappearance for seven years, becoming a recluse, conversion to another religion, cruelty, or desertion for more than three years after commencement of cohabitation, addiction to the intoxicants for more than three years so as not to fulfill marital obligations, matrimonial adultery, bigamy. A wife had the following additional grounds: Impotence from time of marriage to suit, habitually committing an unnatural offence, not allowing the wife to stay with him for more than three years. The husband had the following separate grounds: Wife pregnant by another man at the time of marriage, wife not staying with him for at least three years.

2. Bombay Prevention of Hindu Bigamous Marriage Act, 1946.
3. Bombay Hindu Divorce Act, 1947.[56]
4. The Madras Hindu Bigamy Prevention and Divorce Act, 1949.[57]
5. The Saurashtra Prevention of Bigamous Marriage Act, 1950.
6. The Saurashtra Hindu Divorce Act, 1952.[58]
7. Hindu Code Bill, 1954 (could not be enacted).[59]

---

56. The grounds for divorce were: Impotency at the time of marriage continues till suit, lunacy of seven years, leprosy not contacted from the other party for seven years, continuous desertion for four years, even then if four years of desertion were completed before the said ground; and unknown for seven years, keeping or bringing a concubine, husband married again when wife is still alive. No spouse could ask for divorce however, if the couple had lived in a married life for at least 20 years after attaining majority except on the grounds of desertion or that the husband keeps a concubine, or that the wife was a prostitute or concubine of another person and also the grounds mentioned in section 4 of this Act.
57. The grounds were more comprehensive and available to the spouse over 18 years: keeping a concubine, being a concubine or prostitute, desertion for three years, cruelty in which plaintiff unsafe to live, incurable lunacy, virulent and incurable leprosy and venereal disease from five years, impotency till petition, ceasing to be a Hindu. Wife could also file a petition on the ground that her husband married again, in lifetime of first wife.
58. In the State of Saurashtra two statutes were passed which corresponded to the pair of Bombay Acts, i.e. Saurashtra Act 5 of 1950 and Saurashtra Act 30 of 1952. But that was a result of impatience with what was fancied to be interminable foot-dragging over the Hindu Code Bill.
59. Part II, Chapter II, Section 30 dealt with dissolution of marriage whether it is solemnized before or after the commencement of the Code:
    1. Impotency of either party at the time of marriage and if it continues.
    2. The husband keeping a concubine or the wife becoming a concubine of any other man.
    3. If one of the parties changes his or her religion.
    4. If either party is of unsound mind and continuously under treatment for a period of five years.
    5. If either party is suffering from a virulent form of lunacy.

4.10 DIVORCE PROVISIONS UNDER HINDU MARRIAGE ACT, 1955

Then in 1954 was enacted the Special Marriage Act, 1954[60] and amendments thereto were made by Act 32 of 1963 and sections 27 and 28 of amending Act 68 of 1976 deal with divorce.

Then finally the Hindu Marriage Act, 1955 was enacted wherein section 13 statutorily recognised divorce. Section 13 stipulates various grounds on which the spouses can seek divorce. Section 13B is a further provision by which divorce by mutual consent can be sought.

Under Hindu Law no divorce presents without any one of the five types of the following grounds:

1. Fault grounds.
2. Non-fault grounds.
3. Grounds only applicable to wife.
4. Breakdown of marriage.
5. Divorce by mutual consent.

Some of the other factors were brought as ground for judicial separation:

1. Desertion for at least two years.
2. If one party is so cruel that it is not safe for the other to live with him or her.
3. In case of incurable venereal disease.
4. If one party suffers from leprosy.
5. If one has been habitually of unsound mind since the date of marriage.
6. If one is not faithful.

60. Section 27 speaks of grounds for divorce such as adultery, desertion for a continuous period of not less than two years immediately preceding the presentation of the petition, undergoing imprisonment for seven years or more under an offence as defined in IPC, cruelty, incurable unsound mind, mental disorder. A wife has been given additional grounds for seeking divorce such as, husband guilty of rape, sodomy or bestiality, non-resumption of cohabitation for one year or upwards after the award of decree under section 18 of the Hindu Adoption and Maintenance Act or section 488 of CrPC 1898 non-resumption of cohabitation as between the parties for one year or upwards after the decree of restitution of conjugal rights or judicial separation.

Section 13(1) stipulates eight grounds for seeking divorce, i.e., adultery, desertion cruelty, insanity, leprosy, venereal disease, conversion or renunciation. The first three grounds, i.,e., adultery, desertion and cruelty are the faults or wrongs, attributable to the spouse whosoever he or she is, whereas the other five grounds are not the deliberate or intentional wrongs of the spouse concerned but merely considered as wrongs for the spouse of seeking divorce.

4.10.1 Adultery

Although an English Judge, Karminski, J. observed that "nobody has yet attempted to define adultery and we do not propose to rush in where wiser men have not,[60a] adultery has a fairly established meaning in matrimonial law. In absence of any special definition in the Act, it means 'consensual sexual intercourse between a married person and a person (whether married or unmarried) of the opposite sex, not being the other spouse, during the subsistence of the marriage'.[61] In short, the spouse who engages in extra-marital intercourse is guilty of adultery.

In early English law, divorce was regarded as a mode of punishing the guilty spouse who had rendered himself or herself unworthy of consortium.

The guilt theory further lays down that the party seeking divorce must be an innocent party. In other words, on the one hand, one of the spouses must have committed one or the other matrimonial offence, and on the other, the spouse seeking divorce must be innocent, i.e., in no way party to, or responsible for, the offence of the guilty party.

But sexual intercourse before the marriage is not adultery.[61a] Still, where the adultery was being committed before the marriage by the wife and it had also been

---

60a. Sapsford *v.* Sapsford, (1954) p. 394.

61. Rayden on Divorce 11th edn., p. 178 "Consensual" is used in this context by Bucknill LJ. In Redpath *v.* Radpath and Milligan [1950] 1 All ER 600 for married person. See Charlton *v.* Charlton [1952] 1 All ER 611, 612.

61a. Sudesh Kumari *v.* Chander Parkash, 1978 HLR 670 (Del).

committed, even if once, after the marriage, the marriage, the mischief cl. (i) of s. 13(1) will be attracted.[61b]

In Mallika *v.* Rajendran,[61c] it was established that husband was guilty of adultery and desèrtion; the wife was granted a decree of divorce.[61d] While under the Act husband can sue for divorce on the ground of wife's adultery simpliciter, the wife has to prove that husband is guilty of more than adultery, that to say, adultery should be incest, or coupled with cruelty, or coupled with desertion without reasonable cause for two years or more coupled with bigamy, etc. In Ammim *v.* Union of India[61e] this provision was held to be discriminatory. A special Bench of the Kerala High Court said that this provision was violative of Articles 14 and 21.

Before the coming into force of the Marriage Laws (Amendment) Act, 1976 'living in adultery' was a ground of divorce. On the other hand, a petitioner could obtain a decree of judicial separation, if he could show that his spouse, after the solemnisation of marriage, had sexual intercourse with any person other than his spouse. Now adultery simipliciter has been made ground of divorce as well as of judicial separation.

The earlier expression 'living in adultery' implies a more or less continuous course of adulterous conduct continuing right up to the filing of the petition. These conditions proved too severe for numerous injured spouses[62] and thus the

---

61b. Charanjit Singh *v.* Sandeep Kaur, 1979 HLR 99 (P&H).

61c. Section 10.

61d. Mallika *v.* Rajendran, AIR 1995 Mad 100.

61e. AIR 1995 Ker 252.

62. (i) Mahalingam Pillai *v.* Amsavalli (1956) MLJ 289 wherein the Court distinguished between 'concubine' and 'living in adultery'.
    (ii) Rajani Prabhakar Lokur *v.* Prabhakar Ragvendra Lokur AIR 1958 Bom 264 wherein the Court defined 'living in adultery' means a continuous course of adulterous conduct of life as distinguished from one to two lapses from virtue.
    (iii) Bhagwan Singh *v.* Amar Kaur AIR 1962 Pb 144 a single act of adultery committed before filing an application under section 13 is not sufficient.
    (iv) Chanda *v.* Mst. Nandu AIR 1965 MP 268: 'living in adultery', has in matrimonial cases, a different and wider meaning than in

amendment by which even one act of adultery is sufficient ground for divorce.

So adultery[63] in terms of matrimonial relief means voluntary sexual[64] intercourse[65] between one spouse and a person of the opposite sex, not his or her spouse, during the subsistence of marriage.[66]

Though the stipulation is very specific but still it poses lot of legal problems as to what type of evidence should suffice to warrant the dissolution of marriage. There was a time when our courts following the English precedents, looked to the evidence to be proved beyond reasonable doubt but, however, now the proof is based on the principle of preponderance of probabilities as stipulated by the Supreme Court in Dastane *v.*

---

section 497 of IPC and section 488 of CrPC. It is a sexual relationship, unfollowed by a marriage or a legal union. For that a woman not be the mistress of anybody. She may be the mistress of the adulterer.

(v) Annamilia *v.* Perumayee Ammal AIR 1965 Mad 139 relied upon AIR 1965 MP 268.

(vi) Vardarajalu *v.* Balu AIR 1965 Mad 29.

(vii) Subbarama *v.* Saraswathi (1966) 2 MLJ 263.

(viii) Valliammal *v.* Singaram (1966) 2 MLJ 425.

(ix) Pattayee Ammal *v.* Manickam AIR 1967 Mad 254, the words imply a course of adulterous conduct more or less continuous.

Section 125 (4) Cr.PC says: "No wife shall be entitled to receive an allowance from her husand under this section if she is living in adultery . . . by mutual consent."

Section 125 (5) Cr.PC says: "On proof that any wife in whose favour an order has been made under this section is living in adultery. . . the magistrate shall cancel the order."

63. See sections 23(1)(a) of Special Marriage Act, 1954, Hindu Marriage Act, 1955, section 13(1)(i) and section 10, Parsi Marriage and Divorce Act, 1936 section 32(d). Indian Divorce Act, 1869, sections 10 and 22. However, in the Marriage Laws (Amendment) Act, 1978, Adultery word is not used, but it means the same and made very precise and specific.

64. 'Rape' does not fall under 'adultery', Clarkson *v.* Clarkson (1930) 46 TLR 626; Long *v.* Long & Johnson [1890] 15 PD 218.

65. The act of sexual intercourse need not be complete. Gitabai *v.* Fattoo AIR 1966 MP 130.

66. Pullikkottial Chera *v.* Mary Zechariah AIR 1981 MP 112.

Dastane.[67] This view has been reaffirmed in Manisankar *v.* Radha Devi[68] where adultery was held to be proved by preponderance of probabilities. So the evidence is based on presumptive proof such as circumstantial evidence.[69]

Chastity is the foundation of marriage; marriage is the essence of the family and family is the strongest base of society. It is said that adultery is a sword at the heart of a marriage. Even in a period of undoubted sexual licence, it remains the greatest single cause of matrimonial breakdown as it was considered as the greatest danger to family.

The family performs many functions in a society, among its important functions are regulating and disciplining the sex impulse and giving it stability and durability which is the dominating act in the family psychology drama. Marriage and family are the means used by the society to control promiscuous expression of sex and dissipation of man's energy in undesirable channels even without suppression of sex because our Sastras have rather laid enough stress on Rama along with artha and dharma, leading to the ultimate goal of moksa. Thus, marriage regulates sex in order to make it more meaningful. In marriage sex may become enriched by all the sentiments which association in an enterprise affords. Thus, sex as per Hindu Law and religion occupies a very supreme position as it is the means to have progeny but the sex being talked about is sex with purity and serenity which occurs only between the wife and the husband and any other act of sex beyond this is social, religious and moral taboo and intolerable under all canons.

We find a lot of mention about adultery in the Hindu scriptures. Kane has mentioned that even for adultery, a wife could not be abandoned.[70] We find that even for adultery, not

---

67. AIR 1975 SC 1534.
68. AIR 1992 Raj. 33: Parvati *v.* Shiva Ram AIR 1989 HP 29. Kishore Ghose *v.* Krishna Ghosh AIR 1989 Cal. 327.
69. Sanjukta *v.* Laxminarayan AIR 1991 Ori 39; Arun Kumar *v.* Anita AIR 1993 P&H 33, Subbrama Reddiar *v.* Saraswathi AIR 1967 Mad 85, Chhagan Lal *v.* Sakha Devi AIR 1975 Raj. 8, Ravinder Prasad *v.* Sita Devi, AIR 1989 Pat 128; Chandra Mohini *v.* Avinash Prasad AIR 1967 SC 584.
70. P.V. Kane, History of Dharmasastras, Hindi Smriti, U.P., pp. 322-3.

a very stern view was taken, though the act was considered immoral. Gautama has said that when a woman becomes unchaste, she had to do penitence's, yet; she had the right to receive maintenance. Even Yajnavalkya had spoken to this effect.[71] Manu has also spoken about it.

"In India, it is not usual for a young man and woman to live together in a house when they are neither related to each other. Society being very much more conservative here than elsewhere, it would not be unreasonable to infer adultery from the facts—

(1) that only the respondent and co-respondent stayed in one house together for a long time,
(2) that the respondent had refused to go back to her husband.
(3) That the respondent and the co-respondent had not the courage to come into the witness box to deny the charge of adultery, and
(4) that they had ample opportunity to commit adultery by being alone in the house and their stay together cannot be accounted for on any other reasonable innocent hypothesis."

To establish a state of adultery even this can a circumstance that despite the disruption of the relations between the spouses, the wife gives birth to a child. In the case of Veera Reddi *v.* Kistamma,[71a] Dr. Veera Reddi while still a student married Kistamma who was the daughter of his father's sister. They did not have a happy marital life and there used to be tension on small issues occasionally. The wife brought to an end her every relation with the husband on 17-11-1957 and started living with her parents. After 17-11-1957 there was no meeting between them. On 23-12-1958 after 402 days of the cessation of marital ties the wife delivered a child.

---

71. Yaj, I.70: "The unchaste wife should be deprived of authority, should be unadorned, allowed food barely sufficient to sustain her body, rebuked and let sleep on low bed and thus allowed to dwell."

71a. 1969 Mad 235.

The Madras High Court held the wife guilty of adultery and observed that in absence of her meeting with the husband, wife's delivery this way to a child, was suggestive of adultery of the wife.

In P.V.P. and R[71b] the Bombay High Court held, the presence of wife in the restaurant cabin with her blouse and brassier unhooked and the co-respondent holding her breast in his hands, by itself cannot permit any influence of adultery.

The above decision of the court does not appear correct as a married lady allowing a stranger such an illicit affection and association necessarily leads to a suggestion of adulterous relations with that person.

The act of intercourse to constitute adultery must be voluntary but if it is involuntary for example, rape and on account of misrepresentation, there can be no adultery within the meaning of this Section.

In a proceeding of divorce on the ground of adultery non-appearing of the respondent or non-opposing the charge of adultery, does not mean that adultery is proved. The case must stand on its own merits. The court will refuse to act upon confession alone unless the surrounding circumstances indicate that confession is true.

In Chander Prakash *v.* Sudesh Kumari,[71c] the court held that it is a presumption in law that the respondent charged with adultery is innocent and the burden to prove adultery lies on the party who has alleged it. Where the husband alleged that he had performed the act of sexual intercourse with his wife only once but it was found that she was used to it and the medical examination too confirmed it, the court held that the contention of the petitioner that she was living in adultery could not be accepted. The state of adultery cannot be established by the fact that the lady had every opportunity and freedom to have sexual intercourse with any other person.

Non-access of the husband to his wife and delivery of a child by her will be sufficient to prove adultery on her part and it will entitle the husband to get a decree of divorce.[71d]

71b. AIR 1982 Bom 498.

71c. AIR 1971 Del 208.

71d. Smt Anandi Devi *v.* Raja Rani, AIR 1973 Raj. 14.

It is a pity that in the age of moral degradation, we are expecting a high sense of sex morality. Chastity of the spouses is the sine qua non of marriage, but going astray, a single lapse, is almost civil death for the woman and her social status in the family reaches its lowest ebb and if allowed divorce, she almost gets a civil death in the society and the society has not reached the point of that tolerance that still it will give the same respect to the divorced woman. She is doubly punished, both in the family as well as in the society.

4.10.2 Cruelty

Hindu marriage was considered to be an indissoluble union and as such statutory divorce remained unknown to India even during the British Regime. The Hindu Marriage Act, 1955, wherein cruelty has been prescribed as a ground for Judicial separation only. The Marriage Law (Amendment) Act, 1976 prescribed cruelty is to be a ground for judicial separation as well as for divorce.

Originally, under section 10(1)(b), the petitioner was required to show that the respondent had treated him or her with such cruelty as to cause a reasonable apprehension in his or her mind that it would be harmful or injurious for the petitioner to live with the other party. It is now laid down in section 13(ia) of the said Act that the respondent has treated him or her with cruelty.

Cruelty, either in English Law or in any Indian Law, has not been defined by statute, thus all the law on cruelty is judge made law and must be extracted from the cases.

Lord Stowell in 1790[72] said that no husband could be found guilty of legal cruelty towards his wife unless he had either inflicted bodily injury upon her or had so conducted himself towards her as to cause actual injury upon her or had so conducted himself towards her as to cause actual injury to her mental and bodily health or so as to raise a reasonable apprehension that he would either inflict actual bodily health. But he further said that mere austerity of temper, petulance of manners, rudeness of language, a want of civil attention and accommodation, even occasional sallies of passion, if they do not threaten bodily harm, do not amount to legal cruelty.

72. Evans *v.* Evans 1 Hagg Cons. 35.

In English law in an early case, Russel *v.* Russel,[73] (which contains the earliest formulation of cruelty and to a great extent that formulation is still valid), Lopes LJ cruelty is defined as under:

> "Cruelty is a conduct of such a character as to have caused danger to life or health, bodily or mental, gives rise to reasonable apprehension of such danger which constitute legal cruelty".

However, after the passing of Matrimonial Causes Act, 1950, the definition underwent a change, i.e., "The respondent has treated him or her with cruelty". So the word 'cruelty' was left at the mercy of the judge as to how he infers from the facts of the case. In case like Squire *v.* Squire,[74] Kaslefsry,[75] the view projected was that intention on the part of one to injure another is an essential element of cruelty. However, in Gollens *v.* Gollens[76] it is held that it is not an essential element in matrimonial offences.

In the celebrated English decision King *v.* King,[76a] Lord Normand observed while defining cruelty as under:

> "The general rule in all questions of cruelty is that the whole matrimonial relationship must be considered and that rule is of special value where the cruelty consists not of violent acts but of injurious reproaches, complaints, accusations or taunts. Willful accusations may be made which are not true and for which there are no probable grounds and yet they may not amount to cruelty. To take an obvious example, they may have been provoked by the cruel conduct of the other spouse. There is, in many cases, no such rule, no clear line of demarcation which divides cruelty from something which does not amount to cruelty."

73. [1895] PD 315.
74. [1947] 2 All ER 529.
75. [1950] 2 All ER 398.
76. [1963] 2 All ER 966.
76a. 1952 (2) All ER 584.

The best guide for this class of cases was a passage in the judgment of Bucknill, J. in Horton *v.* Horton,[76b] which reads as follows:

> "Mere conduct which causes injury to health is not enough. If he marries a wife whose character develops in such a way as to make it impossible for him to live happily with her, I do not think that he establishes cruelty merely because he finds that life with her is impossible. He must prove that she has committed willful and unjustifiable acts inflicting pain and misery upon him and causing injury to his health."

In McEwan *v.* McEwan,[76c] Lord Denning held that: "Cruelty being a question of fact, the circumstances of each case must be taken into consideration including the physical and mental condition and the position in life of the parties. However, the conduct complained of must be serious and higher than the ordinary wear and tear of married life."

Before 1976 under the Hindu Marriage Act, section 10(1)(b) which throws light on one aspect that interpretation of the provision entirely lies on the discretion of the Court.

In Shobha Rani *v.* Madhukar Reddi,[76d] the Apex Court states : "Section 13(1)(ia) of the Hindu Marriage Act provides that the party has after solemnization of the marriage treated the petitioner with cruelty. What do these words mean? What should be the nature of cruelty? Should it be only intentional, willful or deliberate? Is it necessary to prove the intention in matrimonial offence? We think not. We have earlier said that cruelty may be of any kind and any variety. It may be different in different cases. It is in relation to the conduct of parties to a marriage. That conduct which is complained of, as cruelty by one spouse may not be so for the other spouse. There may be instances of cruelty by the unintentional but inexcusable

---

76b. (1940) 3 All ER 380.

76c. (1964) 108 Sol. JO 198 (CA).

76d. AIR 1988 SC 121 : 1988 (1) SCR 1010 : 1987 (4) JT 433 : 1988 Cr LR 88 : 1988 SCC (Cr) 60 : 1987 (2) Scale 1008 : 1988 CAR 106 : 1988 MLR 1 : 1988 (1) DMC 12 : 1988 (1) CCC 209 : 1988 (1) SCC 105.

conduct of any party. The cruel treatment may also result by the cultural conflict of the spouse. In such cases, even if the act of cruelty is established, the intention to commit cruelty cannot be established. The aggrieved party may not get relief. We do not think that that was the intention with which the Parliament enacted s. 13(1)(ia) of the Hindu Marriage Act. The context and the set up in which the word 'cruelty' has been used in the section, seems to us, that intention is not a necessary element in cruelty. That word has to be understood in the ordinary sense of the term in matrimonial affairs. If the intention to harm, harass or hurt could be inferred by the nature of the conduct or brutal act complained of, cruelty could be easily established. But the absence of intention should not make any difference in the case, if by ordinary sense in human affairs, the party cannot be denied on the ground that there has been no deliberate or wilful ill-treatment."[76e]

In Bhagwat *v.* Bhagwat[77] the Court held that the question whether the husband was capable of forming an intention to be cruel or actually intended to be cruel is a matter of no consequence. He can relapse into a fit of schizophrenia in which case anything may happen. The apprehension entertained by the wife is well founded. So the Court depended upon the likelihood of the happening which can be dangerous.

In Siddagangiah *v.* Lakshamma,[78] the Court held that the Act speaks is not restricted or confined to acts of physical violence and may extend to behaviour which may cause pain and injury to the mind as well as may create an agonizing ordeal in the matrimonial home and such cruelty is equally within the Act.

In Sreepadachar *v.* Vasantha Bai,[79] the allegation is of

76e. Bhagat *v.* Bhagat, AIR 1994 SC 710 : 1994 (1) SCC 377 : 1993 (6) JT 428 : 1993 (4) Scale 488 : 1994 (1) UJ 70 : 1993 (3) CCC 601 : 1993 (2) DMC 568 : 1994 (1) HLR 74 (SC) ; Surbhi *v.* Sanjay, 2000 (2) HLR 52 (MP-DB).

77. AIR 1967 Bom. 80.

78. AIR 1968 Mys 115.

79. AIR 1970 Mys 232. See also Kondal Rayal Reddiar *v.* Ranganayaki Ammal ILR 46 Mad 791. Soosannamma *v.* Varghese Abraham AIR 1957 Trav. Co. 277. Umrin Bai *v.* Chittar AIR. 1966 MP 205. Anjali Devi *v.* Krushna Chadra AIR 1954 Orissa 117, Sehra Alaraham *v.* Pyli Abraham AIR 1959 Ker 75.

insulting conduct indulged in by the wife in public against her husband and the Court held the view that it amounts to mental pain and agony and prove harmful and injurious to the health of the husband.

Smt. Aloda Dey *v.* Mrinal Kanti Dey,[80] it was a case where the trouble was not entirely due to wife's uncontrollable temper but the other side also contributed to it and there was nothing to suggest that she deliberately intended to upset husband's mental and physical health. Moreover, throughout, there was cohabitation which implicitly shows condonation. Here the court gave weight to intention and condonation and ignored the incidents that sometime do occur in married life and such incidents should not be stressed or taken too far to affect the married life. The Court held that there is no cruelty as warranted under the Act.

Smt. Neera *v.* Kishan Swarup,[81] it is a case of accusation of unchastity of wife. Wherein the Court held that cruelty need not be physical violence inflicted by one spouse on the other, but it may also be in his conduct, demeanour and treatment, but the question of cruelty is to be judged on the totality of circumstances. However, the landmark case of Dastane *v.* Dastane[82] has laid down various propositions:

1. The first step in this process is to fix the probabilities, the second to weigh them. The impossible is weeded out at the first stage and improbable at the second, It is the choice which ultimately determines where the preponderance of probabilities lies and that is the test, 'Proof beyond reasonable doubt' is not to be imported in trials of purely civil nature.[83]
2. Even though condonation is not pleaded as a defence, it is Court's duty, in view of the provisions of section 23(1)(b) to find whether cruelty has been condoned by the appellant. Condonation means forgiveness of the matrimonial offence and the

80. AIR 1973 Cal 393.
81. AIR 1975 All 337.
82. AIR 1975 SC 1534.
83. [1966] 1 All ER 524, [1948] 77 CLR 191 (High Court of Australia).

restoration of the spouse to the same position as occupied earlier.

3. An awareness of foreign decisions could be a useful asset in interpreting our own laws, but the interpretation has to be within the parameter of the specific provision as envisaged in the statute.
4. Condonation is a conditional forgiveness. It does not give the condoning spouse a charter to malign the other spouse. If it is so, the condoned spouse would be required mutely to submit to the cruelty of the other spouse without relief or remedy.[84]

Section 10 (1) (b) contains three ingredients

1. Such cruelty.
2. To cause reasonable apprehension.
3. That it will be harmful or injurious to live with the other spouse.

All these three ingredients follow each other. 'Such cruelty' is not specific in nature. It has been taken in a general form but it must be an act of a nature which may be considered as alien to good human nature which may be called as an act of misconduct in behaviour. But whatever be the nature of this act of misconduct in it must cause apprehension. 'Apprehension' means likelihood of adverse consequences. It is a state of mind which should get, affected with the fear of the likelihood of such consequences and that apprehension must be reasonable. It should not be the thinking of a daydreamer. There should not be hollowness in such thinking. Then this thinking must be in terms of harm or injury by one to another if they live together.

It is worth noting that this provision is for judicial separation and not for divorce.

However, The Marriage Laws (Amendment) Act 1976 brought a drastic change and cruelty has been prescribed as one of the grounds of divorce. Cruelty simpliciter is now a

84. Cooper *v.* Cooper [1950] WN 200 (HL); Bertram *v.* Bertram [1944] p. 59.

ground for divorce as well as judicial separation. Generally there must be an intention to cause suffering to the other spouse. The concept of cruelty has varied from time to time, place to place, individual to individual in its application according to the social status of the parties and their economic conditions etc. culture, temperament, status in life are factors to be considered.[84a] It may be by words, gestures or by mere silence, violence or non-violence.[84b] The question of cruelty must be determined from the whole facts and the matrimonial relations between the spouses. It must be determined as a cumulative effect of all the circumstances.[84c] The question of cruelty is to be judged on the basis of the evidence on record and the totality of the circumstances of the case.[84d] Mere slight acts of violence which any spouse may commit in anger or worry cannot be a ground for holding that legal cruelty exists. Though ordinarily a single act of violence ought not to justify a charge of cruelty,[84e] it is not an invariable rule as it is possible in particular circumstances even for a single act of a grossly violent character being held to constitute legal cruelty. Cruelty by physical violence can be committed both by the husband and wife, though cases of cruelty by the wife must in the nature of things, be rare, Cruelty does not lie in merely beating the spouse.[84f]

In the case of Kalpana Shripati Rao *v.* Shripatdi Rao[85] took the view that cruelty contemplated under section 13(1)(ia) of the Act neither attracts the old English doctrine nor the statutory limits embodied in old section 10(1)(b).

In Ashwini Kumar Sehgal *v.* Smt. Swantantar Sehgal[86] the Court to believe that the relations between the parties had

---

84a. Jia Lal Abrol *v.* Sarla Devi, 1978 J. and K. 69.

84b. Dr. Narayan Ganesh *v.* Mrs. Sucheta, I.L.R. (1969) Bom, 1024: 71. Bom.L.R. 569: 1970 Bom. 312.

84c. Sreepadachar *v.* Vasantha Bai, 1970 Mys. 232.

84d. Neera *v.* Kishan Swarup, 1975 All. 337.

84e. Pranab Biswas *v.* Mrinmayee Dassi, 1976 Cal. 156 (single act follwed by remorse insufficient).

84f. Jagannadhan *v.* Savithramma, (1972) 2 An. W.R. 200: 1972 A.P. 377.

85. [1983] 1 DMC 483.

86. 1979 Mat LR 26 (P&H).

deteriorated to such an extent due to the conduct of one of the spouses that it has become impossible to live together without mental agony, torture or distress.

In Balbir Kaur v.Dhir Dass[87] it was held that cruelty admits in its ambit and scope such acts that might even cause mental agony.

In Londhe *v.* Londhe,[88] Bombay High Court relying upon Report of the Law Commission has treated the petitioner with cruelty' which has been bodily incorporated in section 13(1)(ia), without adding any limiting words. It is cruelty simpliciter.

There is catena of cases which can be broadly categorised as physical cruelty and mental cruelty.

4.10.2.1 Physical Cruelty

Acts of physical violence against another spouse resulting in injury to body, limb or health or causing a reasonable apprehension thereto have been traditionally considered as legal cruelty. What acts of physical violence will amount to cruelty will differ from case to case depending upon the susceptibility or sensibility of the parties, for instance, in the case of a thick skinned person the same act of physical violence may not amount to cruelty as it may be in an average case.[89] There may be series of acts of physical violence or there may be a single isolated act of physical violence of severe nature. This has to be seen with the help of the various case laws as to how the judiciary has visualized it.

In Macho *v.* Manr Singh;[90] It is said that general isolated acts of violence are not sufficient ground to found legal cruelty and in order to establish cruelty againstd the husband the wife must prove more than isolated acts of violence.[91]

In Kaushalya *v.* Wisakhiram,[92] Mr. Justice Dua spoke about the pitiability of woman in the society that woman normally

---

87. AIR 1979 (P&H) 162. See also (i) Dr. Srikant Rangacharya Adya *v.* Smt Anuradha AIR 1980 Kant. 8.
88. Dr. Loudhe *v.* Loudhe AIR 1984 Bom 413 FB.
89. Mohd. Shabbir, "Judicial Interpretation of Cruelty as a ground of Matrimonial relief under Hindu Law", ALT (journal) p. 18.
90. AIR 1928 Oudh 114.
91. Kallan *v.* Kallan AIR 1933 Lah. 728.
92. Kaushallya *v.* Wisakhiram.

submits herself to her fate and bear ill-treatment at the hands of the husband and unless a climax is reached, she usually does not take the desperate step of going to a police station to lodge a report. It was desperate step of going to a police station to lodge a report. It was held in the case that the husband ill treated the wife, beat her, so much so that she had to go to the police station to lodge a report, It was held that even if the injuries on her person are considered not to be so serious as to call for their treatment by a medical practitioner, if she has been actually treated and beaten but it is definitely an act of cruelty.

Saptami *v.* Jagdish[93]

It was a case of physical cruelty coupled with mental cruelty. The husband constantly abused and insulted the wife and ultimately on one day in her father's house he pushed her against wall causing her bruises.

However, one thing is noteworthy that the Court at their discretion, tried to conclude whether the given fact is an act of cruelty or not. A wife living with her husband for just four to five days immediately after the marriage alleged cruelty of the husband. Cruelty of short duration cannot afford ground for divorce especially when the incidents of cruelty quoted by her were in the nature of initial wear and tear of marriage.[94]

In some cases single act of physical violence may be so dangerous as to create a reasonable apprehension of further violence and will itself constitute cruelty.[95]

In A.P. Mary *v.* K.G. Raghwan,[96] the husband assaulted the wife with an iron rod and caused her four injuries, one of them grievous in nature which resulted in fracture of right fibula. Even thereafter his conduct and behaviour was not conducive to healthy atmosphere for maintaining marital relations. The Court, relying upon various case laws, held it a fit case of granting divorce on the ground of cruelty.

In Tapan Kumar *v.* Biva,[97] it is a case where the husband was at the mercy of the wife and she wanted him to live away

93. Saptami *v.* Jagadish.
94. Santosh Kumar *v.* Parveen Kumar AIR 1987 P&H 33.
95. Sulekha *v.* Kamala Kanta AIR 1980 Cal 370.
96. AIR 1979 MP 40.
97. AIR 1988 Cal 223.

from his joint family. On refusal, she even assaulted him physically through her relatives. The Court held it a fit case of cruelty by the wife and granted decree of dissolution of marriage.

It is not limited to only physical cruelty but mental cruelty also comes within the ambit of cruelty as the provision is wide open and Lord Denning has said that the doors of cruelty cannot be shut, but if the doors of cruelty were opened too wide, we should soon find ourselves granting divorce for incompatibility of temperament.

4.10.2.2 Mental Cruelty

In Bhagatd *v.* Bhagat[98] the Supreme Court had the occasion to deal with a matter of divorce on the ground of mental cruelty. In the said decision the Supreme Court observed thus:

> Mental cruelty in section 13(10(1a) can broadly be defined that conduct which inflicts upon the other party such mental pain and agony as would make it not possible for that party to live with the other.

It must be remembered that our Parliament has borrowed the language of English Matrimonial Causes Act, 1950 in our Amendment Act, 1976.

In Horton *v.* Horton,[99] Bucknill J, has said: "Mere conduct which causes injury to health is not enough.

White *v.* White,[100] it was a case where the husband, in spite of wife's protest, consistently practiced coitus interrupts, with the result that the wife who was of a nervous disposition suffered in health. She was examined by a mental specialist who reported that unless the husband could be persuaded to change his attitude, nothing will improve the health of the wife and the husband persisted in the practice. Held that it is a cruelty in law and granted divorce."

98. AIR 1994 SC 710.
99. [1940] 3 All ER 380.
100. [1948] PDA 151.

Westall *v.* Westall,[101] Denning LJ said that although malignity is not an essential element of cruelty......nevertheless intention is an element in this sense that there must be conduct which is, in some way, aimed by one person at the other.

In Evans *v.* Evans,[102] Lord Stowell spoke about the approach of the Courts to be adopted in cases of cruelty: . . . . it is duty of the Court . . . to keep. . . (the definition of cruelty) extremely strict. The cause must be grave and weighty and such as to show an absolute impossibility that the duties of the married life can be discharged.

Gollins *v.* Gollins,[103] the House of Lords dealt in great detail the question of cruelty in matrimonial relationship and made a distinction between 'unequivocal conduct', which is conduct which clearly constitutes cruelty and those involving 'equivocal conduct', conduct which may in certain circumstances amount to cruelty, and in other circumstances amount to not do so. Whether cruelty, as a matrimonial offence, has been established is a question of fact and degree, which should be determined by taking into account the particular individual concerned and the particular circumstances of the case rather than by any objective standard, accordingly, in cases where the two spouses are of normal physical and mental health and the conduct of the respondent spouse, so considered, is so bad that the other should not be called to endure it, cruelty is established, then it cannot be called to endure it, cruelty is established, then it does not matter what was the respondent's state of mind.

Williams *v.* Willams[104] In this case which came to the House of Lords, Lord Evershed talked about insanity and cruelty and said that insanity of a respondent spouse in terms McNaghten Rules, is not necessarily a defence to a suit for divorce on the ground that the respondent treated the petitioner with cruelty but insanity is a factor to be taken into account in applying the test whether in all the circumstances of

---

101. [1949] 65 TLR 337 CA.
102. [1950] 2 All ER 398.
103. [1963] 2 All ER 966.
104. [1963] 2 All ER 994.

the case the respondent's conduct is of such gravity that he has by his acts treated the petitioner with cruelty.

However, Lord Pearce, said that if the conduct were such that it would amount to cruelty only if aggravated by intention to hurt, a spouse who could not form such an intention would not be held to have treated the other with cruelty.

In P(D) *v.* P(J)[105] the wife has not permitted the husband to have normal sexual relationship. Stirling J. has said:

the fact that the wife could not control her psychological inhibition did not in law negative the fact that her conduct in consistently depriving the husband of normal sexual intercourse and the opportunity of becoming a father was unendurable and, as it seriously affected his health, constituted cruelty.

Evans *v.* Evans[106] In this case husband was granted a decree on the ground of cruelty on the finding that the conduct of the wife in refusing to have intercourse was grave and weighty matter and did have an adverse effect on the husband's health and consequently amounted to cruelty.

Sheldon *v.* Sheldon[107] In this case there was refusal by husband of intercourse for six years after normal intercourse for eight years. In spite of the fact that she wanted to have a child, the husband did not oblige though they used to sleep together. In consequence she became ill. This was informed to him by the doctor of her illness. He had no infirmity, She left him and sought divorce. Held that the husband's persistent refusal of sexual intercourse over so long a period without excuse, causing grave injury to his wife's health, amounted to cruelty on his part and granted a decree of divorce.

N. Sreepadachar *v.* Vasantha Bai[108] abusing the husband in public, in a bus and catching hold of his collar, making the husband cook food for her and catching hold of his collar, making the husband in public, and when he served the food, throwing the plate on his head, threatening to burn herself, to give a false complaint to the police so that her husband may

105. [1965] 2 All ER 456.
106. [1965] 2 All ER 789.
107. [1966] 2 All ER 257.
108. AIR 1970 Mys 32.

come into trouble, Stating before others that her husband may be killed in an accident so that she may get his insurance and provident fund amount.

The Honourable Court discussed the matter at length and observed that cruelty need not be only physical but there can be mental cruelty. The question of cruelty must be determined from the whole facts and the matrimonial relations between the spouses. It must be determined as a cumulative effect of all the circumstances.

Smt. Neera *v.* Kishan Swarup[109] It is a case of false accusation of unchastity to wife. The Court discussed as to when and if it amounts to cruelty and what wife has to prove. The essence of the discussion was that she has to establish.

1. The husband had persistently or repeatedly treated her with cruelty.
2. That the cruelty was of such a nature, degree and extent as to cause a reasonable apprehension in her mind that it would be harmful or injurious for her to live with her.

In Smt. Maya *v.* BrijNath[109a] While dealing with cruelty the Court observed thus:

> "Cruelty has not been defined in the Act, But it is now well settled that the conduct should be grave and weighty so as to make cohabitation virtually unendurable. It must be more severe than the ordinary wear and tear of marriage, The cumulative conduct taking into consideration the circumstances and the background of the parties has to be examined to reach a conclusion of cruelty."

In Shobharani *v.* MadhuKar Reddy[110] In this case, the Supreme Court observed thus:

109. AIR 1975 All 337.
109a. AIR 1982 Del 240.
110. AIR 1988 SC 121.

"The word cruelty has not been defined. Indeed it could not have been defined. It has been used in relation to human conduct or human behaviour. It is the conduct in relation to or in respect of matrimonial duties and obligations. It is a course of conduct which is adversely affecting the other. The cruelty may be physical or mental, intentional or unintentional. It is a question of fact and degree . . . . . The cruelty alleged may largely depend upon the type of life the parties are accustomed to or their economic and social condition, their culture and human values to which they attach importance. We, the judges and lawyers, therefore should not import our own notion of life. It would also be better if we less depend upon precedents."

In Nirmala Manohar Jagesha *v.* Manohar Shivram Jagesha[111] the Honourable Court, discussed the concept of cruelty thus:

1. Cruelty in the matrimonial law means conduct of such type that the petitioner cannot reasonably be expected to live with the respondent.
2. The old English Law concept of danger is not applicable in India.
3. The making of wild, reckless and baseless allegations of impotency and lack of manliness itself amounts to cruelty in the matrimonial law.

Debabrata Bhaumik *v.* Smt. Sarmistha San[112] It is a case decided on May 5, 1995. It is a case of mental torture by the husband. The wife was compelled to drink liquor for which she had abhorrence forced to visit hotel which she did not like and to live in unhealthy and unhygienic place. Marital relations became strained so much that it became impossible for the wife to live with her husband. The Court held the marriage between the appellant and the respondent has become dead. In these circumstances it will not be proper for this Court to compel the

111. AIR 1991 Bom 259.
112. 1996 Gauhati 4 FLC.

respondent to live with the appellant. If the Court gives such a direction the consequences may be serious.

Smt. Sova Ghosh *v.* Asit Kr. Ghosh[113] The husband sought divorce on the ground of cruelty alleging that she refused to live in matrimonial home with the family of the husband and refused to perform conjugal obligations without any reasonable cause and that she is insisting to live with the husband separately and not in the joint family. The Court relied upon the reasoning's of the lower Court that the husband left no stone unturned to make the marital life a paradise but the action of the wife is wilful having no relation with rationality. The acts of the wife constitute an unjustifiable interference in the marital life and has brought the matter within the ambit of cruelty. Said that as to how far a wife can go to cause mental agony and torture to the husband and harass him gruesomely.

With the decisions of the Courts in various cases, the following acts of the spouse constitute the ground for divorce under cruelty.

Verbal Abuse and Insults

The continual use of abusive and insulting words spitefully indulged into bring shame and mental agony to the other spouse which will tend to undermine the health of that spouse may in the circumstances of any particular case amount to legal cruelty. Mere trivial incidents which are merely the wear and tear of married life do not constitute cruelty.[113a] In Kamla Devi *v.* Balbir Singh[113b] the court held that using foul and abusive language to the husband and his parents and picking up quarrels tending to disturb husband's mental peace amounts to cruelty.

Excessive sexual intercourse

Demand by the husband of excessive sexual intercourse and compelling the wife to submit to it against her wish and

113. 1996 FLC Cal 176.

113a. Thompson *v.* Thompson, (1957) 1 All. E.R. 161.

113b. 1979 J. & K. 4; Cf., Also see Manjulabai v.Ramachandra, 1975 M.P.L.J. 692; Dr. N.G. Dastane *v.* Mrs. S. Dastana, 1975 S.C. 1534; Sreepadachar *v.* Vasantha Bai, 1970 Mys. 232.

despite her remonstrance resulting in the impairment of her health will amount to cruelty.[113c]

Refusal of Intercourse

Mere refusal of sexual intercourse is not per se cruelty.[113d] But persistent refusal would amount to cruelty.[113e] What has to be found in each case is whether the act is such which the complaining partner should not be asked to endure.[113f]

Neglect

Neglect by the spouse in the discharge of his or her duties of attention and company to the other and forcing the latter to leave the home on account of such neglect would in the circumstances of any particular case constitute neglect amounting to cruelty. Incompatibility of temperament, neglect etc., will not amount to cruelty.[113g] Desertion for a period of less than two years immediately before the presentation of the petition by itself will not constitute cruelty.[113h]

Communication of Venereal Disease

It is well settled that a spouse who knowing that she or he is afflicted with venereal disease has sexual intercourse with the other is guilty of cruelty. Mere addiction to the vice of drink or drug must necessarily result in the cruelty to the other spouse, as cases are not infrequent of such addicts getting on very well with their spouses despite such addiction.[113i]

Refusal to Speak

Where one of the spouses though living under the same roof refuses to speak to the other for a considerably long time

113c. Kusum Lata *v.* Kamla Prasad, 1965 All, 280. See also Holborn *v.* Holboru, 1947 W.N. 70.

113d. Weatherley *v.* Weatherley, (1947) 1 All E.R. 563.

113e. Nighawan *v.* Nighawan, 1973 Delhi 200.

113f. *Ibid.*

113g. See Buchler *v.* Buchler, (1947) 1 All E.R. 319; See also Dr. N.G. Dastane *v.* Mrs. Dastane, supra.

113h. Kaushalya Rani *v.* Vijay Singh, 1973 Raj. 269.

113i. Baker *v.* Baker, (1955) 3 All E.R. 193.

and on that ground the other spouse becomes wretched and worried, such conduct may be a ground for holding that there has been cruelty on the part of the spouse who refuses to speak.

Forcing Association with Improper Persons

The husband inducing his wife to have intercourse with a stranger or inducing her to put up with a lewd woman whom he has brought into her room for his carnal satisfaction, the wife is entitled to resist all such immoral attempts by filing a petition for judicial separation on the ground of cruelty.[113j]

False Charge of Immorality against the Wife

Where a husband falsely charges his wife with immorality and adultery and persists in such charge would support her claim for relief.[113k]

Ill-Treatment of Children

Deliberate and designed ill-treatment of the children in the presence of the mother with a view to give her pain carried to such an extent that it has affected her health and anguished her mind will amount to legal cruelty.[113l]

Cruelty may be inferred from the whole facts and atmosphere disclosed in the proof, and it is a wrong approach to put the various acts or conduct alleged into a series of separate compartments and say of each of them that they by themselves cannot pass the test of cruelty and therefore that totality cannot pass that test. Though actual intention to injure the wife in a case of mental cruelty must be important, and may be decisive in the particular case, it is not an essential factor.

113j. Lalita Devi *v.* Radha Mohan, 1976 Raj. I.

113k. Iqbal Kaur *v.* Pritam Singh, 321 Kuppuswamy Goundan *v.* Alagammal, 322 Umribai *v.* chittar. 323 See also Smt. Bhaga *v.* Bant Sing; 324 Neerc *v.* Kishan Śwarup; 325 Shyam Narayan *v.* Shaila326 [falsely alleging that wife had married again and was living in adultery].

113l. Crawford *v.* Crawford, [1955] 3 All ER 592.

Cruelty during Separation

In Britt *v.* Britt[113m] the wife and the husband were living separately and several months after such separation the husband visited the matrimonial home where the wife was living and gave her a good beating as a result of which she got black eye and again hit her when he subsequently met her in an omnibus. It was held that these acts were sufficient to establish cruelty even though they were committed when the parties were living apart.

Cruelty by Refusal to have Children

Permanent and unreasonable starvation of the maternal instinct in the wife to have children, by the husband deliberately and without good reason, permanently denying his wife of a fair opportunity of having a child, by his practice of *coitus interruptus*, a course which, wile preserving to himself a measure of sexual enjoyment, is a deliberate act contrary to the laws of nature and one which any reasonable husband must realize is likely to affect the wife's health, is cruelty.[113n] Similarly in Forbes *v.* Forbes,[113o] where a wife deliberately and consistently refused to satisfy the husband's craving to have children by insisting on the use of contraceptives and it was found that the wife was not unfit for child birth and that this intentional and persistent conduct on her part had caused the husband anxiety and misery resulting in his mental ill-health to the knowledge of his wife, it was held that the wife was guilty of cruelty to her husband. To the same effect is the decision in Ward *v.* Ward.[113p]

4.10.3 Desertion

Section 13(1)(ib) stipulates:

> Has deserted the petitioner for a continuous period of not less than two years immediately preceding the presentation of the petition.

113m.(1955) 3 All. E.R. 769.

113n. Knott *v.* Knott (1955) 2 All E.R. 305.

113o. (1955) 2 All E.R. 311.

113p. (1958) 1 W.L.R. 693.

Explanation:

In this sub-section, the expression 'desertion as perceived by the other party to the marriage without reasonable cause and without the consent or against the wish of such party, and includes the willful neglect of the petitioner by the other party to the marriage, and its grammatical variations and cognate expressions shall be construed accordingly.

Statutory Hindu Law on divorce is clearly a piece of imitation, having tilting tendency with complete inclination towards English Law on divorce and as such, at least, a faint glimpse of 'desertion' as perceived by English Law needs to be kept in mind along with the Ancient Hindu Law, wherein such concept has been covered very elaborately on the touchstone of dharma.

To speak of English Law, the only remedy, until 1858, for desertion was a suit for restitution of conjugal rights. Desertion was not an offence previously known to the ecclesiastical or common law but the Matrimonial Causes Act, 1857, introduced desertion and later on repealed but replaced by the Supreme Court of Judicature (Consolidation) Act, 1925. However, by Matrimonial Causes Act, 1937 those provisions by making desertion without cause for a period of at least three years immediately preceding the presentation of the petition became a ground for divorce and also a ground for judicial separation. The Matrimonial Causes Act, 1950 which, in relation to desertion, was modified by the Divorce (Insanity and Desertion) Act, 1958 and by the Matrimonial Causes Act, 1965. The Divorce Reforms Act, 1969 provides that desertion for two years is one of the facts showing that a marriage has irretrievably broken down.

Neither the Act nor the Courts have defined 'desertion' but in its essence desertion is the separation of one spouse from the other.[114] This separation is with an intention on the part of

114. Thompson *v.* Thompson [1858] 1 SW * Tr 231, 233.
Graves *v.* Graves [1864] 3 SW & Tr 350, 353.
Frows *v.* Frows [1904] pp. 177, 179.
Pulford *v.* Pulford [1923] pp. 18, 22.

the deserting spouse of bringing cohabitation permanently to an end without reasonable cause and without consent of the other spouse.[115] But desertion may not mean mere physical act of departure by one spouse, as desertion is not a withdrawal from a place, but from a state of things.[116]

For the offence of desertion there must be two elements present on the side of the deserting spouse, namely, the factum, i.e., the physical separation and the animus deserendi, i.e., the intention to bring cohabitation permanently to an end.[117]

But sometimes it so happens that the spouse leaves the matrimonial home because the other's conduct is intolerable. When such complexity appears then Courts have to decide what amounts to justification for leaving, who in fact brought about separation or whether there was consent, So the Courts have to look into the fact of separation, intention behind the separation and justification of the separation, to arrive at whether such a separation amounts to desertion, as such desertion is a matrimonial offence.

Sir Henry Duke, in Pulford *v.* Pulford[118] has said:

> Desertion is not the withdrawal from a place, but from a state of things. The husband may live in a place and make it impossible for his wife to live there, though it is she and not he that actually withdraws; and that state of things may be desertion of the wife. The law does not deal with mere matter of place. What it seeks to enforce is the recognition and discharge of the common obligation of the married state.

Weatherley *v.* Weatherley [1947] AC 628, 631.
Lane *v.* Lane [1951] TLR 1125, 1126.

115. Williams *v.* Williams [1943] 2 All ER 746, 752.
Thomas *v.* Thomas [1923] 39 TLR 520, 521.
Hopes *v.* Hopes [1949] p. 227.

116. Pardy *v.* Pardy [1939] p. 288. Lane *v.* Lane [1951] p. 284.

117. Hopes *v.* Hopes [1949] p. 277, Edwards *v.* Edwards [1948] p. 268, Perry *v.* Perry [1952] p. 203.

118. [1923] p. 18.

In Bartholomew *v.* Bartholomew[119] a husband was refused a decree although he was forced to leave by his wife's persistence in such sluttish behaviour that he could not tolerate the conditions of the home, whereas in Winnan *v.* Winnan[120] a wife who persisted in keeping innumerable cats against her husband's will was held to have driven him out and he was granted divorce.

The main question is that who is entitled to choose the matrimonial home? This is a thorny question. Since the husband has a duty to provide for his wife and family, it might be thought that he would have the right to decide, but it may be true in the past, but now it is not an absolute rule. The Courts have started looking to the reasonableness of the parties. If the role of the husband is important, the role of the wife is equally vital and both are a homogeneous blend called family. The Courts have to see the gravity and weight of the cause, not simply something causing matrimonial unhappiness. Causes like desertion due to adultery or cruelty, excessive or revolting sexual demands[120a] persistent extravagance[121] unjustified refusal of sexual intercourse,[121] insistence on the practice of coitus interruptus[122] are the causes that can lead to desertion. Desertion, basically, is a preliminary act towards disintegration of family and insistence on this state of mind which leads to the final parting and breaking of the spouses or totally forgetting the concept of family, insisting on the individual whims and fancies.

Basically, Hindu Law on divorce is an imitation of English Law but the psychology and philosophy of the Court is pregnant with Hindu cultural heritage and as such there may not be much inspiration derived from English Law but it is also not totally ignorable and the Indian Courts have started laying stress on the old Sastric Law blended with socio-economic prevailing conditions that speak of contrary concepts, i.e.,

---

119. [1952] 2 All ER 1035.
120. [1959] p. 174.
120a. Holborn *v.* Holborn [1947] 1 All ER 32.
121. Synge *v.* Synge (1900) p. 180.
121. Glenister *v.* Glenister [1945] p. 30.
122. G V.G [1930] p. 72.

independence of a woman being now free from the shackles of economic serfdom and armed with constitutional rights of equality. Hindu concept, the obligations of the wife to live under the wing and protection of the husband have always existed. Hindu Law has always spoken of a family and once this concept is recognized as well founded, then the question of desertion on the part of any spouse is unthinkable.

Hindu scriptures did speak of the duties of a wife in its total passivity so much so that Even Manu has gone to the extent of such exhortation that she should worship her husband as a God even though he happens to be a man of bad character and devoid of all good qualities.[123]

Simultaneously, these scriptures did speak of separation (which is now in matrimonial law called desertion) in extraordinary situations. According to Katyayana[124] a lunatic, one guilty of grave sin, a leper, an impotent, a sagotra, one bereft of eyesight and hearing or epileptic, are the persons to be avoided for marriage and if the gift of the daughter is made to such a person, the gift would be null and void, Such views are also quoted by other smrtikaras also.[125] These directions are pre-marriage directions to be obeyed so that there should be no strain of any nature on marital tie in the performance of religious rites.

Hindu Law on divorce covered under section 13(1)(ib) read with Explanation, has been agitated before the Courts wherein the Courts

1. whether there is desertion
2. whether desertion is justified or not

123. Manu, V. 154. "Though destitute of virtue, or seeking pleasure (elsewhere) or devoid of good qualities (yet) a husband must be constantly worshipped as a God by a faithful wife." See also Brhaspati who says that a wife who feels afflicted when her husband is affected and feels happy when he is happy, is truly the devoted wife.

124. Katyayana quoted in Smrtichandrika, 221.

125. Vasistha quoted in Madan-Parijata, 153; Narada, XII 97; Arthasastra XV.

In Bipinchandra *v.* Prabhavati,[125a] a three Judge Bench of the Supreme Court defines 'desertion':

> "In its essence, desertion means the intentional permanent forsaking and abandonment of one spouse by the other's consent, and without reasonable cause. It is a total repudiation of the obligations of marriage."

In Alwar *v.* Sri Devi,[125b] the Supreme Court points out that the essential ingredients to constitute 'desertion' are:

(i) the factum of separation; and
(ii) the intention to bring cohabitation permanently to an end animus deserendi.

Therefore, mere maladjustment between partners cannot be treated to be a case of desertion so as to allow the partners to reach to the extent of seeking a decree of divorce.[125c]

As observed by the Supreme Court in Savitri Pandey *v.* Prem Chand Pandey,[125d] there can be no desertion without previous co-habitation by the parties.

In Rohini Kumari *v.* Narendra Singh[125e] the Supreme Court states: The requirement that the desertion spouse must intend to bring cohabitation to an end must be understood to be subject to the qualification that if without just cause or excuse, a man persists in doing things which he knows his wife probably will not tolerate and which no ordinary woman would tolerate and then she leaves, he has deserted her whatever his desire or intention may have been.

Some of the cases in this regard are :

125a. AIR 1957 SC 176 : 1956 SCR 838 : 1957 SCJ 144 : Gurmel Singh *v.* Ajit Kaur, 1979 HLR 157 (P&H).

125b. Adhyatma Bhattar Alwar *v.* Ahyatma Bhattar Sri Devi AIR 2002 SC 88: JT 2001 (9) SC 429:2001 (8) scale 119: 2001 (8) Supreme 434.

125c. Shimla Devi *v.* Kuldeep Sharma, 2000 (1) HLR 213 (Raj-DB).

125d. AIR 2002 SC 591.

125e. AIR 1972 SC 459 : 1972 (2) SCR 657 : 1972 (1) SCC 1 : 1972 SCC (Cr)1.

1. Nitya Laha (Defdt), Appellant v. Soondaree Dossee (Pltff) Respondent[126]

The ground agitated before the Court is that the wife had incurred the loss of her right of maintenance by reason of having left her husband's house and carried on an independent calling, namely, that she laboured on the railway. The Court held that where a Hindu wife has left her husband's house and carried on an independent calling and the husband did not object to the calling or give her notice and as she was desirous of returning and the husband declined to maintain her, she was entitled to maintenance. The Court relied upon the presumption that a single act of disobedience cannot make her forfeit her right of maintenance forever.

2. Kateeram Dokaneeu v. Mussamut Gendhence[127]

This was suit to recover possession of the person of the plaintiff's wife. The Court observed that according to Hindu Law, after marriage, the husband is the legal guardian of his wife's person and property whether she is a major or a minor. The Court further held that the marriage of an infant being under the Hindu Law a legal and complete marriage, the husband, has the same right as in other cases to demand that his wife shall reside in the same house as himself. The Court cannot deprive the husband of this right except upon some tangible and definite grounds which show that, under the special circumstances of the case, the wife is absolved from this duty.

3. H. Sheenappayya v. Rajamma[128]

It was a case of the husband having a leprosy in a virulent form. The Court held that a Hindu husband suffering from a loathsome disease such as leprosy is a good defence to his suit for the restitution of conjugal rights, and if a leprous husband cannot enforce cohabitation upon an unwilling wife, he equally cannot make his disease a defence to her suit for maintenance so long as he has means to maintain her.

---

126. 1968 WR 475.
127. 1975 WR 178.
128. AIR 1922 Mad. 399.

4. *Perumal Naicker v. Sithalaxmi*[129]

It is a case of dissolution of marriage on ground of desertion by the wife and case came up under Madras Hindu Bigamy Prevention and Divorce Act 1949, wherein desertion has been defined.

Desertion is the active or wilful termination of an existing state of cohabitation without the consent express or implied of the party alleging desertion and against such party's wish. Therefore, be (a) wilful and deliberate, (b) without consent express or implied of the deserted party, (c) against wish of the deserted party, and (d) without reasonable cause.

5. *Tirath Kaur v. Kirpal Singh*[130]

It is a case under section 9 of the Hindu Marriage Act, 1955, wherein the wife was working as a tailoring teacher at a distant place and refused to resign her job whatever may be the position. The Court held that this statement of the wife would be tantamount to withdrawal from society inasmuch as it is the duty of the wife to live with the husband. The Court relied upon the text of Mulla's Hindu Law, para 555 which states:[131]

> A wife's first duty to her husband is to submit herself obediently to his authority and to remain under his roof and protection. She is not, therefore, entitled to separate residence or maintenance, unless she proves that by his misconduct or by his refusal to maintain her in his own place of residence or for other justifying cause she is compelled to live apart from him.

6. *Lachman v. Meena*[132]

This was a case under sections 10(1) and 9 of the Hindu Marriage Act, 1955, wherein the Supreme Court once again reiterated that in its essence desertion means the intentional permanent forsaking and abandonment of one spouse by the other without that other's consent and without reasonable

---

129. AIR 1956 Mad 415.
130. AIR 1964 Punj 28.
131. See Sitanath *v.* Haimabutty [1875] WR 377.
132. AIR 1964 SC 40.

cause. It is a total repudiation of the obligations of marriage. The Supreme Court, said that the burden of proving the 'factum' and animus deserendi is on the petitioner and he or she has to establish beyond reasonable doubt, to the satisfaction of the Court, the desertion throughout the entire period of two years before the petition as well as that such desertion was without just cause.

7. *Gaya Parshad v. Bhaguati*[133]

It was a case under sections 10(1) and 9 of the Hindu Marriage Act, 1955, wherein the most important point for consideration was as to whether the wife had withdrawn from the society of the husband without any reasonable excuse. The Court held that according to the notions of Hindu Society the wife is expected to perform the marital obligations at her husband's residence. She can accept service at a different place but not so to clash with the husband's marital rights which she is duty bound to render and held that the attitude taken by the wife in the instant case amounts to a virtual withdrawal from the society of the husband and it amounts to the matrimonial offence of desertion.

8. *Shanti v. Ramesh*[134]

In this case Katju J. observed that the wife's refusal to resign her job at the instance of the husband is not a sufficient ground for granting a decree of restitution of conjugal rights in favour of the husband, as the wife's taking up of a job even contrary to the wishes of the husband would not amount to withdrawing from the society.

9. *Surrinder Kaur v. Gurdeep Singh*[135]

In this case the wife took up the employment after the marriage at the place of matrimonial home but later on resigned and took a job at a different place, about one hundred miles away from the matrimonial home and the wife categorically stated that she was not willing to join her

133. AIR 1966 MP 212.
134. [1971] All LJ 67.
135. AIR 1973 P&H 134.

husband under any circumstances, apprehending danger to her life from him. Verma J. elaboratting the concept of Hindu marriage and the marital obligations imposed upon the wife and the husband, held that the wife by entering into marriage, places herself under the obligation to reside with her husband wherever he may provide her with a matrimonial home and the wife who does not resign her job at the instance of her husband, held that the wife by entering into marriage, places herself under the obligation to reside with her husband wherever he may provide her with a matrimonial home and the wife who does not resign her job at the instance of her husband, is the wife who has withdrawn from the society of her husband without any reasonable excuse.

10. *Chakar Dhar Mohanty v. Kumunduni Dei*[136]

In this case the question was the burden of proof of desertion. In this case the 'factum' of separation was there but there was no abandonment or animus to bring about an abrogation of duties and obligation of a married life between the couple. The appeal was dismissed for want of animus deserendi.

11. *Rahibni Kumari v.Narinder Singh*[137]

In this case the matter was agitated pertaining to the interpretation of section 10(1)(a) read with the Explanation of the Hindu Marriage Act, 1955. Held that without animus deserendi there can be no desertion within the meaning of section 10(1)(a).

12. *N.R. Radha Krishnan v. N. Dhanalakshmi*[138]

In this case both the husband and wife were employed at different places and the case was under section 9 of the Hindu Marriage Act, 1955. The Court held that under pristine Hindu Law, a Hindu wife's first duty to her husband is to submit herself obediently and to remain under his roof and protection. But then Legislative Enactments like the Hindu Marriage Act

136. AIR 1972 Ori 64.
137. AIR 1972 SC 459.
138. AIR 1975 Mad. 331.

have made considerable inroads upon the unqualified rights that Hindu husband previously enjoyed over the wife. However, in this case the Court could not find animus deserendi and the withdrawal from society of the husband without an intention to shun his company. It was held to be no desertion.

13. *Praveenben v. Sureshbhai*[139]

In this case the wife took the job after the marriage with the full consent of the husband. The parties were posted at different places. There was cohabitation. Later on the husband changed his mind and asked his wife to resign. Shah J. observed that the husband and wife are free to take up a job. It is not a case where the wife had with drawn from the society of the husband.

14. *Kailash Wati v. Ayodhia Parkash*[140]

In this case a question was posed before the Court as to whether a wife, who was gainfully employed at a place away from her matrimonial home, would be justified in law to refuse to leave her job and join her husband to live in the matrimonial home despite the insistent demand of the husband to do so.

15. *Labh Kaur v. Narain Singh*[141]

It is a case under section 13(1)(ib) of Hindu Marriage Act, 1955, and the main point for consideration was animus deserendi, The Court held that desertion means total repudiation of the obligations of marriage and mere factum of living separately does not in itself prove animus deserendi and accordingly the decree of divorce granted by the lower Court is reversed.

***Devi Singh v. Sushila Devi*[142]**

In this case of section 13(1) Explanation of Hindu Marriage Act, 1955, suit for divorce on ground of desertion, the

139. AIR 1975 Guj. 69.
140. ILR [1977] 1 P&H 642.
141. AIR 1978 P&H 317.
142. AIR 1980 Raj. 48.

question was as to the burden of proof and also the applicability of the principle of res-judicata held that the burden of proof lies on the petitioner to show that the respondent has deserted him without reasonable cause and without his consent or against her wishes. The Court held that it is well settled that if one spouse by his words and conduct compels the other spouse to leave the matrimonial home, the former would be guilty of desertion though it is the latter who has physically separated from the other and has the marital home.

16. *Raghuan v. Satyabhama Jayakumar*[143]

This is a case under section 18(2)(a) of the Hindu Adoptions and Maintenance Act, 1956 where the Court held that factum of separation is to be proved. It is not necessary for her to further prove the existence of animus deserendi. The section reads:

> "If he is guilty of desertion that is to say, of abandoning her without reasonable cause and without her consent or against her wish or wilfully neglecting her."

The Court here has taken a humanitarian view and interpreted the section as legislation aiming at the protection and welfare of women who are deserted or neglected and considered the legislation as a beneficent legislation. However, such view cannot be accepted if the question falls under section 13(1)(ib), desertion as a ground of divorce, where the question involved is the breaking of marital tie.

17. *Omwati v. Kishan Chand*[144]

It was a case of divorce on the ground of desertion. There was no difficulty in showing the factum of separation but the animus deserendi had to be inferred was guilty of desertion, as he had totally broken off from his family and had forsaken and abandoned them.

143. AIR 1985 Ker. 193.

144. AIR 1985 Del. 43, See also Asha Handa *v.* Baldev Raj Handa, AIR 1985, Del. 76; Amarjitpal Singh *v.* Kiran Bala, AIR 1985 P&H, 356; Rajendra Kumar *v.* Padam Prakash, AIR 1985 P&H, 232.

4.10.4 No Fault Theory or Other Grounds

We have seen that, adultery, cruelty and desertion have been considered as acts of misconduct and thus fall within the ambit of fault theory. Adultery violates chastity; cruelty is antithesis to love and affection and desertion is contrary to the sanctity of matrimonial home. But there are many other concepts that form the ground for divorce but are not acts of misconduct and thus are kept in the embrace of 'no fault theory', or 'theory of frustration' as envisaged by the Law Commission or 'theory of fait accompli'. Under section 13, various grounds of divorce were recognized both for husband and wife and additional grounds were recognized on which the wife alone could seek divorce. Basically speaking these other grounds are not the acts of misconduct, but an act arising of a state of a thing.

4.10.4.1 Ceased to be a Hindu

Section 13(1)(ii)

Has ceased to be a Hindu by conversion to another religion, or

It is one of the grounds for seeking divorce; this clause speaks of two conditions:

1. Respondent has ceased to be a Hindu, and
2. Respondent has converted to another religion.

One time it was thought that a Hindu is born not made. This means that no one could claim to be governed by Hindu Law simply by professing Hinduism if he was not a Hindu by birth.

This point was agitated in Court of law that the term 'Hindu' means an orthodox Hindu in the strict sense or orthodox believer in Hinduism,[145] in Ran Bhagwan Koer *v.* J.C. Bose[146] the Privy Council said that it is well settled that Hindu does not cease to be governed by Hindu Law by lapses from orthodox Hindu practices or by deviation or dissent from its

145. Raibahadur *v.* Bishandayal [1882] 4 All 39.
146. [1903] 30 IA 249.

control doctrines. Hindu Law applies to Hindus by birth as well as to Hindus by religion.

So we find much elasticity in the concept of Hindu or Hinduism. Hinduism speaks of the ultimate goal of humanity. It is the release and freedom from the unceasing cycle of births and rebirths, moksha or nirvana, which is the ultimate aim of Hindu religion and philosophy, represents the sate of absolute absorption and assimilation of the individual soul with the infinite.

What are the means to attain this end? On this vital issue, there is great divergence of views; some emphasise the importance of jnana or knowledge, while others extol the virtues of bhakti or devotion, and yet others insist upon the paramount importance of the performance of duties with a heart full of devotion and mind inspired by true knowledge. In this sphere again there is diversity of opinion though all are agreed about the ultimate goal. So Hindu, in real sense, is never used in terms of religion, as religion is a very narrow concept in spirituality. Hinduism is a homogeneous amalgamation of various pursuits to seek the ultimate truth and the infinite.

In Ganpat *v.* Presiding Offecer:[147] It is said that when one is born an Hindu, the fact that he goes to a Buddhist temple or a church or dargah, cannot be said to show that he is no more a Hindu unless it is clearly proved that he has changed his religion from Hinduism to some other religion.

This is why the Supreme Court again in Armugam *v.* Rajgopal[148] has said that it is not necessary that there should be any rites or ceremonies whenever there is re-conversion. So a person reconverted to Hinduism is a Hindu. The Hindu Marriage Act, 1955 embraced a very wide definition of a Hindu.

Section 2, Explanation says:

The following persons are Hindus, Buddhists, Jains or Sikhs by religion, as the case may be:

---

147. AIR 1975 SC 420.

148. AIR 1976 SC 939.

(a) any child, legitimate or illegitimate, both of whose parents are Hindus, Buddhists, Jains or Sikhs by religion.

(b) Any child, legitimate or illegitimate, one of whose parents is a Hindu, Buddhist, Jain or Sikh by religion and who is brought up as a member of the tribe, community, group or family to which such parent belongs; and

(c) Any person who is a convert or reconvert to the Hindu, Buddhist, Jain or Sikh religion. Looking to this definition in its vastness and the thoughts expressed on Hinduism as a way of life, a code of conduct, a way to seek Moksha, to seek the ultimate truth, one does not cease to be a Hindu merely because he declares that he has no faith in his religion. A person will not cease to be a Hindu if he does not practise his religion or does not have faith in his religion or renounces his religion or leads an unorthodox life so much so even if he eats beef and insults all Hindu gods and goddesses his faith in another religion and even starts practising another religion.[148a]

In Chandra Sekhar *v.* Kulndaivelu:[149] The Supreme Court stressed on this point that ceasing to be a Hindu is hardly material except in the context of conversion.

Section 13(1)(ii) firstly appears to be superfluous as the petitioner has to prove two things, i.e., that the respondent has ceased to be Hindu and that the respondent has converted to some other religion, which is too difficult a task. Moreover, the conversion of the respondent to a non-Hindu faith does not amount to automatic dissolution of marriage. The petitioner has to file a petition to seek divorce.

4.10.4.2 Insanity

Section 13 (1) (iii)

Has been incurably of unsound mind, or has been

148a. Dr. Paras Diwan, Modern Hindu Law, 9th edn. p. 147.

149. AIR 1963 SC 185.

suffering continuously or intermittently from mental disorder of such a kind and to such an extent that the petitioner cannot reasonably be expected to live with the respondent.

Explanation: In this Clause:

(a) the expression 'mental disorder' means mental illness arrested or incomplete development of mind, psychopathic disorder or any other disorder or disability of mind and includes schizophrenia;
(b) the expression 'psychopathic disorder' means a persistent disorder or disability of mind (whether or not including sub-normality of intelligence) which results in abnormally aggressive or seriously irresponsible conduct on the part of the other party, and whether or not it requires or is susceptible to medical treatment, or

Clause 5 (ii) of Hindu Marriage Act 1955 which stipulates

At the time of marriage, neither party—

(a) is incapable of giving a valid consent to it in consequence of unsoundness of mind; or
(b) though capable of giving consent, has been suffering from mental disorder of such a kind or to such an extent as to be unfit for marriage and the procreation of children; or
(c) has been subject to recurrent attacks of insanity or epilepsy;

This clause is to be read with section 12(1)(b) of the said Act which says that:

(a) the marriage shall be voidable and may be annulled by a decree of nullity on any of the following grounds, namely:
(b) 'that the marriage is in contravention of the condition specified in clause (ii) of section 5.

In Matrimonial Clause Act, 1937, in England, insanity as ground for divorce was introduced.

Section 1(1)(a)(iv): is incurably of unsound mind and has been continuously under care and treatment for a period of at least five years immediately preceding the presentation of the petition;

Section 13(1)(iii): appears to be borrowed from the English Law but the language used is complex, complicate in an inextricable manner that variety of forms of mental illness have been brought in which should result in a situation by which the other spouse fears such company.

To read the legislative mind, a brief history of this provision is required. This provision is substituted by Marriage Laws (Amendment) Act, 1976.

Earlier the provision was:

> Has been incurably of unsound mind for a continuous period of not less than three years, immediately preceding the presentation of the petition.

Also earlier section 10(1)(e) was:

> Has been continuously of unsound mind for a period of two years immediately preceding the presentation of the petition.

Under Section 5 (ii) the stipulation was:

> Neither party should be an idiot or lunatic at the time of marriage.

After the Marriage Laws (Amendment) Act, 1976 the position is:

> Section 5(ii) speaks of (a) unsoundness of mind or (b) is connected with giving of valid consent whereas 5(ii)(a) and (b) is connected with giving of valid consent whereas 5(ii)(c) is itself dependent upon the disease of insanity or epilepsy, but such state of affairs must be existing at the time of marriage.

Grounds for judicial separation as envisaged under section 10 earlier are now to be read as the grounds which are available for divorce, read with section 13A providing alternate relief in divorce proceedings.

Section 13(1)(iii) presently speaks of:

1. incurable of unsound mind or
2. mental disorder of the nature by which the petitioner can not reasonably be expected to live with respondent.

Actually speaking this provision has been borrowed from the English Matrimonial Causes Act, 1973.

In Munishwas Datt *v.* Indra Kumari[150] the Court explained that it is not every form or degree of insanity or lunacy at the time of marriage that invalidates a marriage. The test applied is that a person should have the capacity to understand the nature of contract of marriage and the duties and responsibilities entailed by it and further said that law does not favour annulment or dissolution of marriage and its policy is to uphold the marital status. The Courts will not grant a decree of nullity except on production of clear and convincing evidence.

In Dastane *v.* Dastane,[151] much stress was laid on the concept of schizophrenia in all its aspects. Schizophrenia is a mental disease which is characterised by thought disorders, feelings of persecutions and/or omnipotence social withdrawal and hallucination.[152]

In Bani Devi *v.* A.K.Banerjee,[153] a case under section 13(1)(iii) where the woman was suffering from incurable epilepsy and is also unable to manage herself or her affairs as an ordinary reasonable person, held that such state of mind falls within the expression 'incurably of unsound mind.'

In Alka Sharma *v.* Abhinesh Chandra Sharma.[154] It was a case under sections 5(ii)(b), 12(1)(c) and section 13. Wherein the

150. AIR 1963 Punj. 449.
151. AIR 1970 Bom 312.
152. Roy Hartenstein, Human Anatomy and Physiology.
153. AIR 1972 Del. 50.
154. AIR 1991 MP 205.

Court said that the degree of proof of mental disorder in avoiding a marriage is lighter compared to the degree of mental disorder required for seeking divorce under section 13.

However in Pramath Kumar Nath *v.* Ashina Maiti,[155] the Court said the petitioner has to prove two things:

1. That the respondent is suffering from mental disorder.
2. And that mental disorder is of such a nature that the petitioner cannot reasonably be expected to live with the respondent.

In Santosh *v.* Nandan Singh[156]: The Court was categorical that the expression 'mental disorder' which was explained in clauses (a) and (b) in the Explanation given under this sub-clause requires expert opinion, for the purpose of granting or rejecting the petition.

4.10.4.3 Leprosy

Section 13(1)(iv)

In the original clause, it was stipulated that the party should be suffering from that disease 'for a period of not less than three years immediately preceding the presentation of the petition'. These words have been omitted by the Marriage Laws (Amendment) Act, 1976 and the clause in the present form stands as: 'has been suffering from a virulent and incurable form of leprosy; or

This clause is to be read with section 18(2)(c) of Hindu Adoptions and Maintenance Act, 1956 which states.

(2) A Hindu wife shall be entitled to live separately from her husband without forfeiting her claim to maintenance:

(c) If he is suffering from virulent form of leprosy: Section 18(2)(c), in fact speaks of desertion impliedly but this desertion falls under the preview of section 13(1)(b) read with Explanation thereto and as such does not fall under

155. AIR 1991 Cal. 123.
156. 1983 HLR 528.

the ground of desertion for divorce. Moreover it is merely 'virulent' and incurable is not used herein and as such the spouse had to take recourse for divorce under section l13 (1)(iv) and prove that the respondent spouse is suffering from virulent and incurable leprosy.

Here the petitioner spouse has to prove two things i.e.,

1. It is virulent and
2. It is incurable

Now since the period is omitted, it does not mean that no period is prescribed. Section 13 has to be read with section 14 of the Act which stipulates that no petition for divorce is to be presented within one year or marriage. That period of one year is still mandatory.

In Annapurnamma *v.* Appa Rao,[157] the Court held that it is only in a case where one of the spouses has a virulent and incurable type of leprosy that resort can be had to section (1)(iii). Every form of leprosy is not virulent but that which is malignant or venomous.

Leprosy is defined as chronic contagious granulomatous disease due to infection by mycrobacterium leproe.[158] Leprosy is a chronic disease caused by the acid-fast myhcrobacterium leproe.[159] Leprosy is a disease extremely poisonous; noting a markedly pathogenic microorganism.[160] The main feature of this disease is the formation of granulomata which occurs chiefly in the skin and nerves and causes slowly developing deformities and tropic lesions.

Lepromatous type of leprosy is a severe and malignant form of leprosy. In Dr. G.G. Pama Rao *v.* Swarajya Lakshmi:[161] There was a detailed discussion on the subject and it was held by the Court that lepromatous type of leprosy is malignant and is incurable. The matter was taken in appeal to the Supreme

157. AIR 1963 AP 312.
158. Hanson's Tropical Diseases, 16th edn., p. 478.
159. Rogers and Megaw.
160. Steadman's Medical Dictionary, 19th edn.
161. AIR 1970 AP 300.

Court in Swarajya Lakshmi *v.* Dr. G.G. Padma Rao where the Supreme Court defined malignant as virulent and confirmed the decision of Andhra Pradesh High Court.

So the burden of proof lies on the petitioner to prove that it virulent and incurable. In Annapurna Dei *v.* Narakishore,[162] a typical situation arose where the lower Court passed an order to keep the wife under observation for six months and then report to the Court. The High Court held that such an order is illegal as it militates against the very object of section 13(1)(iv). It is the duty of the petitioner to prove.

Till 1982[163] the patients were traditionally treated with a single drug. Thereafter on the recommendations of World Health Organisation, Multi Drug Therapy (MDA) was introduced in large-scale clinical trials in an attempt to overcome the problem of Dapsone resistance.

So presently, the disease is not dreadful as previously thought over consistently. There has come a sea change due to advancement of medical science and the disease has become curable. Even if deformities are formed that have been curable with corrective surgery.

Besides, the diehard habits have disappeared. There is awakening now among the masses that this disease carried no social stigma. Society has recognised this fact and it is not a disease among many other diseases with no particular emphasis on its specificness. Society has changed in its outlook but law is still static.

4.10.4.4 Venereal Disease in a Communicable Form

Section 13(1)(v)

Originally the ground for divorce was; 'has, for a period of not less than, three years immediately preceding the presentation of the petition, been suffering from venereal disease in a communicable form.' Now after the amendment of 1976 the period of three years is omitted and the clause in the present form is: 'has been suffering from venereal disease in a communicable form.'

---

162. AIR 1965 Ori. 72.

163. Physicians update volume 2, No. 5, Nov./Dec. 1889, Leprosy—Clinical Features and Management by Dr. S. Arunthathi, Vellore.

Now the Section 13(1)(v) is:

(i) Suffering from venereal disease
(ii) In a communicable form

The dictionary meaning[164] of 'venereal disease' is 'a contagious disease that is typically acquired in sexual intercourse. 'Venereal' means 'resulting from or contracted during sexual intercourse and 'communicable' means 'transmittable' 'capable of being communicated'.

Thus, venereal disease is that disease which is contracted during sexual intercourse and which is capable of being transmitted. Syphilis falls within the ambit of venereal disease. There are many diseases connected or caused through sexual intercourse and they are called sexually transmitted diseases (STD), also called venereal diseases.

(i) Syphilis, (ii) Gonorhoea, (iii) Chancorid, (iv) Lymphogranuloma Venereum, (v) Granuloma-inguinale, and (vi) AID, come with the purview of STDs.

No doubt, syphilis is a venereal disease in a communicable form but the disease is curable.

Now the question arises as to whether such a disease should be a ground for divorce. No doubt it is venereal disease and some forms of disease can be in a communicable form, but it is a curable disease.

Judicially speaking even in Birender Kumar *v.* Hemalata Biswas[165] where it was agitated that even if the disease is curable could not be taken as cured until after the lapse of several years.

4.10.4.5 Renunciation

Section 13(1)(vi) stipulates

'has renounced the world by entering any religious order'. Taking up a religious order would mean a person becoming an

164. Werster's Seventh New Collegiate Dictionary, 1971.
165. AIR 1921 Cal 459 later on AIR 1921 Cal. 464 after remand.

ascetic or sanyasi or yati and such transformation would be complete only when one renounces all worldly interests. The Hindu Sastric Law says that one who enters into a religious order severs his connection with the members of his natural family. He is accordingly excluded from inheritance. Neither he nor his natural relative can succeed to each other's property.

In Ramdhan Puri *v.* Dalmer Puri[166] wherein the essentiality of transformation is stated thus: The performance of the viraja homam ceremony was considered necessary for the attainment of the status of perfect and complete sanysi cela.

In Kantal Row *v.* Swamula Varu:[167] It is said that the postulant has to perform his death ceremony and the eight sraddhas, the last of which is his own sraddha, he must then distribute his wealth among his sons and brahmanas reserving enough for the homam (sacrifice in the fire) to be subsequently performed. He then takes leave of his sons and standing in water utters a mantra three times to the effect that he has given up his desire for sons, wealth and world and everything. He does not become a sanyasi till the mantra is pronounced.

Somasundarm Chettiar *v.* Vaithilinga:[168] In this case the question was about a sudra becoming a sanyasi in which a general discussion about the inheritance of sanyasi was held and said that the texts of Hindu Law as to disinheritance applies to a yati or sanyasi to the regenerate classes and thus the concept of sanyasi in terms of religious concept and right to property was underline.

In Baldeo Parshad *v.* Arya Pratinidhi Subha,[169] it is said that the mere fact that a person declares that he has become a sanyasi or that he calls himself or is described by other as such, or wears clothes ordinarily worn by sanyasis would not be sufficient to make him a perfect sanyasi, so as to divest him of all property and amount to his civil death. He must not only retire from all worldly interests and become dead to the world, but to attain this he must perform the necessary ceremonies. For a Hindu of the Sanatana Dharma, the essential ceremonies

166. [1910] 14 CWN 191.
167. [1917] 33 MLJ 63.
168. AIR 1918 Mad. 794.
169. AIR 1930 All 643.

include the performance of prajapati-yesti homam and viraja homam.

In Krishnaji *v.* Hanmaraddi,[170] it is said that renunciation in order to amount to civil death must be complete and final withdrawal from earthly affairs. A man does not become civilly dead because he leaves his family and property. It is necessary that he should enter into a religious order so as to make it certain that he will not change his mind and return to his family.

In Gulab Rao Nathuji Marathe *v.* Nagorao Vishnaji Marathe,[171] the Court held that in order to bring a person under the head sanyasi it is necessary to show absolute abandonment by him of all secular property and a complete and final withdrawal from earthly affairs.

The Supreme Court in Krishna Singh *v.* Mathen Ahir:[172] held that In order to prove that a person has adopted the life a sanyasi, it must be shown that he has actually relinquished and abandoned all-worldly possessions and relinquished all desires for them or that such ceremonies are performed which indicate the severance of his natural family and his secular life. It must also be proved in case of orthodox sanyasi, that necessary ceremonies have been performed such as pindadana or viraja homa or prajapati-yesti without which renunciation will not be complete.

Hindu Marriage Act, 1955 or the amendment thereto in 1976, has nowhere touched the concept of asramas and kept it intact and left it to the discretion of the individual as the said concept is having a religious base and the legislative intention was merely to bring some reforms where needed and not to interfere in the way of life of a Hindu to be regulated by law, so called, the secular law. Moreover, the concept of sanyasi should be couched in and interpreted purely from a religious and social angle.

---

170. AIR 1934 Bom. 385.
171. AIR 1952 Nag. 102.
172. AIR 1980 SC 707.

4.10.4.6 Presumption of Death

Section 13(1)(vii) stipulates

Has not been heard of as being alive for a period of seven years or more by those persons who would naturally have heard of it, had that party been alive.

Section 108 of Indian Evidence Act stipulates:

> Provided that when the question is whether a man is alive or dead and it is proved that he has not been heard of for seven years by those who would naturally have heard of him if he had been alive, the burden of proving that he is alive is shifted to the person who affirms it.

There is no difference between the Law of India as declared in section 108 of the Evidence Act and Law of England which was enunciated In re. Phene's Trusts[173] as follows:

> If a person has not been heard for seven years, there is a presumption of law that he is dead, but at what time within that period he died is not a matter of presumption but of evidence and the onus of proving that the death took place at any particular time within the seven years lies upon the person who claims a right to establishment of which that fact is essential.

But this section is not applicable to proceedings under the Divorce Act[174] and therefore a wife who seeks annulment of marriage on the ground that at the time of her marriage with the respondent, the respondent had a wife alive, is not relieved of the obligation to prove that fact merely by proving that the first wife was alive within thirty years of the petition.

Section 108 of the Evidence Act is to be read in the light of Section 5(1) of Hindu Marriage Act, 1955. Section 5(1) stipulates:

---

173. In re. Phene's Trusts Cl-139.
See Harnam Kaur *v.* Ratna AIR EP 267.

174. Greenwood *v.* Greenwood AIR 1964 Mad 65.

Neither party has a spouse living at the time of the marriage.

So section 5(1), though lays stress on Monogamy, indirectly it also indicates that if either party had a spouse dead at the time of marriage, then there is no difficulty for the next marriage and such marriage is valid under law. Section 108 of the Evidence Act speaks of civil death or presumption of death. It is a legal fiction recognised by law. Thus, if one wants to take shelter under section 108 of the Evidence Act, and wants to have another marriage, a safe measure is to get it recognised by law and not left this presumption to be recognised by the party, because if due to any stroke of bad luck the presumptive dead spouse reappears, legal complications will be in store for the party who married without getting the first marriage dissolved by a decree of divorce under section 13(1)(vii).

But one fact is that if the second marriage is performed on the basis of presumption of death without getting a decree of divorce, no person other than the missing spouse can question the validity of the second marriage.[175] But whatever may be the situation such a provision needs legal recognition, as presumption under section 108 of the Evidence Act is rebuttal.[176]

4.10.5 Irretrievable Breakdown Grounds

Originally divorce was based on the doctrine of the matrimonial offence or the guilt theory under which divorce was viewed as a remedy available to one party for an infringement by the other of the undertakings entered into a marriage. In 1964 by the Hindu Marriage (Amendment) Act, a form of breakdown theory was introduced in Hindu Law by modifying the last two clauses of section 13(1).[177] These clauses were renumbered as clauses (i) and (ii) of Section 13(1A). These clauses were again modified by the Marriage Law

175. Nirmoo *v.* Nikkaram AIR 1968 Del 260.

176. T.R. Rathnam *v.* K. Vardarajulu AIR 1970 AP 246.

177. Section 13(1) (viii) and (ix).

(Amendment) Act, 1976 under which the period of two years has been reduced to one year. Section 13(1A) stipulates:

> Either party to a marriage, whether solemnised before or after the commencement of this Act, may also present a petition for the dissolution of the marriage by a decree of divorce on the ground:
>
> (i) that, there has been no resumption of co-habitation as between the parties to the marriage for a period of one year or upwards after the passing of a decree for judicial separation in a proceeding to which they were parties; or
>
> (ii) that there has been no restitution of conjugal rights as between the parties to the marriage for a period of one year or upwards after the passing of a decree for restitution of conjugal rights in a proceeding to which they are parties.

Section 13(1A) in verbatim is the same as section 27(2) of the Special Marriage Act, 1954 as amended by the Marriage Laws (Amendment) Act, 1976.

We are demonstrably clear to ape the Western concepts and without knowing the consequences. Efforts are further made to make changes and to present the law of divorce in the new fashionable garb. To this effect, the recommendation of Law Commission of India is worth mentioning.

Law Commission took the matter, 'should the irretrievable breakdown of marriage be made a ground for divorce under the Hindu Marriage Act, 1955 as a result of a reference made by the Government of India, Ministry of Law, Justice and Company Affairs. The Law Commission had before it such ground in the laws of a number of countries and various decisions both of Indian and English Courts touching this aspect.

Law Commission recommended 'Irretrievable Breakdown of Marriage[178] as follows which is insertion of new sections 13C, 13D and 13E.

178. 71st Report (7-4-1978).

Section 13C

1. Either party to a marriage may present a petition for the dissolution of a marriage by a decree of divorce to the Court on the ground that the marriage has broken down irretrievably.
2. The Court hearing such a petition shall not hold the marriage to have broken down irretrievably unless it is satisfied that the parties to the marriage have lived apart for a continuous period of at least three years immediately preceding the presentation of the petition.
3. If the Court is satisfied, as to the fact mentioned in sub-section (2) then unless it is satisfied on all the evidence that the marriage has not broken down irretrievably, it shall, subject to the provisions of this Act, grant a decree of divorce.
4. In considering for the purpose of sub-section (2) whether the period for which the parties to a marriage have lived apart has been continuous, no account shall be taken of any one period (not exceeding three months in all) during which the parties resumed living with each other, but no period, during which the parties lived with each other shall count as part of the period for which the parties to the marriage lived apart.
5. For the purpose of sub-sections (2) and (4) a husband and wife shall be treated as living apart unless they are living with each other in the same household, and references in this section to the parties to a marriage living with each other shall be construed as references to their living with each other in the same household.

Section 13D

1. Where the wife is the respondent to a petition for the dissolution of a marriage by a decree of divorce under Section 13C, she may oppose the grant of a decree on the ground that the dissolution of the

marriage will result in grave financial hardship to her and that it should in all the circumstances be wrong to dissolve the marriage.

2. Where the grant of a decree is opposed by virtue of this section, then—
   (i) If the Court finds that the petitioner is entitled to rely on the ground set out in section 13C, and
   (ii) If apart from this section the Court would grant a decree on the petition.

This Court shall consider all the circumstances, including the conduct of the parties to the marriage and the interests of those parties and of any children or other persons concerned, and if the Court is of the opinion that the dissolution of the marriage will result in grave financial hardship to the respondent and that it would in all the circumstances be wrong to dissolve the marriage it shall dismiss the petition or in an appropriate case stay the proceedings until arrangements have been made to its satisfaction to eliminate the hardship.

Section 13E

1. The Court shall not pass a decree of divorce under section 113C unless the Court is satisfied that adequate provision for the maintenance of children born out of the marriage referred to in sub-section (2) has been made consistently with the financial capacity of the parities to the marriage.
2. This section shall apply to—
   (a) minor children;
   (b) unmarried or widowed daughters who have not the financial resources to support themselves; and
   (c) children who, because of special condition of their physical or mental health, need looking after and have not the financial resources to support themselves.

Law Commission, along with this recommended amendments also recommended amendments in Section 21A and section 23 of Hindu Marriage Act, 1955 as follows:

Section 21A[179]

In sub-section (1) clause (a) and clause (b) newly added section 13C should find a mention. In clause (a) after the word and figure 'section 13', the word, figure and letter 'or section 13C', should be inserted. In clause (b) after the word and figure 'section 13', the word, figure and letter 'or section 13' should be inserted.

Section 23(1)(a)[180]

The recommendations of the Law Commission are:

> The petition under the new section 13C would be excluded from the scope of section 23(1)(a). Once divorce is decided to be granted on the basis of irretrievable breakdown of the marriage, any allegation that the fault of a party contributed to the conditions leading to the breakdown of the marriage should be regarded as irrelevant. To allow section 23(1)(a) to operate in all its severity in such cases might defeat the object of the recommended amendment. The general and categorical prohibition contained in section 23(1)(a). The general and categorical prohibition contained in section 23(1)(a) would thus be inappropriate in a case of irretrievable breakdown.

On the basis of this Report,[181] the Marriage Laws (Amendment) Bill 1981 (Bill No. 23 of 1981) was introduced in Parliament but was allowed to lapse. So, presently Hindu Marriage Act, 1955 has no such ground[182] as 'irretrievable breakdown of marriage', but still there is section 13(1A) which does speak of a reflection of irretrievable breakdown of marriage with a difference that firstly, it is a step judicially provided to give chance to the feuding spouses for reconciliation for one year and if still they fail to save their

179. See section 21A of Hindu Marriage Act 1955.

180. See section 23(1)(a) of Hindu Marriage Act, 1955.

181. 71st Report of Law Commission.

182. AIR 1989 Cal 120. The irretrievable breakdown of marriage itself is not a ground for dissolution of marriage under the Hindu Marriage Act, 1955.

marriage, then it becomes one of the grounds to approach the Court for seeking dissolution of marriage by a decree of divorce. It is itself not a ground for divorce. Still the matter will be heard on merit and it is seen that in such matters, the parties to the matrimonial dispute did invoke section 23(1)(a) of the Hindu Marriage Act, 1955.

In Madhukar *v.* Saral,[183] Nain J., observed thus: The enactment of section 13(1A) in 1964 is a legislative recognition of the principle that in the interest of society if there has been a breakdown of the marriage, there is no purpose in keeping the parties tied down to each other.

Jethabai *v.* Manbai:[184] This is a case under sections 13(1A), 10(2), 23(1)(a) of Hindu Marriage Act, 1955. In this case the wife has obtained a decree for judicial separation on the ground of desertion. The husband does not continue to remain under an obligation to co-habit with the wife. Therefore, if he does not make an effort to resume cohabitation, he does not commit a wrong under section 23(1)(a) and would be entitled to get the relief of divorce under 13(1A)(i).

Dastane *v.* Dastane[185] the Supreme Court indirectly points out the section 10 or 9 or section 13(1A) are subject to section 23(1)(a), i.e. section 23(1)(a) has to be looked into.

Bimala Devi *v.* Singh Raj:[186] It is again a case under section 13(1A) and section 23(1)(a). The Court indirectly is of the view that mere non-resumption of co-habitation is not a wrong. There must be a wrong of a nature which can fall under the ambit of section 23(1)(a).

In Gajna Devi *v.* Purushotam Giri[187] again the question agitated was section 13(1A) and section 23(1)(a) and the Court observed that section 23 existed in the statute book prior to the insertion of section 13(1A). Had Parliament intended that a party which is guilty of matrimonial offence and against which a decree for judicial separation or restitution of conjugal rights had been passed, was in view of section 23 of the Act, not

183. AIR 1973 Bom. 55.
184. AIR 1975 Bom. 88.
185. AIR 1975 SC 1534.
186. AIR 1977 P & H 167 FB.
187. AIR 1977 Del. 178.

entitled to obtain divorce, then it would have inserted an exception to section 13(1A) and with such exception, the provisions of section 13(1A) would practically become redundant as the guilty party could never reap the benefit of obtaining divorce, while the innocent party was entitled to obtain it even under the statute as it was before the amendment. Section 23 of the Act, therefore, cannot be construed so as to make effect of amendment of the law by insertion of section 13(1A) nugatory.

In N. Varalakshmi *v.* Hanumantha Rao,[188] it was a case under section 13(1A). It was a case prior to the amendment of section 13(1A). The Court said that there was no cohabitation within two years after the passing of the decree for judicial separation in favour of the husband, the grant of a decree for divorce to the husband would be justified and the fact that the wife's attempts at resumption of cohabitation had been thwarted by the husband would be immaterial. Here the Court shows no concern for section 23(1)(a).

In Anil *v.* Sudhben,[189] it is a case under section 13(1A)(ii) and section 23. The Court held that mere non-compliance per se would not amount to taking advantage of his own wrong. Husband is not precluded from claiming divorce.

Sudershan Kumar *v.* Saroj Rani:[190] In this case a peculiar question as to whether a decree by consent for restitution of conjugal rights can be the basis of divorce proceedings under section 13. The Court held that such a decree is not a nullity and can be the basis of divorce proceedings under section 13.

A different situation arose in Geeta Lakshmi *v.* G.V.R. Sarveshwar Rao[191] wherein sections 9, 13(1A) and 23(1)(a) were agitated. In this case, the husband did not comply with decree but started ill-treating his wife and finally drove her away from the house. The Court held that the husband is not entitled to relief under section 13(1A).

188. AIR 1978 AP 6.
189. AIR 1978 Guj 74. See also AIR 1981 P&H 161, AIR 1983 Kant. 63.
190. AIR 1983 P&H 59. See also AIR 1969 P&H 397 FB.
191. AIR 1983 AP 111. See also AIR 1977 SC 2218.

In Saroj Rani *v.* Sudhershan Kumar,[192] this case was under sections 9, 13, 13B, 23. It was a case of consent decree for restitution of conjugal rights. No cohabitation for one year. The Court held that the husband is not entitled to get a decree of divorce.[193]

The above-cited cases speak as follows:

1. Non-resumption of cohabitation or non-restitution of conjugal rights is a mere ground to present a petition for the grant of divorce.
2. Grant of divorce under section 13(1A) is not automatic. It is still to be decided on merit.
3. It is a step to save marriage and to give time to the spouses to make attempts to reconcile and to nip the evil situation that has unfortunately crept in.
4. Section 13(1A) is subject of section 23(1)(a)
5. Mere non-compliance with the decree is not a 'wrong' under section 23(1)(a). There must be a positive act of 'wrong'.

4.10.6 Special Grounds of Divorce for Wife

Section 13(2) states

> A wife may also present a petition for the dissolution of her marriage by a decree of divorce on the ground.

There are four grounds which can be called wife's special grounds of divorce. Originally section 13(2) of the Act, 1955 provided for only two special grounds on which wife alone could seek divorce. Sub-section (2) was amended by adding two more grounds of divorce at the instance of wife to those contained in the original sub-section (2).[194]

---

192. AIR 1984 SC 1562.
193. AIR 1984 AP 54. See also AIR 1984 All 274, AIR 1988 Cal. 192.
194. The Marriage Laws (Amendment) Act 1976. See 13(2)(iii) & (iv) were added.

Section 13(2)(i) stipulates

In the case of any marriage solemnised before the commencement of this Act, that the husband had married again before such commencement or that any other wife of the husband married before such commencement was alive at the time of solemnisation of the marriage of the petitioner.

Provided that in either case the other wife is alive at the time of the presentation of the petition.

Section 13(2)(i) is in two parts

(i) In the case of any marriage solemnised before the commencement of this Act, that the husband had married again before such commencement, or

(ii) That any other wife of the husband married before such commencement was alive at the time of the solemnisation of the marriage of the petitioner.

Under the first part of this clause a wife whose marriage was solemnised before the commencement of the Act gets the right to seek divorce. In the second part, it is the right of the second wife to seek divorce if the first wife is alive. Thus, both the wives have the right to seek divorce.

In Naganna *v.* Lachmi Bai,[195] there was second marriage by the husband before the commencement of the Act, but that husband divorced his second wife subsequent to filing of petition seeking divorce by the first wife. The Court held that there is no ground for dismissal of the petition as the petition was filed as per the situation and it was clear and unambiguous in view of the section itself. It is the date of the filing of the petition and not the date of the decree.

In Lalithamma *v.* R. Kannan:[196] the Court held that husband cannot plead any conduct of disability on the part of

195. AIR 1963 AP 82: See also AIR 1963 Mys. 118 wherein it is said that the words used in Section 13(2)(i) are unambiguous and clear. The possibility of hardship on a husband on being deprived of the company of both the wives cannot be the ground of taking into consideration in giving effect to a provision of law which does not present any ambiguity.

196. AIR 1966/Mys. 178.

his first wife as a bar to her claim for divorce on the ground of second marriage. In other words even if there is condonation, it will not act as an estoppel.

In Nirmoo *v.* Nikka Ram[197] the Court held that Compromise could not take away the right of the wife under section 13(2)(i) to obtain a decree of divorce and that the compromise could not operate as an estoppel.

However, In Laxmiammal *v.* Alagiriswami,[198] the Court took the stand that section 13(2)(i) is also subject to section 23(1) of the Act and delay of six years after the first marriage, even having two children born after that, was considered as valid for refusing divorce.

Another question arises that if the proceedings are already initiated against the husband under the section 494 of IPC, then what shall be the position of the proceedings also initiated for seeking divorce. The Patna High Court in Raj Kishore Parshad *v.* Raj Kumari Devi[199] held that there is no bar against divorce proceedings.

Now the next question arises as to the efficacy of this provision and the various lacunae inherently present in it.

The legislative intention to make monogamy a law and bigamy not even an exception, as under Hindu Law monogamy was the rule, bigamy was the exception. Various provisions[200] vigorously pursued the enforcement of such law. Here, the legislature totally ignored the circumstances under which the husband resorted the act of bigamy.

Polygamy, as an exception under restraints and constraints, was allowed. It was the unavoidable circumstances that were now completely ignored and even those wives, who have adjusted themselves to a way of life, have also been given the opportunity to disintegrate the family otherwise well settled. Those circumstances were by way of compromise; condonation or necessity, which were well thought of then and now, overlooked which does not speak well of the provision.

This provision has no sanctity under Article 15(3) of the

197. AIR 1968 Del. 260.
198. AIR 1975 Mad. 211.
199. AIR 1986 Pat. 362.
200. Section 5(1), 11, 17 of Hindu Marriage Act, 1955.

Constitution of India which speaks of special provisions for women. Such special provisions should be by way of positive provisions of law and not a provision of negative character.

Art. 15(3) stipulates

Nothing in this article shall prevent the state from making any special provisions for women and children.

Article 51A(e), which stipulates........... to renounce practices derogatory to the dignity of women.

Both provisions read together, it can be safely concluded that any special provision should be consistent with the dignity of women and dignity of women is conclusively intervened with the stability of the marriage and family not otherwise.

This provision is just a namesake provision in the statute book as it has outlived its life. This provision of section 13(2)(i) was incorporated in 1955 and fifty years have passed and is now hit by section 23(1)(d) which stipulates:

> There has not been any unnecessary delay or improper delay in instituting the proceeding, and
> Thus this provision is superfluous and unnecessary.

Section 13(2)(ii) stipulates

The husband has, since the solemnisation of the marriage, been guilty of rape, sodomy or bestiality.

Rape has been defined in section 375 of the Indian Penal Code and its punishment is provided in section 376 thereof. Without going into the legal definition, in common parlance, rape is an act where the woman is ravished and she is the victim of an outrage and it is an injury inflicted on a defenceless and unprotected woman. It is an act of atrocity on a woman amounting to her social death and such act is unpardonable in any civilised society.

Sodomy or bestiality, though covered by section 377 of IPC, but are not mentioned directly.

Sodomy is a felony by the Sexual Offences Act, 1956, section 12[201] for a person to commit buggery with another

---

201. English Law.

person, which means the action of a male person attempting to obtain sexual gratification by means of the anus of human being (sodomy) or with an animal (bestiality) whether per vaginum or per anus.

Sodomy, as per dictionary[202] meaning, means 'an unnatural form of sexual intercourse especially by one male with another'. In B *v.* B[203] the question was referred to a Full Bench of the Punjab Chief Court wherein it was held that husband could be guilty of sodomy on his wife if she was not a consenting party and that this would afford the wife a valid ground to petition for dissolution of marriage. Where the husband used to put his male organ into the mouth or into the anus of the wife and was not prepared to have sexual intercourse at the wife's desire in the usual way, was biting her breasts, coercing her even when she was ill and fell unconscious due to his over indulgence, the wife developed a fear phobia and the husband behaved like a beast, it was held a fit case for divorce.

Bestiality means sexual union by a human being against the order of nature with an animal.[204]

Sodomy or Bestiality are not mere acts of criminality but morally reprehensible too. The modern researches in the disease of AIDS reveal that such type of carnal contact is one of the causes of such a disease.

Adulterous intercourse, rape, sodomy, bestiality are the acts of misconduct and are intolerable in the matrimonial law but instead to make them a ground of divorce, they be made gravely punishable.

Section 13(2)(iii) stipulates

That in a suit under section 18 of the Hindu Adoptions and Maintenance Act 1956 (78 of 1956) or in a proceeding under section 125 of the Code of Criminal Procedure, 1973 (2 of 1974) or under the corresponding section 488 of the Code of

202. Shorter Oxford English Dictionary.

203. 68 PR 1882 referred in (2) DMC 196 (DB).

204. Ganesh *v.* Maya Sundari (1970) 1 Ker. 517 cited in Mayne's Hindu Law and Usage, 13th edn. 254. See also Govindarajulu Naicker (1886) 1 Weir 382.

Criminal Procedure, 1898 (5 of 1898); a decree or order as the case may be, has been passed against the husband awarding maintenance to the wife notwithstanding that she was living apart and that since the passing of such decree or order cohabitation between the parties has not been resumed for one year or upwards.

Section 13(2)(iv) stipulates

That her marriage (whether consummated or not) was solemnised before she attained the age of 15 years and she has repudiated the marriage after attaining that age but before attaining the age of 18 years.

Explanation:

This clause applies whether the marriage was solemnised before or after the commencement of the Marriage Laws (Amendment) Act, 1976.

In Jiviben *v.* Patel Dahyalal Lakhudas,[205] the Court spoke of three essentials of section 13(2)(iv) thus:

1. Marriage before the age of 15 years.
2. She has repudiated the marriage after attaining that age.
3. That she has repudiated the marriage before attaining the age of 18 years.

Savitribai *v.* Sita Ram:[206] In this case she was born on 23rd January 1961. Her marriage was solemnised on 21st April, 1975. The marriage was repudiated on 29th September 1979 and the petition was filed on 25th September 1979. The Court accepted repudiation.

Andhra Pradesh High Court in B. Iylaiah *v.* B.Devamma[207] had gone to the extent that the petition filed immediately after attaining the age of 18 years is maintainable.

205. AIR 1984 Guj. 6.
206. AIR 1986 MP 218.
207. AIR 1981 AP 74.

4.10.7 Divorce by Mutual Consent

In the Indian Divorce Act, 1869, there is no such provision as 'divorce by mutual consent' and same is the case in the Parsi Marriage and Divorce Act, 1936, originally. However, by the Parsi Marriage and Divorce (Amendment) Act, 1988, this provision was introduced.[208] In Muslim Law we have Khula and Mubaraat by which marriage may be dissolved by agreement between the husband and wife. It may take the form of Khula or Mubaraat. In English Law, Divorce Reform Act, 1969 as replaced by Matrimonial Causes Act, 1973 also contains this clause,[209] which is as follows:

> That the parties to the marriage have lived apart for a continuous period of at least two years immediately preceding the presentation of the petition and the respondent consents to decree being granted.

Originally there was no such provision in the Hindu Marriage Act, 1955. Later on by the Marriage Laws (Amendment) Act, 1976, section 13B was inserted which reads as follows:

1. Subject to the provisions of this Act a petition for dissolution of marriage by a decree of divorce may be presented to the District Court by both the parties to a marriage together, whether such marriage was solemnised before or after the commencement of the Marriage Law (Amendment) Act, 1976 on the ground that they have been living separately for a period of one year or more, that they have not been able to live together and that they have mutually agreed that the marriage should be dissolved.
2. On the motion of both the parties made not earlier than six months after the date of presentation of the petition referred to in sub-section (1) and not later than eighteen months after the said date, if the petition is not withdrawn in the meantime, the Court

208. Section 32B of Parsi Marriage & Divorce Act, 1936.
209. Section 2(d).

> shall, on being satisfied, after hearing the parties and after making such inquiry as it thinks fit, that a marriage has been solemnised and that the averments in the petition are true, pass a decree of divorce declaring the marriage to be dissolved with effect from the date of the decree.[210]

Section 14

No petition for divorce to be presented within one year of marriage unless there is exceptional hardship

Reading these sections conjunctively, section 13B(1) cannot override section 14 and as such the period of one year or more should be in addition to the period of one year as given under section 14. So we read these two sections harmoniously, it becomes suffice to reconcile with section 13(1)(ib) which mentions a period of two years.

In Hope *v.* Hope[211] the court held that there is distinction between house and household. It is the household which is the fulcrum point of desertion of living separately.

In Santos *v.* Santos[212] the Court said that household essentially refers to people held together by a particular kind of tie and if that tie is broken, only roof remains. The concept here is sharing of domestic life.

In Sullivan *v.* Sullivan,[213] Turner J. said

> Living apart does not begin until that date on which, if the spouse in question were compellingly asked to define his or her attitude to cohabitation, he (or she) would express an attitude averse to it. Until that stage is reached co-habitation is not broken. When it is reached living apart begins.

---

210. See Section 28 of Special Marriage Act 1954 which is verbatim present in section 13B.
211. [1949] p. 227. See also Hollens *v.* Hollens [1971] 115 SJ 327.
212. [1972] Fam 247. See also Fuller *v.* Fuller [1972] Fam 1247 where living together and living in same household has been distinguished.
213. [1958] NZLR 912.

Bombay High Court in Leela Mahadeo Joshi *v.* Mahadev Sitaram Joshi[214] explained the concept that the term 'have been living separately' has to be read in conjunction with 'not having been able to live together',

> Thus, two ingredients, i.e., 'that they have been living separately for period of one year or more' and 'that they have not been able to live together' are not two differentconcepts but one follows the other. Firstly, there is repugnance and secondly complete disappearance of any change of removal of this repugnance and to come closer. Rather these two ingredients should further go to put it into concrete shape of resolve to dissolve the marriage once for all.

The third ingredient i.e. 'that they have mutually agreed 'that the marriage should be dissolved.'

Some of the High Courts have devised a new approach of granting divorce by mutual consent under Section 13B of the Act on the basis of compromise deeds or mutual agreements without complying with the provisions of Section 13B of the Act.

The Supreme Court in *Renold Rajamani* v. *Union of India*[215] while deciding the case under the Indian Divorce Act, 1869, section 10, held that Court couldn't add new grounds by interpretative process.

The question that has arisen is that once the petition is filed under section 13B, can one party withdraw it?

In *Jayashree* v. *Ramesh*,[216] the Court held that the very object of Section 13B would be frustrated if one of the parties at a subsequent state refuses unreasonably to join in the petition and granted a decree of divorce.

In *Nachhator Singh* v. *Harcharn Kaur*,[217] it was held that the petition couldn't be dismissed as withdrawn at the instance of one party. Both the parties must ask for withdrawal.

---

214. AIR 1991 Bom 105.
215. AIR 1982 SC 1261.
216. AIR 1984 Bom 302.
217. AIR 1986 P&H 201.

In *Chander Kanta v. Hans Kumar*[218] the Court held that unilateral withdrawal of consent without proving that consent was obtained by force, fraud or undue influence, not allowed.

In *Dhanjit Vadra v. Beena Vadra,*[219] the Court held that section 13(B)2 is a matter of formality. Decree can be granted without waiting for prescribed period.

Andhra Pradesh High Court also held that section 13(B) 2 is directory and not mandatory.[220]

On the other side of the judicial picture, the decisions of some of the Courts are contrary to the opinions of other Courts as given above.

In Harcharan Kaur *v.* Nachhatar Singh[221] the Court held that withdrawal of consent by either party is permissible. Either party is at liberty to revoke its consent any time before petition is finally disposed of.

The Supreme Court at length discussed this matter in Sureshta Devi *v.* Om Prakash[222] and reversed the decision of Himachal Pradesh High Court which held that the wife gave her consent to the petition without any force, fraud or undue influence and therefore she was bound by that consent.

The Supreme Court analysed the section and held that the filing of the petition with mutual consent does not authorise the Court to make a decree for divorce. Mutual consent to the divorce is a *sine qua non* for passing a decree under section 13B. Mutual consent should continue till the divorce decree is passed then alone can divorce be called a divorce by mutual consent.

4.11 BARS TO MATRIMONIAL RELIEF

There are certain bars under matrimonial Hindu Law for relief to the parties. They are:

---

218. AIR 1989 Del 73.
219. AIR 1990 Del 146.
220. AIR 1986 AP 167.
221. AIR 1988 P & H 27. See also K.I. Mohan *v.* Jeejabai AIR 1988 Ker 28; N.G. Parshad *v.* B.C. Vanamala AIR 1988 Karn 162; Smt. Prakash Kaur *v.* Bikramjit Singh, AIR 1989 P&H 46.
222. AIR 1992 SC 1904. In this case AIR 1984 Bom 302, AIR 1989 Del 73, [1984] 2 DCM 388 (MP) overruled and AIR 1988 Ker 28, AIR 1988 P&H 27 and AIR 1986 Raj. 128 approved.

1. The matrimonial action can be initiated only by a party to the matrimony, that is to say, the husband or the wife. Under Section 13 of the Hindu Marriage Act either the husband or the wife has to present the petition. Section 9, 10, 11, 13B, 24, 26 reiterates the same.
2. The standard of proof in matrimonial cases has to be beyond reasonable doubt. The Supreme Court accepted the rule of beyond reasonable doubt in the case of matrimonial offences.[223] It means it must carry a high degree of probability.[224] The matrimonial offences may be proved by mere preponderance of probability.[225] Of course, the degree of probability shall depend on the subject matter.
3. The Action for a matrimonial relief is for a purely personal right must be brought by the party injured only, and is not transmissible to his representatives. However, the maxim Actio personalis cum moritur per sona, "a personal action dies with the person," is not applicable as the judgement passed in matrimonial action is a judgement in rem and not merely a judgement in personam.
4. Events subsequent to institution of proceedings should taken into account by the court wherever possible to mould the relief in accordance therewith and avoid multiplicity and protraction of proceedings not only in the interest of the parties to the proceedings but also in the interest of the society in general.
5. The well established rule of matrimonial law is that a decree of dissolution of marriage is to be obtained upon 'satisfaction of the Court' which entails 'strict proof' of the ground or grounds for relief. Consent, connivance, collusion, delay, taking advantage of one's own wrong, etc. stand in the way of Courts satisfaction.

---

223. Bipin Chandra *v.* Provabati, AIR 1957 SC 176.
224. Veerareddi *v.* Kistamma, AIR 1969 Mad. 236.
225. Dastane *v.* Dastane, AIR 1975 SC 1535.

6. Principles of *resjudicata* are applicable in appropriate cases of matrimonial relief. The Supreme Court observed that though *estoppel* is described as a rule of evidence and *resjudicata* as a species of *estoppel*, the whole concept is more correctly viewed as substantive rule of law.[226]
7. Condonation or forgiveness of conjugal offence with full knowledge of all the circumstances is the bar for getting matrimonial relief. Where there is no breach of condonation after condonation or forgiveness stands complete, absolute and irrevocable. Therefore, condonation consists of a *factum* of reinstatement and *animus remittendi*.
8. Connivance, as applicable to matrimonial causes, is the willing consent to a conjugal offence or a culpable acquiescence in a course of conduct reasonably likely to lead to the offence being committed is the bar to obtain relief by reason of an offence to which he himself has consented.
9. Collusion is an agreement between the spouses or the petitioner and co-respondent for the purpose of procuring the initiation of matrimonial action is a bar for obtaining the relief under matrimonial cases. However, once collusion established, does not stand as a bar for all time. The party may again bring a fresh petition which is free from collusion.[227]
10. Advantage of one's own wrong is also a bar for seeking matrimonial relief. This rule is based on the principle that a wrongdoer cannot be allowed to take advantage of his or her own wrong or disability for the purpose of obtaining relief through the Court.

---

226. Guda Vijayalakshmi *v.* G.R. Sekhara Sastry, AIR 1981 SC 1143.
227. Emanuel *v.* Emanuel (1946) p. 115.

CHAPTER

Judicial Attitude

5.0 JUDICIAL DECISIONS

The decisions of Courts on various grounds of divorce reveal the attitude of the Judiciary from time and again. The Judicial decisions on various grounds of divorce detailed below shows the attitude of Courts from time to time. At the very outset, doubts are to be cleared as to whether standard of proof in divorce proceedings is one of "proof beyond reasonable doubt" as applicable in criminal cases or one of "Preponderance of probabilities" as applicable in civil matters, because the courts are in conflicting views on the ground that the proceedings in the matrimonial causes are of civil nature. Nature of proceedings will not conclusively decide the standard of proof because the divorce proceedings are meant to dissolve marriage between parties which may not only have adverse effect on the parties themselves but also on the offspring from the wedlock.

Standard of proof in divorce proceeding must be stricter than that in proceedings for judicial separation. This is so because a decree of divorce can also be obtained on the ground that there has been no resumption of cohabitation between the parties to the marriage for a period of one year or upwards after the passing of a decree for judicial separation in proceeding to which they are parties.[1] Therefore, the allegations constituting the ground(s) for dissolution of marriage will have to be proved by the party seeking a decree for divorce beyond any reasonable doubt notwithstanding that the proceedings are of civil and not of criminal or quasi-criminal nature. Therefore, the Punjab and Haryana High Court,[2] the Calcutta High Court,[3] the Supreme Court[4] and the M.P. High Court[5] are right in their views that the allegation, e.g., adultery or voluntary sexual intercourse with non-spouse, must be proved beyond reasonable doubt and the views of the Supreme Court,[6] the Karnataka High Court[7] and of other High Courts, following the Supreme Court in Dastane *v.* Dastane[8] before the 1976 amendment of the provisions. There can be no doubt that the 1976 amendments are of far-reaching consequences, because before the said amendment, "living in adultery" was one of the grounds for divorce where after amendment, it is "voluntary sexual intercourse with non-spouse", i.e., a single act of voluntary sexual intercourse with non-spouse, if proved, is sufficient to declare dissolution of marriage and, therefore, of necessity, a stricter proof is required.[9]

1. See s. 13(1A)(i).
2. See Dassi *v.* Dhani Ram, AIR 1969 P&H 25 (DB) : ILR (1969) 2 Punj 365.
3. See Sachindranath *v.* Nilima, AIR 1970 Cal 38 (DB) : 74 CWN 168.
4. See Bipinchandra *v.* Prabhavati, AIR 1957 SC 176 : 1956 SCR 838 : 1957 SCJ 144; White *v.* White, AIR 1958 SC 441 : 1958 SCR 1410: 1958 SCJ 839 and Chandra Mohini *v.* Avinash Prasad, AIR 1967 SC 581 : 1967 (1) SCR 864.
5. See Hargovind *v.* Ramdulari, 1986 (1) HLR 543 (MP).
6. See Dastane *v.* Dastane, AIR 1975 SC 1534 : 1975 (3) SCR 967 : 1975 (2) SCC 326 : 1975 HLR 111.
7. See Sham Prabha *v.* Chandra Sekhar, 1983 HLR 288 (Kar-DB) and Subhashini *v.* Uma Kanth, 1985 (1) HLR 285 (Kar-DB).
8. AIR 1975 SC 1534 : 1975 (3) SCR 967: 1975 (2) SCC 326 : 1975 HLR 111.
9. The point on "standard of proof" will also be elaborated in the context of the relevant grounds for divorce, where necessary.

5.1 ADULTERY

The Courts cannot grant divorce on guilty of adultery of the spouse of a petitioner unless there is sufficient positive proof or presumptive proof such as circumstantial evidence to prove the guilty. Courts did not accept mere allegations that one of the spouses is in adultery. The decisions of the Courts in various cases proved the same.

In Dalbara Singh *v.* Mohinder Kaur[10] Divorce sought on ground of unchastity of wife. Parties' were cohabitated in Ludhiana district till 6-5-1975. The husband serving in Army and joined duty in NEF but wife did not accompany him. Husband remained in NEFA till 10-1-1976. The child born on 7-5-1976 but the husband had disowned the child. The husband could not prove that the child was born on 7-5-1976 and that he had no access to his wife during the crucial period while posted to a station from where he could not visit his wife and that the child could not be conceived between 6-5-1975 to 10-1-1976. Trial court dismissed his petition. The Appellate court allowed husband to produce certificate of date of birth of the child and the wife to lead evidence in rebuttal. Evidence also found lacking in material particulars, i.e., non-access of husband to wife from his place of posting on one or two gazette holidays without formal authorized leave, from the proper authority and that the child could be given birth to by the wife from the loins of the husband after the expiry of 280 days from her conception. The Court had rejected the plea of the husband and no divorce was granted.

In Rabindra Prashad *v.* Sita Devi[11] the marriage sought to be dissolved by husband on the ground of adultery committed by wife. The husband alleging that wife was seen in the company of two persons in a cinema hall and also some where else and in the presence of her mother wife went upstairs with the persons in a hotel room and stayed there for an hour. But neither the owner of the hotel was produced nor was the reservation of any room on that day by the alleged adulterers proved. Mere allegation that wife was seen in the company of

10. 1978 HLR 647 (Punjab and Haryana).
11. 1985 (2) HLR 69 Pat.

the alleged adulterers not sufficient in the absence of positive proof that they were caught in any compromising situation. Witnesses produced by husband being a chance witness, a hawker of monkey-nuts and a friend of his not found reliable. Suit for dissolution of marriage was not sustainable.

Broken marriage on account of adulterous conduct of husband. No self-respecting wife can tolerate adulterous conduct of her husband and by rejecting divorce petition; it would be perpetuating serious crime on the womanhood. Decree of divorce granted in favour of wife.[12]

In Mohinder Singh *v.* Smt Murti[13] the wife leading an unchaste and adulterous life. By commission of sexual intercourse with somebody, gave birth to a child. The Court held that the husband was entitled for decree of divorce.

In Smt Maya Chatterji *v.* Shiv Chandra Chatterji[14] the Divorce Petition of the husband was rejected. The petitioner alleged desertion by wife as well as allegations of adultery on the part of wife with named correspondent. But the husband maintained sexual relations with his wife even after discovery of such adultery. Husband in fact himself deserted his wife and then filed petition for divorce. Husband not entitled to a decree of divorce in such circumstances.

In Kewal Rain *v.* Jiji Bai[15] the wife had sexual intercourse with some person other than her husband after solemnization of marriage. No information regarding birth or death of the presumed illegitimate child conveyed to the Kotwar or to any other authority. This circumstance only probabilities the fact that the child is not legitimate and granted Divorce.

In M. Akkamma *v.* M. Jagannadham[16] the wife was seen sleeping in night with her sister's husband. Also given birth to a son as a result of adulterous intercourse. Disinterested testimony of three witnesses in that regard proved the adultery.

---

12. Smt Chandrakanta *v.* Rajesh 1985 (1) HLR 426 (Raj.).
13. 1977 HLR 420 P&H.
14. 1984 HLR 160 Allahabad.
15. 1984 HLR 609 MP.
16. 1981 HLR 646 (D.B.) AP.

In Raj Pal Malhotra *v.* Tripta Malhotra and another[17] the husband and wife residing with his parents, brother, sister and uncle in a house consisting of 3 rooms-Respondent No. 2 was on visiting terms with wife. Husband alleged adultery against wife by respondent No. 2. Wife averred that Respondent No. 2 was just like brother to her and he had arranged for her marriage ceremonies. Husband failed to prove adultery. Held, that it was incredible that in a small house with such a large number of persons present, wife and respondent No. 2 indulged in adultery.

Husband has made an allegation of adultery against wife. Husband alleged that the child born to her was not from his loins and wife had illicit relations with a person of 70 years of age and Municipal Commissioner. That person himself appeared as a witness to prove the allegation to be wrong. Evidence established that wife was of good character and the child was born from the loins of the husband. Husband failed to produce any person from the locality to support his allegation against wife. Held that wife was not guilty of adultery.[18]

In Jaswati Gordhanbhai Vaghela *v.* Priyakant Meghjibhai Vaghela and another[19] the wife stayed with her husband for a very short while as his wife. Witness is a disinterested witness and as social worker she is lady of good will who had done her best to see that wife and husband forgive and forget what had happened in the past and live together as husband and wife. When reconciliation tried through one medical practitioner and social worker, wife eloped with second respondent had known each other since childhood as they are neighbours. Mere fact of woman going away with another man to a different town and be away from her father's house as well as her husband's place does not necessarily and conclusively establish that there was adulterous relationship between the two. Something more is required to show that relationship between the two has reached a point where adultery could be inferred.

17. 1981 HLR 168 Del.
18. Guldev Raj *v.* Mohan Kaur, 1985(1) HLR 250 P&H.
19. 1986(1) HLR 93 Guj.

The husband would be guilty of adultery where the wife herself saw the husband sharing bed with his brother's wife[20] or where the husband is having sexual intercourse with his second wife because second marriage during the lifetime of the first wife is a nullity[21] or where the husband is having a second wife, whether marriage valid or not[22] or where the husband is living with another man's wife and children,[23] or where the husband is keeping a woman in his house, committing voluntary act of sexual intercourse with her and out of this illegal union, two children are born.[24] But the husband would not be guilty of adultery where the wife fails to give name of any lady with whom adultery is alleged against the husband.[25]

While the finding of the respondent's wife in the company of a person other than her husband having been dragged by him into a shed by holding her hand would not amount to having sexual intercourse with any person other than her husband.[26] If an unrelated person is found alone with a young wife after midnight in her bedroom in actual physical juxtaposition, that circumstance unless explained in manner compatible with innocence would justify inference of adultery.[27]

The sexual intercourse had by the respondent with a stranger need not have been committed within India, and though the operation of the Act is confined to India, the fact that one of the grounds for the relief had its habitat outside India does not prevent a petition being presented in India for the necessary relief based upon that ground, Gerald *v.* Esid.[28]

---

20. Karnail Singh *v.* Balbir Kaur, 1980 HLR 24 (P&H).
21. Darsabai v.Ganga Prasad, 1988 (2) HLR 294 (MP).
22. Satya Narain *v.* Mamta, 1997 (1) HLR 732 (Raj-DB).
23. Amit Kumar *v.* Sefali, 1998 (1) HLR 196 (Cal-DB).
24. Mam Kaur *v.* Ram Sarup, 2001 (1) HLR 596 (P&H).
25. Prem Chand *v.* Savitri, 1998 (2) HLR 666 (All-DB).
26. Sadhu Amma *v.* Satyanarayana, (1967) An, W.R. 179.
27. Subba Rama Reddiar *v.* Saraswathy, (1966) 2 M.L.J. 363: 1967 Mad, 85. Cf. Chandra Mohini *v.* Avinash, 1967 SC 584 (mere fact of male relation writing improper letters to a married woman does not necessarily prove illicit intimacy between them).
28. [1956] 2 MLJ 289.

Adultery committed before marriage is not a ground for relief Coleman *v.* Coleman.[29]

The birth of a child to the wife when there was no access to her by the husband during the possible period of conception shows the adultery of the wife.[30] Mere suspicion and opinion cannot take the place of proof and there must be evidence to show not only opportunity to commit the adultery, but also desire or inclination to commit it.[31]

The rules governing human conduct and known to common observation and experience are applied in these cases as in all other investigations of fact. The early view was (but not now) that proof should be proof beyond reasonable doubt.[32] Proof beyond reasonable doubt is a requirement of criminal law, and even there it is only a guideline and not a fetish.[33] Direct proof however is not an imperative.[34] It is highly improbable that any person could be witness to such act; hence direct proof will be very rare and even if forthcoming the Court would regard it with disfavour.[35] Normally adultery is expected

29. (1955) All E.R. 617.
30. Anthony *v.* Mery, ILR 62 Cal, 1080.
31. Mahalingam Pillai *v.* Amsavalli (1956) 2 MLJ 289.
32. See Bipin Chandra *v.* Prabhavati; 1957 S.C. 176; Varadarajulu *v.* Baby Ammal, 1965 Mad.29; Bhagwanti *v.* Sadhu Ram, 1961 Punj. 181; Harish Chandra *v.* Rama Gowri, 1969 B.L.J.R. 999; Narayanan *v.* Parukutty, 1973 Ker, L.T. 80: 1973 Ker. L.J. 120; Kunhikannan *v.* Malu, 1973 Ker. L.T. 431; Chhaganlal *v.* Sakkha Devi, 1975 Raj. 8. Cf., Whirte *v.* white, 1958 S.C. 441 (case under the Divorce Act). Cf., however Prem Masth *v.* Kumudani Bai, 1974 M.P. 89 (case under the Divorce Act), bolding that the view that the standard of proof required in order to be satisfied is proof beyond reasonable doubt does not now hols the field and the civil standard of proof alone will have to applied now, in view of the changed interpretation of the law in England in Blyth *v.* Blyth,(1966) 1 All E.R 524. Cf. also champa Gowri v.Jannadas Amirchand, Supra holding that adultery must be proved by a preponderance of probability and Dr. N.G. Dastene *v.* Mrs. S. Dastane, 1975 S.C. 1534; Shyam Narain *v.* Shail, (1978) 4 A.L.R. 882.
33. Inder Singh *v.* The State, (1979) 2 S.C.J. 10, 11.
34. Chandra Mohini *v.* Asinash, 1967 S.C. 384; Vedavathi *v.* Ramaswamy, 1964 Mys. 280; Devyani *v.* Kauntilal, 1963 Bom. 98.
35. Simon Lakra *v.* Bakla, I.L.Rl 11 Pat. 627; Phillips *v.* Emperor, 1925 Oudb 508.

to be established by circumstantial evidence. It is not possible to lay down a rule of thumb as to what circumstances would be sufficient to establish adultery. The only general rule is that the circumstances must be such as would lead to a guarded judgment of a reasonable and just man to that conclusion. The Court would not as a general rule infer adultery from evidence of opportunity alone but would require some more satisfactory proof.[36] Evidence of a guilty inclination or passion is needed in addition.[37]

To establish adultery it is not necessary to prove the direct fact or even an act of adultery in time and place, or even necessarily the name of the person with whom the respondent is alleged to have committed adultery.[38] The birth of a child 11 months and 20 days after final parting company with husband would go a long way to establish adultery on the wife's part.[39]

Likewise the birth of a child 402 days after final severance of ties was proof that the child was born only as a result of the wife's sexual intercourse with someone other than the husband and no other evidence is needed to prove this.[40]

In Tribhat Singh *v.* Vimla Devi,[41] the facts found were that the wife had been frequently absenting herself from her house for days at a stretch and during such periods of her absence was found in company with a total stranger and no explanation had been forthcoming for the woman being found in the stranger's company at several places, and it was held that these facts would be consistent with a finding that she had been living in adultery with that man. The degree of proof need not reach certainty but must carry a high degree of probability.[42]

---

36. Pushpa Devi *v.* Radheshyam, 1972 Raj, 260; Chhaganlal *v.* Sakkha Devi, supra. See further. Subbarama Reddiar *v.* Saraswathi, 1967 Mad. 85; Pattayee *v.* Manickam, 1967 Mad. 254; Barker *v.* Barker, 1955 M.B. 103; Hearsey *v.* Hearsey, 1931 Oudh 259.
37. Champa Gowri *v.* Jannadas Amir Chand, supra.
38. Champa Gowri *v.* Jannadas Amirchand, supra; Barker *v.* Barker, supra; Heaesay *v.* Hearsey, supra.
39. Kamlesh Kumari *v.* Balvir Singh Bedi, 1973 P. & H. 152.
40. Vira Reddi *v.* Kistamma, 81 L.W. 490: 1969 Mad. 235: (1969) 1 M.L.J. 366.
41. 1959 J. and K. 72.
42. Baby Ammal *v.* Varadarajulu, (1969) 82 L.W. 18.

Proof beyond reasonable doubt does not mean proof beyond a shadow of doubt or that it should reach certainty reversed by Supreme Court on another point.[43]

Green *v.* Green[44] where a husband against whom a decree for judicial separation has been passed at the instance of the wife, commits adultery, subsequently, the wife is entitled to a decree of divorce on the ground that the husband has been living in adultery. The judicial separation does not amount to immunity for matrimonial offence and it is no argument for the respondent to urge that he or she being separated under an order of judicial separation, the petitioner ought not to bother as to how the respondent conducts himself or herself.

The petitioner for a decree of divorce is expected to come with clean hands, and the question may therefore arise if he or she has been guilty of adultery, whether a petition on the ground of respondent's adultery should be viewed with favour. The answer is provided by section 23(1)(a), which vests a discretion in the Court to consider all the circumstances of such a case and see if the petitioner should be given the relief. No doubt, there is no express provision in the Act and certainly not in this particular section to the effect that the petitioner who is guilty of adultery cannot submit a petition for divorce against the respondent. But the wide and comprehensive qualification embodied in section 23(1)(a) will meet the justice of any particular case.

5.2 CRUELTY

It is evident that the concept of cruelty has not remained the same, as it was some hundred or even fifty years back. Before the acceptance of the irretrievable breakdown of marriage as a ground, for that if a marriage has broken down by any act or conduct of the respondent, it was considered to be covered under "cruelty": And, despite Lord Denning's warning in 1950 "if the doors of cruelty were opened too wide,

---

43. Vira Reddi *v.* Kistamma, 81 L.W. 490: 1969 Mad. 235: (1969) 1 M.L.J. 366.
44. L.R. 3 Prob. 121.

we should soon find ourselves granting divorce for incompatibility of temperament."

Cruelty is a course of conduct of one which is adversely affecting the other. Isolated incidents where the parties may have quarrelled, by itself, would not amount to cruelty.[45] In order to find whether the behaviour of erring spouse falls within ambit of cruelty a cumulative effect of all acts and conduct has to be taken into consideration. Even subsequent events can be taken into consideration.[46]

The following cases are proved that the said instances on the part of the wife against the husband constitute the ground of cruelty for divorce.

1. Refusal of wife to come back to the matrimonial home and to keep the child of two months left by her, which resulted in the death of the child.[47]
2. False complaint by wife against husband resulting in investigation and enquiry by government[48] or wild allegations against husband in criminal complaint under SS. 494 and 120B, IPC, even though complaint was dismissed[49] or complaint against husband under SS. 294 and 323, IPC, was found without substance and complaint under SS. 494/34, IPC[50] or complaint against husband to police resulting in his arrest, remand to judicial custody and suspension from employment.[51]
3. Callous indifference of wife towards husband.[52]
4. False allegation of molestation by elder brother of husband.[53]

---

45. Deepak *v.* Manisha, 2001 (2) HLR 398 (P&H).
46. Surbhi *v.* Sanjay, 2000 (2) HLR 52 (MP-DB).
47. Gurucharan Singh *v.* Sukhdev Kaur, 1979 HLR 155 (P&H).
48. M.K. *v.* Keerthi, 1987 (1) HLR 199 (Del.).
49. Balram Singh *v.* Sukhvant Kaur, 1988 [1] HLR 307 (P&H).
50. Rama Devi *v.* Ashok Kumar, 1994 [1] HLR 591 [MP-DB].
51. Vijayalakshmi *v.* Bheem Reddy 1988 [2] HLR 688 [AP-DB].
52. Rajendra Singh *v.* Tharavathi, 1980 HLR, 534 [Del.].
53. Nirmal *v.* Brij Mohan, 1981 HLR 106 [P&H].

5. Wife being of nagging type, constantly insulting her husband in presence of her friends.[54]
6. Wife writing threatening letters to husband, for pressing him live apart on account of ill-treatment of her mother-in-law, using intemperate language to insult him in his office and before his superiors and making unsubstantiated allegations of illicit relationship.[55]
7. Wife launching proceeding against husband under s.107/116, Cr. P.C and also leveling allegations in course of her statement that the husband had illicit relations with the wife of someone else.[56]
8. Wife keeping insinuating husband to be guilty of three misdeeds, i.e., murder of their daughter, attempted murder of wife and bigamous conduct of husband.[57]
9. False allegations against husband of his being drunkard, gambler and characterless.[58]
10. Unsuccessful prosecution in criminal case of her husband and relations.[59]
11. False allegations regarding illicit connection against her husband made not only to the employer of husband but also to police authorities, resulting in his demotion from the post of foreman to the post of an engine driver.[60]
12. Wife making complaints or getting the complaints addressed to the employers of husband and to persons in authority and also to the police found to be baseless on enquiry.[61]

---

54. Krishna *v.* Chunilal, 1982 HLR 30 [P&H-DB].
55. Urmila *v.* Devender Kumar, 1983 HLR 529 [Del.].
56. Krishna *v.* Prabhu Dayal, 1983 HLR 540 [P&H].
57. Sukhwinder *v.* Shinjara Singh, 1985 [1] HLR 9 [P&H-DB].
58. Urmila *v.* Ravi Prakash, 1985 [1] HLR 310 [Del.].
59. Surjit Kaur *v.* Veerender 1986 [1] HLR 417 [P&H].
60. Narain Dutt *v.* Santosh, 1986 [1] HLR 573 [Del.].
61. Vinod Kumar *v.* Nutan Sharma, 1986 [1] HLR 625 [Del.].

13. Disobedience by wife, her refusal to cook, insulting the husband in presence of others, ill-treatment, threatening to commit suicide, refusal to cohabitation, not allowing access in the house and keeping the husband waiting outside the house for hours, slapping husband in the presence of others.[62]
14. Allegation of adultery against husband amounts to legal cruelty when found false.[63] Further, baseless imputation by wife that husband had illicit connection with his own married elder sister is an instance of cruelty.[64]
15. Where beating was given to husband by his father-in-law and brothers-in-law in the presence of his wife, the wife also insulted the husband and did not come forward to rescue her husband and she used to insult husband with the object of humiliating and degrading him.[65]
16. Birth of illegitimate child.[66]
17. Wife leaving matrimonial home and leaving two minor children in a room and not caring to look after them.[67]
18. Baseless allegations against husband in letters and pleadings (written statements) resulting in mental torture.[68]

---

62. Haribhajan *v.* Amarjit Kaur 1986 [1] HLR 634 [MP].
63. Gomukh Singh *v.* Balvinder Kaur, 1985 [1] HLR 116 [P&H]; Manjit Kaur *v.* Avtar Singh 2001 [1] HLR 614 [P&H).
64. Ashim *v.* Anusree, 1991 (1) HLR 611 (Cal-DB); Chanderkala *v.* Dr.S.P.Dwivedi, 1993 (2) HLR 264 (SC); 1993 (4) SCC 232: 1993 (4) JT 644: 1993 (2) UJ 538 : 1993 (3) scale 541: 1993 (2) DMC 271 : 1993 (3) CCC 205; Rajan *v.* Shobha, 1995 (2) HLR 656 (Bom – DB). But see Selvi *v.* Arumugam, 1990 (2) HLR 605 (Mad.) for the view that a false allegation against husband living in extra marital relationship with another woman does not amount to cruelty.
65. Surender *v.* Tejender, 1987 [1] HLR 86 [P&H].
66. Madanlal *v.* Sudesh Kumari, 1987 [1] HLR 583 (Del.); Rekha *v.* Narendra Mohan, 1995 [2] HLR 228 [P&H].
67. Gopallal *v.* Gayetri Devi, 1989 [2] HLR 149 [Raj.- DB].
68. S.P.Thrivedi *v.* Chandra Kal, 1990 [2] HLR 67 [Bom.].

19. Constant threat of wife to commit suicide and to entangle her husband and her relatives for the same[69] or propensity of wife to commit suicide[70] or several attempts by wife to commit suicide,[71] however, allegations that wife gave threats to immolate herself and commit suicide, when not proved to be true, would not prove cruelty.[72]
20. Wife depriving the husband of all the pleasures of married life by not coming to matrimonial home.[73]
21. Unsubstantiated allegations of cheating, criminal breach of trust of criminal misappropriation against the husband and mother-in-law and filing of criminal case on such allegations.[74]
22. Incorrigible conduct of wife, e.g., when wife told that her father-in-law had died and her husband told her to return, but she did not rejoin him in the moment of despair and melancholy and on being informed that Bhog ceremony was to be performed of her late father-in-law, she again did not join her husband at the moment of need.[75]
23. Use of offensive language such as "Fauji Gadha" or "Fauji Tatto" would not be acceptable by any self-respecting husband.[76]
24. Wife asking the husband soon after marriage to shift to some other place and get separated from his parents without there being any extraordinary

---

69. Gurdip Kaur *v.* Balbir Singh, 1991 [2] HLR 309 (P&H); Daya *v.* Krishna Lal, 1992 (1) HLR 273 (MP); Sushila *v.* Om Parkash, 1992 (1) HLR 517 (P&H); Parimi Mehar *v.* Parimi Nageswara, 1993 (2) HLR 222 (AP-DB); Sudha *v.* Narayan, 1994 (2) hlr 633 (Bom-DB). But see contra Chinmoy *v.* Bharati, 1990 (2) HLR 128 (Cal.-DB).
70. Krishna *v.* Alok Ranjan, 1985 [5] HLR 759 [Cal.-DB].
71. Rangarao *v.* Vijayalakshmi, 1990 [1] HLR 610 [Mad.].
72. Krishna *v.* Bhooribai, 1996 [2] HLR 36 [MP].
73. Meena Rani *v.* Madan Lal, 1995 [2] HLR 97 [P&H]; Sunil Kumar *v.* Sasibala, [1995] 2 HLR 332 [P&H].
74. Sukhdev Kaur *v.* Ravindra Singh, 1996 [2] HLR 296 [Cal.-DB].
75. Rani *v.* Amarnadh, 1997 [1] HLR 707 [P&H].
76. Mahabir *v.* Nirmala, 1998 [1] HLR 292 [P&H].

situation and circumstances especially when they are living jointly under the same roof and in the same mess and using abusive language and being rude in behaviour towards the husband and members of the family.[77]

25. Where the wife quarrelled with the husband generally and abused other members of his family, threw a cup of tea at the husband, on several occasions when the husband returned from this official work, the wife shut the husband out and did not open the door with the result that the husband was compelled to stay with his friend at night.[78]
26. Where the wife did not permit any sexual contact to the husband and the story of abortion created by her was not justified by her conduct.[79]
27. Where the behaviour of wife with her husband was far from satisfactory, she was quarrelling with him, assaulted him and abused not only the husband but members of the family also and husband was humiliated and insulted by wife.[80]
28. Where the wife left the matrimonial home after two and a half months after the marriage, she rushed to the police implicating her in-laws in criminal proceedings and had threatened the husband and his family of dire consequences.[81]
29. Where the wife put a false version regarding consummation of marriage and pregnancy, etc. and she was unable to sexually co-operate with the husband and she did not co-operate even to get medical treatment.[82]
30. Where the wife did not behave in a responsible manner when she levelled bald allegations that her husband was carrying on with a woman without

77. Manisha Jah *v.* Koonal Kanti, 1998 [1] HLR 518 [Cal.-DB].
78. Monika *v.* Samaran, 2001 [2] HLR 136 [Gau.].
79. Satrupa *v.* Basant Kumar, 2000 (2) HLR 580 (MP).
80. Kaushalya *v.* Daggulal, 2000 (2) HLR 611 (MP).
81. Praveen *v.* Surindar, 2001 (1) HLR 353 (Del.).
82. Indrajeet *v.* Praveen, 2000 (1) HRL 370 (P&H).

disclosing name, etc. of that lady and she got the husband beaten in her presence for accepting her demands without any criminal act on the part of the husband.[83]

31. Where the wife leaves matrimonial home without the consent of her husband did not return thereafter.[84]

Though, the instances as above[85] may also constitute mental cruelty, because it is very difficult to dissect mental cruelty from physical cruelty, the following specific instances of mental cruelty may be noticed, because mental cruelty is that which must have adverse effect on the mind of the complaining spouse,[86] namely, the husband:

1. Wife, right from the beginning finding herself uncomfortable in the house of her husband, leaving matrimonial home after 12 days of marriage with entire jewellery and dowry articles and thereafter followed a series of offensives and defensives including lodging of false criminal complaint by wife.[87]
2. Wife launching a criminal prosecution against husband under s. 494, IPC for an offence of marrying again during her lifetime, but allegation proving to be false.[88]

If any imputations against the character of any spouse is alleged either by the wife or by the husband without any foundation and the same is based on mere suspicion, such baseless allegations of illicit relationship amount to mental

83. Harpal Kaur *v.* Balbir Singh, 2000 (1) HLR 265 (P&H).
84. Rakesh *v.* Surbhi, AIR 2002 Raj 138 (DB).
85. See discussion under sub-healding (viii) above.
86. Shobha Rani *v.* Madhukar Reddi, AIR 1388 sc 121, 1988 [1] SCC 105; 1988 [1] SCR 1010: 1987 (4) Jt 433: 1988 Cr LR 88: 1988 SCC (Cr) 60: 1987 (2) Scale 1008: 1988 CAR 106: 1988 MLR 1: 1988 (1) DMC 12: 1988 (1) CCC 209: 1988 (1) HLR 169.
87. Sashi Lata *v.* Chetan, 1984 HLR 710 (P&H).
88. Raj Kishore *v.* Raj Kumari, 1987 (2) HLR 36 (Pat.).
89. Namai Kumar *v.* Mita, 1986 (2) HLR 71 (Cal.-DB).

cruelty.[89] But a single Judge of the Madras High Court has rightly analysed the matter from social perspective: "In a Hindu society, if an allegation of unchastity is made against a woman falsely, it would certainly amount to cruelty on the part of the husband. But the converse will not be correct. The court can certainly take judicial notice of the fact that even though bigamy is made an offence under the Penal Code and bigamy is prevented by legislation from 1949 onwards, there are numerous instances where men are living with more than one woman in extramarital relationship. If an allegation is made against a man that he is living with another woman in illicit intimacy, that will not by itself amount to cruelty. It is here the principle set out by the Punjab and Haryana High Court in Balbir Kaur's Case[90] becomes relevant. If the customs and traditions by which the parties are governed as also the public opinion in the locality are taken into account, it cannot be said that an allegation that a man is living in illicit intimacy with another woman, even if such allegati0on is false, will amount to cruelty. Such an allegation cannot be placed on the same pedestal as a false allegation of unchastity made against a Hindu woman".[91]

3. Persistent abuses and insults by wife to husband.[92]
4. Any man with reasonable self-respect and power of endurance will find it difficult to live with a taunting wife, when such taunts are in fact insult and indignities. Human nature being what it is, a reasonable man's reaction to the conduct of the offending spouse is the test and unending accusations and imputations can cause more pain and misery than physical beating.[93]
5. Rude and insulting attitude and behaviour of wife towards husband.[94]

---

90. AIR 1979 P&H 162: 1979 HLR 118: 81 Punj. LR 113: 1979 Marri LJ 286.
91. Tamizh *v.* Arumugam, 1990 (2) HLR 605 (Mad.).
92. Bhagwant *v.* Sheela Devi, 1987 (1) HLR 536 (P&H).
93. Kiran *v.* Mohini 1989 (1) HLR 565 (P&H-DB).
94. Sumiti *v.* Aroon, 1992 (2) HLR 30 (P&H):

6. To call husband 'danab', 'kukar' and 'saitan' coupled with allegation of husband having extra-marital relations with his sister-in-law.[95]
7. Allegations by wife against husband in written statement and also in deposition before court that husband was having illicit connections with other girls, but allegations are not substantiated. It is now well-settled that such false allegation against the character of any spouse made by the other spouse constitutes mental cruelty and that such mental cruelty will be valid ground for passing a decree of divorce. The allegation made in the written statement and in the deposition can and should be taken note of in matrimonial proceeding without driving the petitioner to another proceeding on the ground of such cruelty.[96]
8. Where, therefore, on a petition for divorce brought by the husband that the wife was leading adulterous life, the wife alleges in her written statement that her husband was not a normal person but was a mental patient and required psychological treatment to restore his mental health, it will definitely, as pointed out by the Supreme Court in Bhagat *v.* Bhagat, amount to mental cruelty of husband by the wife.[97] However, allegations made by the wife in the written statement filed in an earlier petition will not constitute mental cruelty to the husband in a subsequent petition when the allegations are not repeated.[98]

95. Sumiran *v.* Menoka, 1992 (2) HLR 574 (Cal.-DB).
96. Amarendranath *v.* Krishna, 1993 (1) HLR 606 (Cal.-DB), Following Harendranath *v.* Suprova, AIR 1989 Cal. 120: (1988)93 Cal WN 102: 1989 (1) HRL 228: 1989 (1) Cal. LT 104 (DB) and Shikhar Chand *v.* Digambar Jain, AIR 1974 SC 1178: 1974 (3) SCR 101: 1974 (1) SCC 675: 1974 UJ 153.
97. Bhagat *v.* Bhagat, AIR 1994 SC 710: 1994 (1) SCC 377: 1993 (6) JT 488: 1994 (1) UJ 70: 1993 (3) CCC 601: 1993 (2) DMC 568: 1994 (1) HLR 74 (SC).
98. Ramesh Chander *v.* Savitri, 1994 (1) HLR 624 (P&H-DB).

9. Wife having left matrimonial home not informing the husband about the illness of the child and her death and husband experiencing mental shock on account of the conduct of the wife.[99]
10. Refusal of wife to fulfil her matrimonial obligations coupled with her making of false complaints.[100] Wife levelling unfounded scandalous allegations that there was a threat to her life from her husband and proceedings under Sec. 107/150 Cr.P.C. also initiated against husband in which he was discharged.[101]
11. Wife in her letter to husband severely criticizing her husband, his parent's brother and sister and also writing to husband that instead of marrying her, he should have married his sister or his mother.[102]
12. Husband and his parents are always crazy to have a child in the family but the wife always dashing their hopes by resorting to termination of pregnancy.[103]
13. Referring to a husband in letters as the incarnation of 'Ravana', calling him a person of mean mentality and cheap character, making unsubstantiated allegations regarding illicit relationship.[104]
14. Continuous contempt and disrespect and misbehaviour of wife towards husband and members of his family causing mental agony.[105]
15. Unfounded allegations, scandalous in nature, levelled by wife against her husband.[106]
16. Injurious reproaches, taunts and accusations especially alleging incestuous relationship of husband

---

99. Jyotsna *v.* Utpal, 1999 (2) HLR 43 (Cal-DB).
100. Shakuntala *v.* Om Parkash, AIR 1981 Del 53: 1981 Raj LR 121: 1981 (19)DLT 64: 1981 Marri LJ 197: ILR (1980) 2 Del 1609.
101. Kiran Kapoor *v.* Surinder Kumar, 1982 HLR 379 (Del).
102. Gopal *v.* Neelam, 1982 HLR 545 (P&H).
103. Satya *v.* Siri Rama, 1983 HLR 177 (P&H).
104. Urmila Devi *v.* Devinder Kumar, 1983 HLR 120 (Del.).
105. Manorama *v.* Karan, 1983 HLR 172 (P&H).
106. Kiran *v.* Surinder, 1983 HLR 195 (Del.).

with his cousin sister, coupled with the deprivation of social and sexual intercourse.[107]

17. Wife failing to go back to her husband for two years[108]
18. Wife writing letters and stating that husband is 'rascal' and his mother, sister and his brother's wife have given birth to bastards.[109]
19. Murder of minor child by mother by throwing into a deep well is infliction of mental cruelty of worst sort on husband.[110]
20. Disturbance of mental peace of husband as a result of abnormal behaviour of wife.[111]
21. Conduct of wife towards her husband such that he could not sleep for nights and wife also wanted to commit suicide by sprinkling kerosene oil on her body for which she was convicted by court.[112]
22. Wife in an attempt to resist the petition for divorce levelling baseless allegations which amounted to moral turpitude on the part of husband.[113]
23. Wife never living peacefully with her husband, great enmity between parties and criminal complaints filed against each other still pending.[114]
24. Where the wife voluntarily deprived the husband of the society and cohabitation for years, the husband could legitimately be said to be under the strain of the wilful separation for years and complete denial of the conjugal relationship amounting to mental cruelty by wife.[115]
25. Where the wife wrote letter to her bother-in-law

---

107. Uma *v.* Anil Kumar, 1983 HLR 319 (Del.).
108. Rekha *v.* Nathu Ram, 1984 HLR 355 (P&H).
109. Amarjit *v.* Chainsingh, 1984 HLR 352 (P&H).
110. Mohana *v.* Thankamani, 1995 (2) HLR 174 (Ker-DB).
111. Uma *v.* Arjan, 1995 (2) HLR 334 (P&H).
112. Navin *v.* Veena Rani, 1995 (2) HLR 532 (P&H-DB).
113. Jayakrishna *v.* Surekha, 1996 (1) HLR 289 (AP-DB).
114. Nathu Lal *v.* Nathi Bai, 1998 (1) HLR 264 (Raj.-DB).
115. Gayatri *v.* Pramod Kumar, 2000 (1) HLR438 (Ori-DB).

about the impotency of her husband, it would cause mental cruelty to the husband.[116]

26. Where the husband is a double doctorate Polder Worly in USA alleged that attitude of wife was not cordial and co-operative causing him mental cruelty, the wife returned to India prevented entry of the husband in house when he came to persuade her to return and also filed criminal complaint against the husband and his mother, the incidents threw inside in the past conduct of the wife and his mother, and it was clear that the married life of the parties even as per the wife was not happy. Therefore, the husband was entitled to a decree of divorce.[117]
27. Where the wife makes false and scandalous allegations against the husband of demand of dowry and regarding his adulterous life.[118]

However, the wife will not be guilty of having caused mental cruelty to the husband in the following cases:

1. Allegations of general nature, e.g., wife being of quarrelsome nature, threats of suicide by her and complaint to police against him, being denied by wife and husband failing to prove allegations.[119]
2. Removal of Mangalsutra and bangles by wife in privacy at the instance of husband or preservation of copies of letters by wife written by her to husband or representation by wife to the Women Protection Cell to bring about reconciliation between parties even though husband and members of his family seeking anticipatory bail out of panic, for which wife not to be blamed.[120]

---

116. Padmini *v.* Sivananda, 2000 (2) HLR 99 (AP-D.
117. Kameshra Rao *v.* Jabilli, AIR 2002 SC 576.
118. Rakesh *v.* Surbhi, AIR 2002 Raj.138 (DB).
119. Anil *v.* Aruna, 1994 (1) HLR 362 (Cal.-DB).
120. Hanumantha Rao *v.* Ramani, AIR 1999 SC 1318: 1999 (3) SCC 620: 1999 (2) jt 451: 1999 (2) Scale 338: 1999 (3) Supreme 358: 1999 (3) SLT 318: 1999 (4) SRJ 422: 1999 (1) DMC 628: 1999 (2) KLT 17 (SN) 1999 (1) HLR 418 (SC).

3. If a husband, admitting his company with wine and women, also becomes a scare to his wife, what else would be left in the mind of the wife other than to call him immoral? Hence, the accusation of the wife against the moral character of the husband is not baseless or unfounded. The principle is that accusation against moral character would constitute cruelty only when those were baseless and unfounded meaning thereby that if such allegations were not unfounded and if those could be entertained by a spouse of ordinary prudence in some given facts and circumstance of an individual case, that would not be taken to be an act of cruelty.[121]

5.2.1 Cruelty by Husband

In the following cases, the husband would be guilty of treating the wife with cruelty:

1. Wife maltreated and subjected to beating more than once by the husband[122] or severe beating by husband wanting to kill wife,[123] though cruelty does not lie merely in beating[124] or in minor injuries suffered by wife in a scuffle with the husband,[125] still a single act of violence may be cruelty if violence is of a grievous and inexcusable nature.[126]
2. False allegations of adultery against wife.[127] The allegation that the wife had sexual intercourse with a person other than the husband is a serious allegation

---

121. Surjit *v.* Anita, 1996 (2) HLR 345 (Cal.-DB).
122. Mohinder *v.* Chanda, 1978 HLR 562 (P&H).
123. V.K. Rampal *v.* Chand, 1980 HLR 65 (P&H).
124. Jagannadham *v.* Savithramma, AIR 1972 ap 377: 1972 (1) Andh LT 133: 1972 (2) Andh WR 200.
125. Ram Murti *v.* Sohan Lal, 1980 HLR 65 (P&H).
126. Mary *v.* Raghavan, 1979 HLR 771 (MP-DB), Barker *v.* Barker, (1949) 1 All ER 247; Russel *v.* Russel, (1897) AC 395.
127. Jiwan *v.* Krishan Kumar, 1979 HLR 599 (P&H); Jasbir Kaur *v.* Jaswant Singh, 1997 (2) HLR 691 (P&H-DB).

against the wife and shows the cruel conduct of the husband.[128]

3. Failure or inability or refusal to effectuate sexual intercourse by husband without any reason on the part of wife.[129]
4. Beating by husband and demand of sufficient dowry[130] or taunts by husband for bringing insufficient dowry causing wife to cry for taunts every day[131] or persistent demand of dowry by husband which her parents are not able to satisfy[132] or in laws constantly pestering her to bring more and more dowry for which she was harassed and beaten by in laws.[133] In Sobha Rani *v.* Madhukar Reddi,[134] the Final Court points out that harassment of the women where such harassment is with a view to coercing her or any person related to her to meet any unlawful demand from any person related to her to meet any unlawful demand for any property or valuable security would constitute cruelty.[135] If a wife resents unfair or unreasonable demand for dowry and decides to keep away from the husband on account of the persistent and dubious approach to compel her parents to yield, the wife cannot be faulted because cruelty by husband is writ large.[136] Therefore, demand for dowry amounts to cruelty to wife and

---

128. Balasubramanian *v.* Vijayalakshmi 1999 (2) HLR 411 (SC).
129. Srikant *v.* Anuradha, 1980 HLR 265 (Kar-DB).
130. Surjit *v.* Amjer, 1981 HLR 148 (P&H).
131. Sudesh Kaushal *v.* Darshan Bala, 1984 HLR 567 (Del.).
132. Om Prakash *v.* Rajni, 1987 (1) HLR 316 (Del.).
133. Rameshwari *v.* Ram Narayan, 1987 (1) HLR 345 (All).
134. AIR 1988 SC 121: 1988 (1) SCC 105: 1988 (1) SCR 1010: 1987 (4) JT 433: 1988 CrLR 88: 1988 SCC (Cr) 60: 1987 (2) scale 1008: 1988 CAR 106: 1988 MLR 1: 1988 (1) CCC 209: 1988 (1) HLR 169 (SC).
135. See also Kamalijit *v.* Nimrat Preet, 1991 (1) HLR 231 (HP-DB), where allegations of demand of dowry were not proved and such allegations were held to amount to legal cruelty to husband.
136. Rajani *v.* Subramanian, 1990 (1) HLR 635 (Ker-DB).

she is entitled to get a decree of divorce on this ground.[137]

5. Husband being a habitual drunkard and wife coming from a family of teetotallers, suffering unhappiness of living with such husband.[138] Drinking alcohol by itself may not be more than a person's weakness resulting from diverse factors. But it becomes injurious to the wife when the husband, enslaved by alcohol, ceases to be a partner in life. His depressed state of mind sulken isolation and distressing that matrimony becomes an empty shell without the substance of cohabitation. Thus, the distress, pain and suffering of the mind resulting from continuous drinking by the husband transforms his individual weakness into such injury to the mind of a wife whose susceptibilities, broken aspiration and other circumstances of her life, make matrimonial life impossible. It is in such circumstances that drinking alcohol becomes matrimonial cruelty.[139]
6. Husband misbehaving and giving beatings to wife and wanting to kill her.[140]
7. Husband gambler and drunkard and giving merciless beatings to wife under influence of drink and not giving her anything for the household expenses.[141]
8. Wife conceiving thrice but the conceptions terminated due to ill-treatment of the husband, being ill-treated because she was unwilling to part with her salary, husband imputing unchastity to his wife, suspecting that she had illicit relations with her brother-in-law who was instigating her to separate from husband who was a poor teacher.[142]

---

137. Navodita *v.* Dinesh Singh, 1993 (1) HLR 16 (P&H); Ramesh Kumar *v.* State of Punjab, 1987 (1) HLR 189 (P&H).
138. Satinder Lal *v.* Swarna Lata, 1981 HLR 580 (Del).
139. Geeta *v.* Mohan 1992 (1) HLR 367 (Ker-DB), following Rita *v.* Bri Kishore, AIR 1987 Del 291: 1984 (2) DMC 262 and Collins *v.* Collins, (1963) 2 All ER 966; Debo *v.* Jagir Singh, 1985 (1) HLR 582 (P&H).
140. Prabhati *v.* D.K.Mitra, 1982 HLR 397 (Del.).
141. Raj Rani *v.* Sukh Raj, 1982 HLR 475 (Del.).
142. Gopilal *v.* Pushpa, 1983 HLR 315 (MP).

9. Husband asking her to do household work while she, being lame, unable to do, used to beat her, extorted her from his house by beating her.[143]
10. When wife protested to the husband about two facts i.e. the non-disclosure of the off springs of the previous marriage and the illicit liaison with her elder sister, she was given a thrashing and was turned out of the house.[144]
11. Husband being a man of bad temper, has quarrelled and still quarrels not only with the wife but also with the children.[145]
12. Wife alleging maltreatment by husband which forced her to leave the matrimonial home.[146]
13. Husband being habitual drunkard, continuing wasting income in gambling and drinking and continuing abusing wife and beating at times and also giving brutal injury.[147]
14. Conduct of husband not only overbearing, harsh and abusive but he resorted even to violence on occasions.[148]
15. Wife finding that brothers of her husband wanted to share the bed with her to which she objected and ultimately per force was compelled to leave the matrimonial home.[149]
16. Filing of a false criminal complaints against wife and the letter written to her superiors containing false and baseless allegations causing a great deal of embarrassment and agony to her.[150]
17. Husband used to kick wife, give her fists and blows, apart from abusing her in most filthy language and at times, she was not provided with food.[151]

---

143. Mangila *v.* Kalabai, 1983 HLR 324 (MP).
144. Kartar *v.* Rattanjit, 1984 HLR 179 (P&H).
145. Atmaram *v.* Jaibala, 1985 (1) HLR 440 (Bom.).
146. Mohinder *v.* Surinder 1985 (1) HLR 584 (P&H).
147. K.V.Sallappan *v.* Kamala, 1985 (1) HLR 734 (Del).
148. Asha *v.* Baldev, 1985, 1985 (1) HLR 351 (Del).
149. Amarjit *v.* Govind, 1986 (1) HLR 259 (P&H).
150. Jorden *v.* Swaranjeet, 1986 (2) HLR 174 (Del-DB).
151. Jagadish *v.* Dipali, 1986 (2) HLR 374 (Cal-DB).

18. There can not be more insulting injury to the wife than her own husband doubting her chastity. The mental cruelty resulting from such insult is a matter of judicial inference.[152]
19. Husband treating wife with cruelty not only by constant beatings but also by accusations of infidelity, which had persisted since long and even making attempt on her life with a knife which incident was reported to the police.[153]
20. Wife being maltreated by her husband for the reasons best known to him and when she failed to comply with his wishes, she was turned out of the house, people of bad character used to visit the husband's house and she was forced to satisfy their lust.[154]
21. Husband living in adultery with other woman and perpetrating mental cruelty on the wife, wife never attended to by the husband during her pregnancy and husband not caring for the newly born male child.[155]
22. Husband being drunkard and gambler used to visit his doctor wife in drunken state so as to cause annoyance to her, her visitors and the landlady, he also used to extricate money from her and wife never getting affection of husband but he was a person who wanted money out of her every time.[156]
23. Impotency of husband falls within the ambit of legal and mental cruelty.[157]
24. Husband avoiding normal sex with wife.[158]
25. Beating given by husband to wife, demand of money by husband and husband turning her out of the house and making no effort to bring her back.[159]

152. Jaishree *v.* Mohan Govind, 1987 (1) HLR 395 (Bom.).
153. Roop Chand *v.* Uma Bai, 1987 (1) HLR 406 (MP).
154. Sukhwinder *v.* Harnek, 1988 (1) HLR 432 (P&H).
155. Sarbjit *v.* Maninder, 1988 (2) HLR 199 (P&H).
156. Madan *v.* Savita, 1989 (1) HLR 40 (Raj.).
157. Parbti *v.* Fakkar, 1991 (2) HLR 233 (P&H).
158. Kanta *v.* Suresh, 1993 (2) HLR 434 (P&H).
159. Bhagsingh *v.* Surjan, 1994 (1) HLR 387 (P&H).

26. Husband aged about 55 years marrying a girl of 20-22 years of age brings untold miseries to a young, illiterate and innocent girl deserving severe condemnation.[160]
27. Husband turning out his wife from matrimonial home for want of dowry and cash and wife apprehending well founded danger to her life and not prepared to go to husband.[161]
28. Husband creating such circumstances which made the life of wife miserable.[162]
29. Wife alleging maltreatment towards her by her husband and father-in-law and demand of dowry by both of them and husband and her father-in-law both confessing their guilt when prosecuted under Sec.107/151 Cr.P.C.[163]
30. Husband making allegations against wife in written statement regarding her deformities and that she was unable to satisfy him physically and also doubting character of wife.[164]
31. Husband intentionally made false allegations of physical deformity of wife denying restitution of conjugal rights to wife and not cohabiting with her.[165]
32. Living apart and depriving husband of cohabitation is an act of cruelty. But where wife has proved that as she could not bear a child, she was treated cruelly by the husband and he used to call her a barren woman and used to beat her on that account, this testimony by the wife does not require any corroboration as it is duly corroborated by the allegations made by the husband in his earlier divorce petition. A plain perusal of the allegations made in the earlier divorce petition makes it evident that he levelled this false allegation against his wife that she was not a normal

160. Moti Singh *v.* Charanjit Kaur, 1995 (1) HLR 339 (P&H).
161. Satya *v.* Gian, 1995 (2) HLR 307 (P&H).
162. Raghubir *v.* Surjit, 1995 (2) HLR 637 (P&H).
163. Baldev *v.* Karamjit, 1996 (1) HLR 53 (P&H).
164. Kankana Rani *v.* Samir Kumar, 1996 (1) HLR 550 (Cal-DB).
165. Tuhin *v.* Arati, 1996 (1) HLR 569 (Cal.-DB).

woman. Thereby, he slashed her womanhood and caused a deep mental injury to her. During the pendency of that divorce petition, she was medically examined and the doctors opined that she is capable of enjoying normal sexual life. Thus it is apparent that by levelling such inhuman and insulting allegation against her, he caused her mental cruelty.[166]

33. Husband keeping wife only for a period of four months after marriage till she was turned out from matrimonial home, publicly abusing her and stating that she was very ugly and there was no place in the house for her and that he was a dowry greedy man, only after 10 days of marriage husband started beating her for not bringing sufficient dowry, keeping her even without food and water and trying to strangulate her.[167]
34. Under the influence of liquor, the husband and his relations beating the wife and attacking her with weapons like sword and knife and husband also trying to pour kerosene oil on her.[168]
35. Where the husband has contracted the second marriage.[169]

However, the following case would afford instances where it cannot be said that the husband "treated the wife with cruelty":

1. Where wife alleges beating by husband and turning her out of matrimonial home for want of dowry, but parties lived together for 3 years, the husband was a cleaner and the father of the wife was a labourer, it was impossible that husband would demand more dowry and if husband had started treating her

166. Raj Kumar *v.* Ram Dulari, 1997 (1) HLR 32 (P&H).
167. Bula Devi *v.* Ram Kumar, 1997 (1) HLR 460 (P&H).
168. Anita *v.* Babloo, 1999 (2) HLR 555 (MP).
169. Sunner *v.* Madhulata, 2000 (1) HLR 290 (Ker-DB).

> cruelly soon after marriage, wife would have not stayed with him for such a long time.[170]

As pointed out by the Supreme Court in Dastane,[171] what is required is that the petitioner must prove that the respondent has treated the petitioner which cruelty. Cruelty may be inferred from the whole facts and matrimonial relations of the parties and interaction in their daily life disclosed by the evidence. The question whether the respondent treated the petitioner with cruelty is a single question, only to be answered after all the facts have been taken into account.[172]

The allegation of cruelty has to be proved by cogent and convincing evidence, mere probabilities will not suffice. If the evidence falls short of proving the charge, relief of divorce on the ground of cruelty cannot be granted.[173] The spouse coming to the court to seek dissolution of the marriage on the ground of cruelty will have to prove his/her case. The court cannot be expected to help him/her on "preponderance of probabilities". Hence, there is no purpose in insisting that divorce can be granted on "preponderance of probabilities."[174] Cruelty is not a ground which can easily be inferred from certain averments. For establishing it, there must be cogent material constituting legal proof.[175] In the absence of any acts of cruelty proved beyond reasonable doubt, it would not be justified to grant a decree of divorce.[176]

5.3 DESERTION

In the matrimonial jurisprudence, desertion means,

---

170. Jeet Ram *v.* Channo, 1981 HLR 180 (P&H).
171. AIR 1975 SC 1534: 1975 HLR 111: 1975 (2) SCC 326: 1981 (1) DMC 293.
172. Kamaljit *v.* Nimrat Preet, 1991 (1) HLR 231 (HP-DB).
173. Sushila *v.* Bharorao, 1984 HLR 638 (MP).
174. See Krishna *v.* Alok Ranjan, 1985 (1) HLR 759 (Cal-DB): Ramchand *v.* Mohini, 986 (2) HLR 20 (MP): Somasekharan *v.* Thankamma, 1990 (1) HLR 373 (Ker-DB); where rule of "preponderance of probabilities" has been followed.
175. Karthikeyan *v.* Sarojini, 1998 (2) HLR 536 (Ker-DB).
176. Rajeswara *v.* Revathi, 2000 (1) HLR 361 (AP-DB).

desertion of one spouse by the other without reasonable cause and without the consent of the other. But what is sought to be emphasized is that a state of affairs, which would otherwise amount to desertion, would cease to be so if there is reasonable cause therefore or if the other party has consented thereto. However, consensual desertion or desertion by consent would almost amount to contradiction in terms as a state of affairs emanating from consent of both the parties can never amount to desertion of the one by the other and therefore, it seems that the provision providing that desertion must be without consent has been incorporated ex *abundanti cautela*, unless what is meant is that desertion would cease to be so if the deserted spouse has subsequently consented thereto.[177]

The following cases will illustrate desertion of the husband by wife:

(1) Where the marriage has not been consummated due to willful refusal of the wife to submit to sexual intercourse.[178] However, mere refusal of matrimonial company by wife is not desertion, nor is it desertion to neglect opportunity of consorting with the husband.[179]

(2) Where the wife withdrew from the society of the husband on the ground that he failed to attend the marriage of her sister and willfully neglected the husband for a period of more than two years. If one of the spouses does not attend the marriage of a relation of the other, it does not entitle the other spouse to break the matrimonial accord for such a reason, nor can under the law her withdrawal in such circumstances be deemed to be a reasonable cause.[180]

(3) Where the wife left the matrimonial home, did not come back despite the efforts of the husband and

177. Kamal *v.* Kalyani, 1988 (2) HLR 25 (Cal-DB).

178. Brij Vallabh *v.* Sumitra, 1975 HLR 521 (Raj), following F.v.P., (1896) 75 Lt 192 : G.c. G, (1924) AC 349.

179. Bhagwanti *v.* Sadhu Ram, AIR 1961 Punj 181.

180. Harbans Singh *v.* Kuldip Kaur, 1979 HLR 47 (P&H).

even did not come at the *bhog* ceremony of the husband's mother.[181]

(4) Where the wife hotly contested the husband's suit for restitution of conjugal rights filed before the petition for divorce, initiated proceedings against the husband under s. 107/151, Cr. P.C. and also filed complaints against him to his officers, alleged maltreatment by her mother-in-law, but did not join the husband after the death of the mother-in-law and continued contesting petition for restitution of conjugal rights.[182]

(5) Where the husband wrote many letters to the wife to come and reside with him and the wife promised to come but did not come on one pretext or the other.[183]

(6) Where the wife developed abhorrence for the husband and had shunned his company.[184]

(7) Where it is proved that the husband was always willing to keep the wife but wife was reluctant to live with him.[185]

(8) Where the wife took away all jewellery from the joint-locker, made complaints to the authorities of the husband in the Army and showed her unwillingness to live with the husband any longer.[186]

(9) Where the wife took away all her valuables from the matrimonial home got herself admitted at a distant place for nursing course against the wishes of the husband and disclosed herself as unmarried and did not allege any misbehaviour or an unbecoming conduct on the part of the husband.[187]

(10) Where the marriage was not consummated since the very inception and the wife was reluctant to go to the husband's home, allegation of the wife that the husband was living with another woman

181. Jagir Kaur *v.* Jagtar Singh, 1979 HLR 89 (P&H).
182. Chander Prabha *v.* Chander Mohan, 1979 HLR 533 (P&H).
183. Umesh *v.* Shakuntala, 1979 HLR 584 (Del).
184. Kalpana *v.* Ranjit, 1980 HLR 787(Pat-DB).
185. Daljit Kaur *v.* Balwant singh, 1983 HLR 98 (Raj).
186. Suresh Bala *v.* Gurmohinder, 1983 HLR 405 (Del).
187. Jasinder *v.* Gurbaksh, 1983 HLR 509 (P&H).

notwithstanding. The conduct of the husband living with a concubine or marrying a second time will not operate ipso facto as a reasonable cause. It must be proved that the conduct of the husband has produced an impact on the mind of the wife so as to cause her to continue to live apart and continue the desertion. If a desertion has already taken place by the deserting spouse, the subsequent conduct of the deserted spouse cannot constitute a reasonable cause to justify the conduct of deserting spouse.[188]

(11) Where the efforts of the husband to bring back the wife proved futile, her allegation of remarriage by the husband was wrong and the wife refused point-blank to live with the husband.[189]

(12) Where the petition for divorce by mutual consent was withdrawn, parties had been living apart for six years and no attempt was made by the wife for reconciliation.[190]

(13) Where the wife voluntarily lived separately from the husband and never wanted to join him.[191]

(14) Where the wife always quarrelled with the husband on account of his refusal to financially help her parents and she finally went to her parents not to return.[192]

(15) Where the wife left the matrimonial home on the pretext of medical treatment, did not return even after persistent requests by the husband and even did not join him in his days of grief.[193]

(16) Where the wife left the matrimonial home and made no effort to go and join it.[194]

---

188. Lakshmi *v.* Siva, 1984 HLR 30 (AP-DB), following Rohini Kumari *v.* Narendra Singh, AIR 1972 SC 459 : 1972 (2) SCR 657 : 1972 (1) SCC 1 :1972 SCC (Cr)1.

189. Chaman *v.* Sita, 1985 (1) HLR 638 (P&H).

190. Asha *v.* Gurchain, 1986 (1) HLR 462 (P&H).

191. Anil *v.* Indira, 1986 (1) HLR 584 (MP).

192. Prakash *v.* Radha, 1986 (2) HLR 282 (MP).

193. K. *v.* S., 1989 (2) HLR 356 (Raj.-DB)

194. Sanat *v.* Nandini, AIR 1990 SC 594 : 1990 (1) JT 90 : 1990 (1) SCC 475: 1990 (1) DMC 377 : 1990 (1) Scale 76 : 1990 (2) UJ 358 : 1990 (1) CCC 331 : 1990 MLR 142 : 1990 (1) HLR 567 (SC).

(17) Where the wife was living with her parents neglecting her husband on the ground that she was in service at a place near the residence of her parents, thus wife willfully withdrawing from the society of her husband without sufficient cause.[195]

(18) Where the wife lived with her parents without the consent of the husband, there was no cohabitation for more than four years and the evidence showed that she had no intention to resume cohabitation and to lead family life with her husband.[196]

(19) Where the husband proved the refusal of the wife to live with him for a long time, the fact that the parties lived together for a short duration at the intervention of the court for reconciliation would not disprove desertion by the wife.[197]

(20) Where the wife left her matrimonial home and preferred to live with her parents, their relationship got sour on account of unreasonable demand and desire of wife and her father that the husband should live with them as "Gharjamai", there was no intention on the part of wife to resume cohabitation unless and until her husband acceded to her demand and thus, there was abandonment and non-performance of marital obligation by the wife with an intention to do so.[198]

(21) Where despite the efforts made by the husband, the wife refused to discharge her marital obligation and failed to return to the matrimonial home and the wife was not interested in resuming marital ties.[199]

(22) Where the wife filed a petition under s. 498-A, IPC and also under s. 125, Cr.P.C. it indicated that the wife had decided to abandon the matrimonial home permanently.[200]

---

195. Sundari *v.* Ram Lal, 1994 (2) HLR 84 (P&H-DB).
196. Mahadev *v.* Yadabai, 1995 (2) HLR 29 (AP-DB).
197. Om Prakash *v.* Sareshta, 1993 (2) HLR 72 (HP-DB).
198. Gajendra *v.* Madhu Moti, AIR 2001 MP 299.
199. Gyatri *v.* Pramod Kumar, 2000 (1) HLR (Ori-DB).
200. Padmalatha *v.* Sudershan Rao, 2000 (2) HLR 70 (AP-DB).

In the following cases, the wife cannot be said to have deserted the husband:

(1) A wife is not deserter where she refuses to live with the husband who has another wife living.[201]
(2) Where the wife went to her parental home in connection with delivery of a child and she often remained ill but willing to live with the husband.[202]
(3) Where the wife made all out efforts for reconciliation to preserve the marriage, even with her relations, the wife could not be said to have animus deserendi against the husband.[203]
(4) Where the wife lived with her parents with the husband's consent till she refused to join service under the Haryana Government under which the husband was serving, it could not be said that she had exhibited permanent intention to abandon or desert the husband when she accepted appointment in Punjab State.[204]
(5) Where the husband maltreated and turned the wife out of house.[205]
(6) Where the wife was turned out and the husband married another girl, wife had reasonable cause for not returning to matrimonial home.[206]
(7) Where the wife, being turned out from marital home after being beaten, resided with her parents and made serious efforts to go to the husband but the husband made no efforts to bring her back.[207]

---

201. Mallappa *v.* Neelawwa, AIR 1970 Mys 59 : 1969 (2) Mys LJ 332. This proposition is unaffected by what is stated by the Supreme Court in Rohini Kumari *v.* Narendra Singh, AIR 1972 SC 459 : 1972 (2) SCR 657 : 1972 (1) SCC 1 : 1972 SCC (Cr)1.
202. Asari *v.* Piara, 1978 HLR 754 (P&H).
203. N.v.V., 1979 HLR 37 (Del).
204. Rajinder *v.* Kanta, 1979 HLR 443 (P&H).
205. Angrez Kaur *v.* Baldeo, 1979 HLR 561 (P&H), where decree of divorce converted into decree of judicial separation.
206. Kalawanti *v.* Jeet, 1980 HLR 45 (P&H).
207. Surjit *v.* Tirath, 1980 HLR 52 (P&H), See also Rajinder *v.* Rama, 1980 HLR 122 (P&H).

(8) Where the wife left marital home when relations between her and husband were not strained and with no intention not to resume cohabitation.[208]

(9) Where the husband wrote letters to father-in-law that wife, being illiterate, could neither come upto his standard nor could she lead a family life with him any time, husband also advised wife to seek divorce and wife made efforts to go to husband but husband was reluctant to bring her back.[209]

(10) Where the wife was in service at a place other than that of her husband, husband ignored seeing wife when a child was born but wife was willing to live with husband and leave service and the husband refused to keep her even after she left service.[210]

(11) Where the wife alleged maltreatment by husband as cause of leaving matrimonial home and the husband never made an attempt to bring her back.[211]

(12) Where the husband alleged that wife had developed a liaison with the domestic servant and matrimonial offence was condoned after she had confessed her guilt and parties continued living together but the wife denied the allegations saying that husband got certain papers signed by her under threats without disclosing their contents and thereafter turned her out of the house.[212]

(13) Where the attitude of the husband is hostile who is persisting with allegations and insinuations against wife, wife has reason to leave and stay away.[213]

(14) Where the evidence established that it was husband who was at fault in deserting the wife and wife was quite willing to accompany the husband but husband was reluctant to take her with him.[214]

---

208. Parshotam *v.* Sushila, 1980 HLR 149 (P&H).
209. A.C. Poswal *v.* Parkashwati, 1980 HLR 189 (P&H).
210. Ritu *v.* Dharampal, 1980 HLR 355 (P&H).
211. Virinder Kaur *v.* Surinder, 1980 HLR 366 (P&H).
212. Narinder *v.* Khushpal, 1980 HLR 620 P&H-DB).
213. Sarla *v.* Krishan, 1982 HLR 420 (Raj).
214. Vijay Kumar *v.* Rita Kumari, 1982 HLR 539 (P&H).

(15) Where the evidence proved that wife was living separately because of the misconduct and misbehaviour of the husband and the husband himself stated that he had no intention to keep her, there was no animus deserendi on the part of wife.[215]

(16) Where the husband himself was guilty of explosive conduct of leveling charges of unchastity, which compelled the wife to leave him and the wife thus separated from him with reasonable excuse.[216]

(17) Where the wife used to write to husband although expressing her desire to live with him if he lived apart from his brother and sister, there was no animus deserendi on the part of wife.[217]

(18) There will be no animus deserendi on the part of wife where she has not left matrimonial home without the consent of the husband and the husband fails to show any reasonable cause in not bringing her back when he has turned her out[218] or where the wife lived separately with a view to avoiding further ill-treatment by the husband[219] or where the wife, though turned out of matrimonial home and was living separately, attended the marriage of her husband's sister[220] or where the wife was living with her parents on account of ill-treatment by the husband and his relations[221] or where the mother of the husband who ill-treated the wife and even burnt her with hot press, was responsible for the wife to live away from matrimonial home and the husband was not prepared to bring her back[222] or where the wife left for her parental home in advanced stage of pregnancy for having a baby and returning thereafter

215. Devi Singh *v.* Sushila, 1982 HLR 600 (Raj-DB).
216. Sarla *v.* Krishan, 1982 HLR 670 (Raj).
217. Bajinder *v.* Shashi, 1983 HLR 160 (P&H).
218. Hari Kumar *v.* Suman, 1984 HLR 196 (Del).
219. Rukmini *v.* Srinivasa, 1984 HLR 210 (Kar-DB).
220. Triveni *v.* Tej Singh, 1984 HLR 675 (MP).
221. Radha *v.* Harinarayan, 1986 (1) HLR 340 (MP).
222. Ram *v.* Mohini, 1986 (2) HLR 20 (MP).

and the husband did not bother to come and take her back or make any arrangement for her and the baby, financial or otherwise[223] or where the wife appeared as a witness against her husband in a murder case and the husband was sentenced to life imprisonment[224] or where the wife is willing to return to matrimonial home after admitting her fault in leaving it but the husband is insisting upon a written undertaking.[225]

(19) Where the husband levelled false charge of adultery against the wife or suspected her character, it would afford a reasonable cause to the wife to refuse to live with the husband or to cohabit with him.[226]

(20) Where the wife was beaten with cruelty and was turned out of house by the husband, she would be justified in living away from the husband.[227]

(21) Where the options given by wife as to how to accommodate living together while she retaining her job were not acceptable to the husband.[228]

(22) Where the wife has been maltreated and beaten and the husband has imputed unchastity to her, the wife will be justified in not going and living with the husband.[229]

(23) Where the wife left the matrimonial home with the consent of the husband and was willing to come back but the husband was insisting through letters that he was not ready to keep his wife and would seek divorce.[230]

---

223. Ram Chander *v.* Adarsh, 1986 (2) HLR 167 (Del).
224. Jai Bhagwan *v.* Madhu, 1994 (1) HLR 152 (Del).
225. Chandrashekhar *v.* Rohini, 1994 (1) HLR 395 (Bom-DB).
226. M.v.S., 1984 HLR 160 (All); A.v. G., 1985 (1) HLR 313 (Del); G.V.R., 1986 (1) HLR 5 (MP); Rajaram *v.* Urmila, 1986 (2) HLR 124 (MP); Kamala *v.* Nitya Gopal, 1991 (1) HLR 604 (Cal-DB).
227. Krishnaswamy *v.* Lalita, 1984 HLR 375 (P&H).
228. Krishan Lal *v.* Bimla, 1984 HLR 455 (P&H).
229. Gurdev Kaur *v.* Balbir Singh, 1985 (1) HLR 201 (P&H).
230. Govil *v.* Govil, 1985 (1) HLR 224 (Del).

(24) Where the husband turned the wife out of matrimonial home, as she was unable to satisfy his dowry demands.[231]

(25) Where the wife was turned out of the matrimonial home and when the husband went to Germany for four years, she tried to live in the matrimonial home even during his absence but was not accepted there.[232]

(26) Where the wife was sent by her husband and his parents to her parental home and was ready to come back but the husband refused to take her back as she was incapable of bearing child.[233]

(27) Where the husband turned the wife, after beating, out of house and the wife was repeatedly asserting that despite all sufferings which she had to undergo at the hands of her husband, she had never refused to live with him.[234]

(28) Where the husband and other members of his family have no love for wife although they have their love and lust for monthly income earned by her as schoolteacher.[235]

(29) If the husband, by his own acts, is responsible for the wife living separately, he cannot complain of desertion by wife, rather it is he who must be guilty of desertion.[236]

(30) Where the wife repeatedly appeared before the court with the child and expressed her readiness and willingness to resume cohabitation by going to the husband's house but the husband remained absent and kept himself away from the court despite repeated opportunities, inference was irresistible that the husband and not the wife was guilty of desertion.[237]

---

231. R. *v.* K., 1985 (1) HLR 707 (Del); H. *v.* G., 1986 (1) HLR 485 (MP).
232. Nirmala *v.* Prem Nath, 1985 (1) HLR 785 (P&H).
233. Manorama *v.* Ramesh, 1986 (1) HLR 208 (MP).
234. Vinod *v.* Asha, 1986 (1) HLR 508 (MP).
235. Ashis *v.* Namita, 1986 (1) HLR 672 (Cal-DB).
236. R. *v.* R., 1987 (1) HLR 476 (AP-DB).
237. Ratan *v.* Sheela, 1988 (1) HLR 620 (MP).

(31) Where the wife was tortured physically and mental cruelty was also meted out to her, she could not be held guilty of desertion because animus deserendi on her part was lacking.[238]

(32) Where the wife had no intention to bring the cohabitation permanently to an end, because it was petitioner who took the wife to her parents and left her there without any effort to bring her back.[239]

(33) Where the wife was compelled to leave her husband because of his being a vagabond and also not in a position to maintain her and she had no intention to bring cohabitation permanently to an end.[240]

(34) Where the letters written by husband himself showed that it was not the wife who had deserted the husband, but, in fact, it was the husband who had forced her to leave the matrimonial home.[241]

(35) Where the wife is willing to come to matrimonial home provided the internal dispute between husband's sister and wife's brother is settled but no effort is made by husband to bring wife to his matrimonial home.[242]

(36) Where the notice by the husband to wife to return home, was certainly not a simple reminder to the wife to return to the matrimonial home, but a preemptory call, fraught with threatening legal consequences and preceded by such allegations which no self-respecting woman, howsoever financially humble her parents or brothers may have been, would have pocketed, particularly when the insinuations were patently false and mischievous. The tone and tenor of the notice is such that no other inference can commend to any discerning mind, but

238. Purna Chandra *v.* Ranu, 1988 (2) HLR 99 (Cal-DB).

239. S. Venugopal *v.* Chandra, 1988 (2) HLR 310 (Ker-DB).

240. Sachindra Nath *v.* Kalpana, 1988 (2) HLR 507 (Cal-DB).

241. Bhallabha Das *v.* Sushila, AIR 1988 SC 2089 : 1988 Supp SCC 720 : 1988 (3) JT 422 : 1988 (3) JT 422 : 1988 (2) Scale 283 : 1988 (2) UJ 313: 1988 MLR 314 : 1988 (2) DMC 385 : 1988 (2) CCC 581 : 1988 (2) HLR 654 (SC).

242. Narayanan *v.* Sreedevi, 1989 b(2) HLR 29 (Ker-DB).

that the husband was bent upon discarding the wife, and had deliberately worded notice, which he served through a lawyer, in such a manner that the wife could take no other decision but not to those delicate feelings which add meaning, and lend charm to matrimonial relations.[243]

(37) Where the wife was in service before marriage and she continued to reside at the place of her service till transfer to another place and no permanent matrimonial home was agreed to and settled between the parties as the husband was residing with his parents, there was no obligation on the wife to reside in her matrimonial home. Insistence of the husband that she should leave service and reside with him was, therefore, not warranted. Hence, the attitude of the wife that she is ready and willing to continue arrangements of visiting each other at their places shows that there is no desertion on her part[244]

(38) A wife cannot be compelled to live in the same house under the same roof with another woman not related to husband and her refusal to live is not desertion.[245]

(39) Where no effort is made by the husband to bring the wife back and he fraudulently contracts second marriage.[246]

(40) Where the husband has created such an atmosphere as to compel the wife to leave the matrimonial home.[247]

(41) The wife will have good reason for leaving her matrimonial home specifically in view of the fact that her fine sentiments and susceptibilities as educated

243. Nitu *v.* Krishan Lal, 1990 (1) HLR 571 (Del-DB).

244. Prabhakar *v.* Managal, 1991 (2) HLR 317 (Bom). See also Teerath *v.* Parvati, 1995 (2) HLR 233 (Raj-DB) where wife living separately for 11 years and demanding establishment of independent matrimonial home was held having no intention to break matrimonial tie.

245. Madan *v.* Chitra 1993 (2) HLR 38 (Cal-DB).

246. Rajinder Singh *v.* Balbir Kaur, 1993 (2) HLR 85 (P&H).

247. Surinder *v.* Chander Kanta, 1993 (2) HLR 157 (P&H).

and cultured lady were mortally wounded by the acts of the parents of husband.[248]

(42) Where the wife was maltreated and turned out of the matrimonial home and she was ready and willing to join her husband though he was not inclined, the reason being that he had remarried and was blessed with two children.[249]

(43) Where the wife shows sufficient cause for having left the house of the husband and animus deserendi on her part is not established.[250]

(44) Where the wife is willing to rejoin the husband but the husband denies to take her back and that shows that husband has no liking for her and, therefore, by hook or crook, he wants to get rid of her by taking advantage of his own wrong.[251]

(45) Where the husband demanded Rs. 16,000 from wife, she would have reasons to withdraw from the society of the husband.[252]

(46) Where the wife was compelled to leave the matrimonial home due to the ill-treatment meted out to her by her husband who, in addition thereto, had also kept a mistress in the matrimonial home.[253]

(47) Where the husband is himself leading life of adultery by living separately with another lady.[254]

(48) Where the wife was ill-treated by her mother-in-law and brother-in-law, was turned out of the house of husband and the husband neglected her thereafter,

---

248. Sudeshna *v.* Abhijit, 1995 (2) (Cal-DB).

249. Pawan Kumar *v.* Chanchal Kumari, 1996 (1) HLR 213 (P&H). See also Kailash Rani *v.* Kimti Lal, 1997 (1) HLR 174 (P&H).

250. Vijayalakshmi *v.* Balasubramanian, 1997 (1) HLR 664 (Mad-DB), following A. *v.* G., (1995) 1 LW 113 (Mad) and S. *v.* R., (1996) 2 LW 288 (Mad-DB).

251. Surender *v.* Laxmi, 1998 (2) HLR 437 (P&H-DB).

252. Srinivas *v.* Pydithalli, 1998 (2) HLR 437 (AP-DB).

253. Kanchan *v.* Premananda, 1999 (1) HLR 187 (Ori-DB).

254. Swapna *v.* Viplav, 1999 (1) HLR 433 (MP); Sanjhi Ram *v.* Mohindro, 1999 (1) HLR 569 (P&H-DB).

wife was thus forced to live away from her husband.[255]

(49) Where the reasons given by the wife for keeping away from the company of her husband had illegal relations with another woman were found to be valid.[256]

(50) Where the husband expelled the wife from the house and did not agree to reconcile the matter and he levelled irresponsible allegations of adultery against the wife.[257]

(51) Where the wife was given such harsh and cruel treatment by the husband that she was compelled to take the shelter of the police by lodging a report and a case was registered against the husband and the members of his family.[258]

(52) Where mental and physical cruelty was proved to have been caused by the husband to the wife and, therefore, there was cogent reason for the wife to stay away from the matrimonial home.[259]

(53) Where the evidence of the wife established that the husband had developed illicit relationship with another lady, she was justified to keep away from the husband and the plea of the husband that the wife deserted him without any justifiable reason was untenable.[260]

(54) Where the wife expressly stated before the court that she was willing to return to the society of her husband, it showed that she had no animus deserendi to desert the husband and end her marital relationship.[261]

---

255. Urmila Devi *v.* Deepak Kumar, 1999 (2) HLR 205 (MP).
256. Chetan Dass *v.* Kamla Devi, AIR 2001 SC 1709 : 2001 (4) SCC 250 : 2001 (5) JT 21 : 2001 (3) Scale 399 : 2001 (3) Supreme 403 : 2001 (3) SLT 420 : 2001 (5) SRj 334 : 2001 (1) HLR 418 (SC).
257. Kulwinder Kaur *v.* Jagdish Singh, 2001 (1) HLR 472 (P&H).
258. Ram Khelawan *v.* Seeta, 2001 (1) HLR 667 (MP).
259. Swapan Kumar *v.* Smiritikana, AIR 2002 Cal 6 (DB).
260. Laxmi *v.* Mayadhar, AIR 2002 Ori 5 (DB).
261. Nanak Ram *v.* Santoshibai, 2000 (1) HLR 211 (MP-DB).

(55) Where the evidence showed that the wife was willing to cohabit.[262]

(56) Where the husband was misbehaving with the wife after the birth of a daughter and therefore, the wife left the house of her husband.[263]

5.3.1 Desertion by Husband

The following cases illustrate where the husband will be guilty of deserting his wife:

(1) Wife alleging maltreatment, denial of medical treatment and turning her out of matrimonial home by husband on her first arrival at her husband's home, husband taking warrants under s. 97, Cr. P.C. to get the wife recovered and wife, when produced before a Magistrate, refusing to reside with husband.[264]

(2) Evidence establishing that husband had illicit relations with some other lady which forced the wife to leave the matrimonial home.[265]

(3) The husband committing theft of jewellery worth Rs. 15,000 from wife's parents' house, not proper to disbelieve her simply because she did not care to lodge a report with the police and evidence showing that the husband has deserted her without any reasonable excuse for more than two years.[266]

(4) Husband having knowledge of the death of the child but not coming to the wife's house to attend the funeral of the child, conduct of husband showing that he has nothing to do with the child, event of child's death is proof presumptive of the husband's animus and establishing "willful neglect" on the part of husband.[267]

---

262. Priyamvaba *v.* Sharad, 2000 (1) HLR 473 (Bom-DB)
263. Kamla *v.* Suresh Kumar, 2000 (1) HLR 605 (Raj-DB).
264. Balbir *v.* Dhir Dass, 1979 HLR 118 (P&H).
265. Satish Kumar *v.* Gayatri, 1981 HLR 309 (P&H).
266. Veena *v.* Makhan Lal, 1984 HLR 261 (Del).
267. Om Wati *v.* Kirshan, 1984 HLR 519 (Del).

(5) Husband driving away his wife after beating her and thereafter deserting the wife without reasonable cause and without her consent.[268]

(6) If a wife returns to the matrimonial home on the persuasion of her parents, with whom she is seeking shelter, during the early years of her marriage, it does not mean that she should not be granted a decree of divorce, when she is subsequently and finally turned to the matrimonial home. This is especially so, when numerous attempts at reconciliation between the parties have failed.[269]

(7) Where the wife was a teen aged girl, and the husband, being over 50 years of age, by his obnoxious behaviour and beating, meted out to her with the maltreatment more than she was called upon to bear, she could not live with the husband with safety to life and limb.[270]

(8) Where the husband left matrimonial home due to having love affair with another lady.[271]

(9) Where the husband went to England in 1976 and returned to India on a temporary visit in 1981, Parties were living separately for more than 25 years and there was no material on record to show that husband ever tried to take the respondent-wife to England and she refused to go there.[272]

(10) Where the husband seeking divorce himself failed to discharge marital obligations for over 18 years, leaving the wife with the child to live in her parental home.[273]

(11) Husband staying separately for the last 12 years and contracting second marriage, it is the husband who has deserted and not the wife.[274]

---

268. Shantaben *v.* Damsang, 1986 (1) HLR 505 (Guj).
269. Paramjit *v.* Rajinder, 1986 (2) HLR 312 (P&H).
270. Prem Pati *v.* Ranbir Singh , 1987 (1) HLR 160 (P&H).
271. Kanai Lal *v.* Rama, 1988 (1) HLR 118 (Cal-DB).
272. Major *v.* Gurdev, 1994 (2) HLR 591 (P&H-DB).
273. Sulochana *v.* Rajagopal, 1997 (2) HLR 183 (Mad-DB).
274. Ashwani *v.* Anita, 1999 (1) HLR 28 (All-DB).

(12) Where the husband is having relations with another woman, the wife goes to live with him during the pendency of the appeal but she is turned out.[275]

However, there would be no desertion on the part of the husband, where the wife was living with her brother and sister and never cared for the husband and the request made by the wife to set-up a separate family in a different place was turned down by the husband, when wife was not co-operating with the husband for running the family smoothly.[276]

Where the spouses were living separately since January, 1963 and Petition for divorce was filed by the husband on 11.10.1991, such inordinate delay in filing the petition, when remaining unexplained by the husband, would entail dismissal of petition for unnecessary and improper delay.[277]

It is well settled that the person who actually withdraws from cohabitation is not necessarily the deserting party. Desertion is a matter of inference to be drawn from the facts and circumstances of each case. But the burden of proving desertion i.e., the factum of separation as also the animus deserendi is always on the petitioner. He or she has to establish that such desertion was without just cause.[278] The petitioner for divorce bears the burden of proving the elements of desertion in the two spouses respectively and their continuance throughout the statutory period.[279] A three-Judge Bench of the Supreme Court in Bipinchandra *v.* Prabhavati[280] has laid down that in the proceedings for divorce, the plaintiff must prove the offence of desertion beyond all reasonable doubt. A five-judge Bench in Lachman *v.* Meena[281] has approved this statement of law. But a subsequent three-Judge Bench of the Supreme Court

275. Ram Dayal *v.* Uma, 1991 (1) HLR 41 (P&H-DB).

276. Sarada *v.* Satyamurthi, 2000 (1) HLR 298 (Mad-DB).

277. Rajesh *v.* Rukmani, 2000 (2) HLR 104 (MP-DB).

278. Sudarshan *v.* Daya, 1981 HLR 587 (Del).

279. Alwar *v.* Sri Devi, AIR 2002 SC 88 : JT 2001 (9) SC 429 : 2001 (8) Scale 119 : 2001 (8) Supreme 434.

280. AIR 1957 SC 176 : 1956 SCR 838 : 1957 SCJ 144.

281. AIR 1964 SC 40 1964 (4) SCR 331; Gurcharan Kaur *v.* Prithipal Singh, 1977 HLR 523 (P&H).

in Datane *v.* Dastane,[282] without noticing the aforesaid decisions in Bipinchandra *v.* Prabhavati and Lachman *v.* Meena, speaking through Chandrachud, J. in the context of 'cruelty' laid down that the proof beyond reasonable doubt was not required and the proof on "preponderance of probabilities" was sufficient. It goes without saying that the proposition laid down in Dastane *v.* Dastane is not a binding precedent, but without deeply analyzing the matter, some of the High Courts have been following Dastane *v.* Dastane.[283]

5.4 CONVERSION TO ANOTHER RELIGION

The language of S.13 (1)(ii) is very clear that divorce may be granted on a petition presented by a spouse for a decree of divorce on the ground that the other party "has ceased to be a Hindu by conversion to another religion." There is a clear bar on the husband or wife to file a petition for divorce on the

282. AIR 1975 SC 1534 : 1975 (3) SCR 967 : 1975 (2) SCC 326 : 1981 (1) DMC 293 : 1975 HLR 111.

283. See Gopala *v.* Pushpaveni, 1983 HLR 4 (Ker-DB), where the reasoning is : It is no doubt true that the learned Civil Judge relied upon a decision of the Supreme Court in the case of Lachman Utamchand *v.* Meena, AIR 1964 SC 40 : 1964 (4)SCR 331. that was based on a decision of the House of Lords in the case, Preston Jones *v.* Preston Jones, 1951 (1) All ER 124, laying down that in a matrimonial offence, the standard of proof necessarily is similar to one required in a criminal trial, But, subsequently the House of Lords changed its view in 1966 in the case, Blyth *v.* Blyth, 1966 (1) All ER 524 at p. 536. Accordingly, in 1975 in the case of Dr. N.G. Dastane *v.* Mrs. S. Dastane AIR 1975 SC 1534 : 1975 (3) SCR 967 : 1975 (2) SCC 326 : 1981 (1) DMC 293 : 1975 HLR 111, the Supreme Court changed its view by laying down that the standard of proof necessary in a proceeding under the Hindu Marriage Act is as in a civil case being preponderance of probability and not of "beyond reasonable doubt" as in criminal trial, But the fact is that Preston Jones *v.* Preston Jones has not at all been referred to in Lachman Utamchand *v.* Meena, AIR 1964 SC 40 : 1964 (4) SCR 331; Lakshmi *v.* Siva, 1984 HLR 30 (AP-DB0, though the other High Courts have rightly been insisting upon proof "beyond reasonable doubt", See Gurcharan Kaur *v.* Prithipai Singh, 1977 HLR 523 (P&H); Archna *v.* Ajay, 1999 (1) HLR 229 (MP).

ground of his or her changing religion.[284] Hence, only the aggrieved party is entitled to seek relief of divorce and the party guilty of conversion to another religion cannot seek such relief.[285]

5.5 INCURABLE UNSOUNDNESS OF MIND OR MENTAL DISORDER

In Whysall *v.* Whysall,[286] it was held that "in deciding whether a person is "incurably of unsound mind", the test to be applied is whether by reason of his mental condition, he is capable of managing himself and his affairs and, if not, whether he can hope to be resorted to a state in which he will be able to do so. It was also held that the above test the rider that the capacity to be required is that a reasonable person."

The following cases illustrate absence of mental disorder:

(1) Swooning of wife on particular shocking incidents.[287]

(2) Merely the fact that wife suffered from 'schizophrenia' prior to the marriage and that fact was not brought to the knowledge of the husband or his relations before the marriage would not be a ground to say that the mental disorder was of a kind and extent as envisaged in cl. (iii) of s. 13(1).[288]

(3) Where the doctor in plain terms admitted that the wife was otherwise healthy, physically and mentally and that her ailment of hysteria could be cured.[289]

(4) Where the husband sought divorce on the ground that wife was suffering from schizophrenia but disease was curable and the wife recovered from the ailment and could remain in that state of mind by continuous treatment.[290]

---

284. Neelaveni *v.* Venkateswara Rao, 1989 (1) HLR 410 (AP).
285. Rasna *v.* Arun, 1997 (2) HLR 546 (MP)
286. (1959) 3 All ER 389
287. Vinod *v.* Surinder, 1984 HLR 508 (P&H).
288. Gurminder *v.* Surjit, 1981 HLR 24 (P&H).
289. Bhaskar *v.* Meerabai, 1983 HLR 584 (Bom).
290. Joginder *v.* Surjit, 1985 (1) HLR 378 (P&H).

(5) Where the mental disorder of wife in 1971 was cured in 1983 and the parties lived as husband and wife peacefully and five children were born out of the wedlock.[291]

(6) Where the wife had appeared in court and on putting questions, the impression left was that she was a simpleton with an I.Q. of a little lesser degree but not the slightest impression was created if she was suffering from any mental disorder of a kind and to such an extent that it was not reasonable for the husband to live with her. Her statement was recorded in court. Even a reading of that statement showed that she understood every question and made coherent and correct replies.[292]

(7) Where the case of the wife was that the ill-treatment extended to her by her in-law right from the time of marriage told upon her mental state and she became very irritative and apprehensive and the husband failed to adduce any evidence that could prove beyond reasonable doubt that the mental disorder of the wife was of such a kind and to such an extent that the husband could not live safely with her.[293]

(8) Where no symptom of mental disorder was found either by the court or by witness.[294]

(9) Where the husband failed to prove that the wife had been suffering or was suffering from schizophrenia or that she was behaving abnormally as alleged in the petition and the doctor admitted that the wife could be rehabilitated after due treatment and could continue the marital life.[295]

---

291. Raj Rani *v.* Hardish, 1985 (1) HLR 704 (P&H).

292. Surinder *v.* Kamlesh Rani, 1987 (1) HLR 19 (P&H).

293. Rameshwari *v.* Ram Narayan, 1987 (1) HLR 345 (All) affirmed in Ram Narayan *v.* Rameshwari, AIR 1988 SC 2260 : 1988 (4) SCC 247: 1988 (3) JT 621 : 1988 (2) Scale 670 : 1989 (1) UJ174 : 1988 Supp (2) SCR 913 : 1988 MLR 374 : 1988 (2) DMC 364 : 1988 (2) CCC 737 : 1988 (2) HLR 557 (SC).

294. Parmeshwar *v.* Vimala, 1987 (1) HLR 455 (Raj).

295. Gopal Chandra *v.* Hira, 1988 (1) HLR 498 (Gau).

(10) Where the wife was allegedly suffering from epilepsy and the wife, while admitting the disease, pleaded that it was curable if proper treatment was given and there was no evidence to show that the disease was incurable and of such a kind and nature that the husband could not be reasonably expected to live with his spouse.[296]

(11) Where mental disorder of the wife was alleged by the husband as to endanger the safety and security of not only himself but also parents but the parents were not examined to support the allegation and the doctors allegedly treating the wife for mental disorder also not examined as witnesses.[297]

(12) Where the evidence of the doctor shows that the wife-patient did respond to the treatment given by him and the frequency of the attacks of hysteria as also the severity thereof both came to be actually reduced and the husband also admitted that he had come to know that his wife, after she went back to the parental home, had attended a college and at the date of his evidence, the wife was, to his knowledge, doing some job also. All these facts, therefore, very clearly show that the wife was not suffering from any such mental disorder which was of such a kind and was to such an extent as to make it reasonably not possible for the husband to continue to live with her.[298]

(13) It is apt to notice that there is no single test for determining as to whether a person is suffering from mental disorder. It is the total clinical picture and history of development of symptom which has to be studied. Thus, where two children were born out of the wedlock and the wife was looking after the children to the best of her ability, the possibility that allegations were made against her on the very first day of the marriage might have affected her for a

296. Kadambani *v.* Reshamlal, 1990 (1) HLR 292 (MP).

297. Pramatha Kumar *v.* Ashima, 1991 (1) HLR 399 (Cal-DB).

298. Sanjeevani *v.* Anil, 1994 (1) HLR 529 (Bom-DB).

while. She might be feeble-minded person but then this cannot be taken to mean that she is suffering from mental disorder which makes her incapable of knowing concept of marriage as well as the consequences of a marriage tie.[299]

(14) A person who is suffering due to psychomotor cannot be said to be of unsound mind always, but it can be said that such person will be of unsound mind only during the time of attack, Therefore, ailment of psychomotor epilepsy due to which the wife is suffering cannot be termed as continuous unsoundness of mind within the meaning of cl. (iii) of s. 13(1).[300]

(15) Where the wife, when summoned by the court, intelligently answers the question put to her by the court.[301]

(16) Where there was no evidence that wife was of incurably unsound mind on the date of marriage nor was any evidence that her mental condition was such that the husband could not reasonably be expected to live with her and the wife was admitted in hospital and the diagnosis at the time of discharge was mental retardation, schizophrenic along with paranoid ideas but basis for forming such an opinion was neither mentioned in any of the files nor in the statement of the doctor.[302]

(17) When the petition for divorce by the husband was dismissed by the trial Court in 1994, but in 1992 the wife was informed that the divorce was granted and the custody of the child was given to the husband, it would certainly upset any ordinary human being and especially a woman. If any ordinary lady hears about such news, certainly she will go mad. Such are the attempts made by the husband to spoil the life of the wife and make her mentally upset by giving such

299. Usha *v.* Santosh, 1996 (1) HLR 233 (MP).

300. Rajagopalan *v.* Usha, 1997 (2) HLR 170 (Mad).

301. Pratap Lal *v.* Kundana, 1998 (1) HLR 153 (Raj-DB).

302. Baldev *v.* Bimla, 1998 (1) HLR 354 (P&H-DB).

false news. Therefore, it is the husband who had been inflicting cruelty on the wife making her unhappy at times and the plea of mental disorder or schizophrenic is not at all made out.[303]

5.6 RESPONDENT SUFFERING FROM VIRULENT AND INCURABLE FORM OF LEPROSY

In Swarjya Lakshmi *v.* Padma Rao,[304] a three-Judge Bench of the Supreme Court states that leprometous leprosy is malignant and contagious and all medical authorities have recognized it. But it is true that a great advance on the previous methods of treatment of leprosy but it does not guarantee complete cure. Even the experts do not yet consider that with all the advances in physiotherapy, surgery or orthopedic surgery, it is possible either to cure the disease completely or to correct the deformities and mutilations that are often produced by the disease.[305]

Though, medical science has made tremendous advances since the judgment of the Supreme Court in Swarjya Lakshmi *v.* Padma Rao,[306] still it has not been possible to declare leprosy as a completely curable disease despite the fact that its treatment takes a very long time.

5.7 VENEREAL DISEASE IN COMMUNICABLE FORM

The petitioner spouse will be entitled to a decree for divorce on the ground that the respondent has been suffering from venereal disease in communicable form.

In Gurdev Singh *v.* Balbir Kaur,[307] the husband alleged that the wife had suffered from venereal disease due to her own fault and had got her uterus removed with the result that she had become incapable to produce any child and was, therefore,

303. Sudhakar *v.* Vrinda, AIR 2001 Kar 1 (DB) : 2001 (2) HLR 416 (Kar-DB).
304. AIR 1974 SC 165: 1974 (2) SCR 97: 1974 (1) SCC 58: 1973 UJ 903.
305. Padma Rao *v.* Swarajya Lakshmi, AIR 1970 AP 300 (DB), affirmed.
306. AIR 1974 SC 165: 1974 (2) SCR 97: 1974 (1) SCC 58: 1973 UJ 903.
307. 1993 (2) HLR 55 (P&H).

guilty of cruelty towards the petitioner, refusal to direct the medical examination of the wife cannot be faulted with, because the medical examination of the respondent could not have served any purpose. In absence of any evidence on record to show that the wife ever suffered from any venereal disease, the husband would have to be content with refusal of relief.

5.8 RENUNCIATION OF WORLD

A marriage may be dissolved on the petition of one spouse on the ground that the other spouse has renounced the world by entering any religious order. If any religious order does not insist upon the severance of all relations from the family and the property, adoption of this order will not attract this ground of divorce.

5.9 CIVIL DEATH

One spouse is entitled to get dissolution of the marriage on the ground that the other spouse has not been heard of as being alive for a period of seven years or more by those persons who would normally have heard of him/her, had he/she been alive.

The rules framed by the High Court under the Act may require the petitioner to give particulars of the last date and place of cohabitation of the parties, circumstances under which ceased to cohabit, the date and place where the respondent was last seen or heard of and the steps taken to trace the respondent.[308]

5.10 NO RESUMPTION OF COHABITATION ON DECREE FOR JUDICIAL SEPARATION

Either party to the marriage may present a petition for divorce on the ground that there has been no resumption of cohabitation as between the parties to the marriage for a period of one year or upwards after the passing of a decree for judicial

308. See Rule 8 (vii)(b) of the Rules of the Patna High Court.

separation in a proceeding to which they were parties. But either party to the petition for decree for judicial separation is entitled to seek a decree of divorce irrespective of in whose favour the decree for judicial separation has been granted.[309] No petitioner is allowed to take advantage of his or her own wrong.[310] A Division Bench of the Gujarat High Court hold that 'wrong' in the context of judicial separation, if any, must be one of substantial degree occurring after the decree for judicial separation and not one continuing from before.[311]

5.11 NO RESUMPTION OF COHABITATION ON DECREE FOR RESTITUTION OF CONJUGAL RIGHTS

Either party to the marriage may present a petition seeking divorce on the ground that there has been no restitution of conjugal rights as between the parties to the marriage for a period of one year or upwards after the passing of a decree for restitution of conjugal rights in a proceeding to which they were parties. Where the husband has obtained a decree for restitution of conjugal rights, but does not take any steps to enforce the decree, he can still maintain an application for divorce under s. 13(1A)(ii). Order 21, Rule 32(1), CPC will not affect this right. The decree-holder may have a right to enforce his decree in a civil court by preferring an execution petition. Still, if the statute gives him a specific and independent right to seek a relief de hors his right to enforce the decree for restitution of conjugal rights by filing an execution petition in an execution court, he cannot be barred, by his conduct in not enforcing the decree, from seeking that relief under the statue.[312]

The language of s. 23(1)(a) cannot be strained to import "reprehensible conduct" of the defaulting spouse to constitute

309. Kumud *v.* Mahender, 1998 (1) HLR 325 (P&H-DB). Where decree of divorce was granted to the husband whereas decree for judical separation was passed in favour of the wife.

310. See Gajna Devi *v.* Purushotam, AIR 1977 Del 178.

311. See Balmani *v.* Jayantilal, AIR 1979, Guj.209 (DB).

312. Suryakantham *v.* Laxmichand, AIR 1968 Bom 332 : 70 Bom LR 80 : 1968 Mah LR 338.

"wrong" within the meaning of that provision. The word "wrong" does not and cannot always carry with it "reprehensibility" of conduct. Therefore, the conclusion is irresistible that the defaulting spouse, i.e., the spouse against whom decree for restitution has been passed, is not entitled to the decree of divorce.[313]

A two-Judge Bench of the Supreme Court in Hirachand *v.* Sunanda[314] has considered the proposition laid down in Dharmendra *v.* Usha,[315] and expressed:

> "The decision cannot be read as laying down a general principle that a petitioner in an application for divorce is not entitled to the relief merely on establishing the existence of the ground pleaded by him or her in support of the relief nor that the decision lays down the principle that the Court has no discretion to decline relief to the petitioner in a case where the fulfillment of the ground pleaded by him or her is established."

313. See Jeevan Lata *v.* Darshan Kumar, 1984 HLR 469 (P&H), where Dharmendra *v.* Usha, AIR 1977 SC 2218 : 1977 HLR 605 (SC) : 1987 (1) SCR 315 : 1977 (4) SCC 12 : 1977 UJ 568 : 1977 MLR 160 was noticed but it was held that defaulting spouse was not entitled to decree of divorce. See also Saroj Rani, *v.* Sudarshan Kumar, 1984 (4) SCC 90 : 1985 (1) SCR 303 : 1984 MLR 306 : 1984 (2) Scale 118 : 1984 CAR 346 : 1984 (2) DMC 325 : 1985 (1) CCC 127 : 1984 HLR 713 (SC), where divorce was granted in favour of the husband against whom a decree for restitution of conjugal rights was passed by consent which was held not to be collusive but the plea of 'wrong' of the husband in not allowing the compliance with the decree was not accepted as there was no pleading in that behalf primarily because the marriage had broken down, the parties could no longer live as husband and wife and it was better to close the chapter. But this decision cannot be taken to lay down the proposition that even a defaulting spouse is entitled to decree of divorce.

314. AIR 2001 SC 1285 : 2001 (4) SCC 125 : 2001 (3) JT 620 : 2001 (2) Scale 514 : 2001 (2) Supreme 435 : 2001 (2) SLT 783 : 2001 (2) SCJ 412 : 2001 (4) SRj 323.

315. AIR 1977 SC 2218 : 1997 HLR 605 (SC) : 1978 (1) SCR 315 : 1977 (4) SCC 12 : 1977 UJ 568 : 1977.

5.12 IRRETRIEVABLY BROKEN DOWN MARRIAGE

In Chetan Dass *v.* Kamla Devi, the Supreme Court points out that matrimonial matters are matters of delicate human and emotional relationship. It demands mutual trust; regard, respect, love and affection with sufficient play for reasonable adjustments with the spouse. The relationship has to conform to the social norms as well. The matrimonial conduct has now come to be governed by statute framed, keeping in view such norms and changed social order. It is sought to be controlled in the interest of the individuals as well as in broader perspective, for regulating matrimonial norms for making of a well knot, healthy and not a disturbed and porous society. Institution of marriage occupies an important place and role to play in the society, in general. Therefore, it would not be appropriate to apply any submission of 'irretrievably broken marriage" as a straightjacket formula for grant of relief of divorce. This aspect has to be considered in the background of the other facts and circumstances of the case.[316]

In Saroj Rani *v.* Sudarshan Kumar,[317] it has been laid down by the Supreme Court that the right of the husband or the wife to the society of the other spouse is not merely a creature of the statute. Such a right is inherent in the very institution of marriage itself. The essence of marriage lies in sharing of common life, a sharing of all the happiness that life has to offer and all the misery that has to be faced in life, an experience of the joy that comes from enjoying, in common, things of the matter and of the spirit and from showering love and affection

316. Chetan Dass *v.* Kamla Devi, AIR 2001 SC 1709 : 2001 (4) SCC 250 : 2001 (5) JT 21 : 2001 (3) Scale 399 : 2001 (3) Supreme 403 : 2001 (3) SLT 420 : 2001 (5) SRJ 334 : 2001 (1) HLR 418 (SC), explaining and distinguishing chanderkala *v.* S.P. Trivedi, 1993 (4) SCC 232 : 1993 (2) HLR 264 (SC) ; Romesh *v.* Savitri, AIR 1995 SC 851 : 1995 (1) JT 362 :1995 (1)Scale 177 : 1995 (1) UJ 434: (1) HLR 325 (SC) ; Saroj Rani *v.* Sudarshan Kumar, 1984 (4) SCC 90 : 1984 HLR 713 (SC): 1985 (1) SCR 303 : 1984 MLR 306 : 1984 (2) Scale 118 : 1984 CAR 346 : 1984 (2) DMC 325 : 1985 (1) CCC 127.

317. AIR 1984 SC 1562 : 1983 (1) SCR 303 : 1984 (4) SCC 90 : 1984 (2) Scale 118 : 1985 (1) CCC 127 : 1984 (2) DMC 325 : 1984 MLR : 1984 HLR 713 : 1984 CAR 346.

of one's offspring. Living together is a symbol of such sharing in all its aspects. Living apart is a symbol indicating the negation of such sharing. It is indicative of disruption of the essence of marriage—'break down' and, if it continues for a fairly long period, it would indicate destruction of the essence of marriage—"irretrievable break down". Where therefore, the parties are living separately for the last about 17 years and have in fact spent the prime of their life without the company of each other, and as the grounds under s. 13(1)(ia) and 13(1)(ib) are made out, decree for divorce deserves to be granted.[318] Similarly, if the conduct of the wife is such that it is impossible for the husband to share marital life with her and the marriage has badly broken down, a decree for divorce will be just and eminently proper.[319]

5.13 RECENT DEVELOPMENTS ON IRRETRIEVABLE BREAKDOWN THEORY

The Supreme Court has in the past granted divorce based on irretrievable breakdown of marriage, but a recent judgement dismisses it. In Naveen Kohli *v.* Neelu Kohli,[320] A three-Judge bench of the Supreme Court headed by Justice B.N. Agarwal granted divorce precisely because of irretrievable breakdown of marriage and also recommended an amendment to the Hindu Marriage Act, whereby either spouse can site irretrievable breakdown of marriage as a reason to seek divorce. Expressing the concern that divorce could not be granted in number cases where marriages were virtually dead due to the absence of the provision of irretrievable breakdown, the Court strongly advocated incorporating the concept in the law in view of the change of circumstances.

But recently in Vishnu Dutt Sharma *v.* Manju Sharma,[321] a two Judge bench headed by Justice Markandy Katju refused to grant divorce on that ground dispite the precedent set by a larger bench. Taking a conservative position, Justice Katju said

318. Gajendra *v.* Madhu Mati, AIR 2001 MP 299.
319. Manga *v.* Venkata Ramana, 2000 (2) HLR 178 (AP-DB).
320. 2006 (3) SCALE 252.
321. 2009 (3) SCALE 424.

that since the Hindu Marriage Act was silent on irretrievable breakdown, the Court could not "add such a ground to Section 13 of the Act as that would be amending the Act, which is a function of the Legislature."

There is an ongoing debate about whether divorce should be granted solely on the basis of the "fault of the party", or whether it should be based on the breakdown of marriage. Opinions remain divided among sociologists, lawmakers, reformers and even activists and feminists. The judicial trend seemed to be moving towards an acceptance of "irretrievable breakdown" as ground for divorce. Earlier in many cases, the Supreme Court granted a divorce on these grounds by observing that where the marriage had been wrecked beyond any hope of salvation, public interest and the interest of all concerned lay in the recognition, in law, of this fact.

The Law Commission in its 71st report, submitted in 1978, dealt with the concept of irretrievable breakdown of marriage. The Report mentions that as far back as 1920, New Zealand was the first of the Commonwealth Countries to introduce the provision that a three-year or more separation was ground for filing a petition in the courts for divorce. The New Zealand Court while granting divorce in the first case on these grounds laid down that when matrimonial relations have, in fact, ceased to exist it is not in the interest of the parties or in the interest of the public to keep a man and woman bound as husband and wife in law. In the even of such a separation, the essential purpose of marriage is frustrated and its further continuance is in no use. This classic formulation has become a classic enunciation of the breakdown principle in matrimonial law.

The Law Commission observed that restricting divorce to matrimonial disability results in an injustice in cases where neither party is at fault, or if the fault, or if the fault is of such a nature that the parties do not wish to divulge it and yet the marriage cannot be worked out. The Commission concludes that where a marriage has ceased to exist both in substance and in reality, divorce should be seen as a solution and an escape route out of a difficult situation.

Taking into consideration of the Law Commission's recommendation, a Bill was introduced in the year 1981, to give effect irretrievable breakdown as a ground for divorce, but it did not accept the Parliament. Some scholars apprehended that unscrupulous husband would desert their wives and take advantage of this provision. They opined that there is a risk in giving recognition to a situation where the marriage would be deemed to have been broken. Such a unilateral act, unless made an issue by the wronged spouse cannot be deemed to be a valid ground to take away the legal right, which has accrued by solemnization of marriage at the instance of the spouse who is found guilty of any wrong.

Now the Union Cabinet has cleared the Bill which has been prepared on the recommendations of the Law Commission as well as the Supreme Court that "irretrievable breakdown of marriage" should be incorporated as "another ground for grant of divorce". The Marriage Laws (Amendment) Act 2010 seeks to amend the Hindu Marriage Act 1955 and the Special Marriage Act 1954. Under the new amendment, a couple can seek divorce on the basis that either or both spouses do not want to live with each other and the relationship has ended with no hope of resumption. The bill would provide safeguards to parties to marriage who file petition for grant of divorce by consent from the harassment in court if an of the party does not come to the court or wilfully avoids the court to keep the divorce proceedings inconclusive.

The amendments proposed under the Hindu Marriage (Amendment) Act 2010 are as follows:

Amendment to Section 13B

In Section 13B, in sub-section (2), for the words, brackets and figure "on the motion of the parties made not earlier than six months after the date of the presentation of the petition referred to in sub-section (1) and not later than eighteen months after the said date, if the petition is not withdrawn in the meantime", the words, brackets and figure "upon receipt of a petition under sub-section (1)" shall be substituted.

Insertion of New Sections 13C, 13D and 13E

After Section 13B of the Hindu Marriage Act, the following sections shall be inserted, namely:

Divorce on Ground of Irretrievable Breakdown of Marriage

13C(1)A Petition for the dissolution of marriage by a decree of divorce may be presented to the district court by either party to a marriage [whether solemnized before or after the commencement of the Marriage Laws (Amendment) Act, 2010] on the ground that the marriage has broken down irretrievably.

(2) The court hearing a petition referred to in sub-section (1) shall not hold the marriage to have broken down irretrievably unless it is satisfied that the parties to the marriage have lived apart for a continuous period of not less than three years immediately preceding the presentation of the petition.

(3) If the court is satisfied, on the evidence, as to the fact mentioned in sub-section (2), then, unless it is satisfied on all the evidence that the marriage has not broken down irretrievably, it shall, subject to the provisions of this Act, grant a decree of divorce.

(4) In considering, for the purpose of sub-section (2), whether the period for which the parties to a marriage have lived apart has been continuous, no account shall be taken of any one period (not exceeding three months' in all) during which the parties resumed living with each other, but no other period during which the parties lived with each other shall count as part of the period for which the parties to the marriage lived apart.

(5) For the purposes of sub-sections (2) and (4), a husband and wife shall be treated as living apart unless they are living with each other in the same household, and reference in this section to the parties to a marriage living with each other shall be construed as reference to their living with each other in the same household.

Wife's Right to Oppose Petition on Ground of Hardship

13D (1) Where the wife is the respondent to a petition for the dissolution of marriage by a decree of divorce under section 13C, she may oppose the grant of a decree on the ground that the dissolution of the marriage will result in grave financial hardship to her and that it would in all the circumstances be wrong to dissolve the marriage.

(2) Where the grant of a decree is opposed by virtue of this section, then,—

(a) if the court finds that the petitioner is entitled to rely on the ground set out in section 13C; and

(b) if, apart from this section, the court would grant a decree on the petition, the court shall consider all the circumstances, including the conduct of the parties to the marriage and the interests of those parties and of any children or other persons concerned, and if, the court is of the opinion that the dissolution of the marriage shall result in grave financial hardship to the respondent and that it would, in all the circumstances, be wrong to dissolve the marriage, it shall dismiss the petition, or in an appropriate case stay the proceedings until arrangements have been made to its satisfaction to eliminate the hardship.

Restriction on Decree for Divorce Affecting Children

13E. The court shall not pass a decree of divorce under section 13C unless the court is satisfied that adequate provision for the maintenance of children born out of the marriage has been made consistently with the financial capacity of the parties to the marriage.

Explanation.— In this section, the expression "children" means—

(a) Minor Children;

(b) Unmarried or widowed daughters who have not the financial resources to support themselves; and

(c) Children who, because of special condition of their physical or mental health, need looking after and do not have the financial resources to support themselves.

Amendment of Section 21A

In section 21A of the Hindu Marriage Act, in sub-section (1), after the word and figures "section 13", at both the places where they occur, the words, figures and letter "or section 13C" shall be inserted.

Amendment of Section 23

In section 23 of the Hindu Marriage Act, in sub-section (1), in clause (a), after the word and figure "section 5", the words, figures and letter "or in cases where the petition is presented under section 13C" shall be inserted.

The Bill was introduced in the Rajya Sabha in August 2010 and then it was referred to the Parliamentary Standing Committee on Personnel, Public Grievances, Law and Justice due to woe and cry of the public representatives and women activists. The Committee was submitted its report in March 2011. The Committee was in agreement with the broad objective that 'irretrievable breakdown of marriage' should be introduced as new ground for granting a divorce. However, the Committee felt that there are certain important social and legal issues that need to be addressed before introducing this new ground of divorce. The Committee in its report recommended the following:

1. The Bill proposes to remove the six months waiting period required before moving a joint motion in case of divorce by mutual consent. The Committee was of the view that there is no connection between proposed amendment and the main objective of the Bill. Therefore, the existing waiting period should be retained in order to protect the institution of marriage.
2. The Committee was of the opinion that the Bill should provide additional safeguards in order to prevent the misuse of the new ground of divorce. The Committee also recommended that the term 'irretrievable breakdown of marriage' should be defined.
3. Under the proposed Bill, the wife has been given a right to oppose the grant of divorce on the ground

that would result in 'grave financial hardship' to her. The Committee noted that the said term was ambiguous and capable of different interpretations. It therefore, recommended that the term 'grave financial hardship' should be defined. It further recommended that there should be a review of the provisions of the Bill to protect the interests of women in divorce proceedings.

4. As per the proposed Bill, the Court before granting the divorce has to satisfy itself that adequate provisions has been made for maintenance of 'children born out of marriage.' The Committee opined that this provision could exclude 'adopted children' and therefore, the government should clarify the position regarding adopted children.
5. The Committee recommended that the government should make adequate provisions in the matrimonial laws to ensure that the courts at the time of divorce decide upon the women their share in the matrimonial property, to which they have contributed during the marriage.
6. The Committee despite being the agreement with the main objective of the bill felt that the some of the provisions could be misused again women. It recommended that the government should reconsider the various clauses of the Bill in view of the Committee's apprehensions and introduces a revised comprehensive bill.

Partly accepting the recommendations of the Parliamentary Committee, the government has redrafted the bill on Marriage Laws (Amendment) Act 2010 and cleared by the Cabinet. In the redrafted Bill the government has included the following four key recommendations of the Committee.

1. The Courts will decide the cooling off period.
2. Adopted children have rights on par with biological children of a couple in case the parents go for a divorce.

3. The women should have a share in the property of her husband in case of a divorce. But the courts on case-by-case basis will decide the quantum of share.
4. A wife can oppose a husband's plea for a divorce under the new "irretrievable breakdown of marriage" clause, the husband will have no such rights to oppose if the wife moves court on the same grounds.

The re-drafted Bill could be introduced afresh in the Parliament and yet to be approved to make effect of the same.

In this respect on 17th May, 2012 the Union cabinet hsa resolved to make necessary amendments to the proposed bill with the following :

1. The women and Childern have a fixed share int he property of her husband in case of divorce. But the purpose she has to file a separate case after granting of divorce by the court.
2. It is also resolved to keep the provision of compulsory six month waiting period required before filing of a case for divorce by any spouse as it is. But it is proposed to waive it if moving a joint motion for divorce by mutual consent.

5.14 RECONCILIATION

In V.K. Gupta *v.* N. Gupta[322] the Supreme Court emphasizes that it is fundamental that reconciliation of a ruptured marriage is the first essay of the Judge, aided by counsel in this noble adventure. The sanctity of marriage is, in essence, the foundation of civilization and, therefore, court and counsel owe a duty to society to strain to the utmost repair the snapped relations between the parties. This task becomes more insistent when an innocent offspring of the wedding struggles in between the disputing parents.

322. 1980 (1) SCR 506 : 1979 (4) SCC 258 : 1979 UJ 722 : 1980 HLR 290 (SC).

5.15 COMPROMISE DECREE

There is nothing wrong in granting a compromise decree of divorce,[323] particularly when s. 13B allows divorce by mutual consent.[324] In Jayashree *v.* M. Srinivasa,[325] differences between the husband and wife were sorted out by their written memo and the Supreme Court granted two years as outer limit for sorting out problems.

323. Krishan Lal *v.* Rakesh Kumari, 1982 HLR 486 (Del) Davender *v.* Lavleen, 1982 HLR 135 (P&H); Avinash *v.* Tarunbala, 1984 HLR 360 (Del); Chaandrakanta *v.* Rajesh, 1985 (1) HLR 426 (Raj).

324. Pratibha *v.* Prabhakar, 1985 (1) HLR 361 (Bom).

325. 1995 Supp (3) SCC 525 : 1995 (4) Scale 850 (1): 1995 (2) HLR 451 (SC).

CHAPTER

6

Critical Appraisal

As per Hindu culture and tradition from time immemorial or Vedic times Marriage is considered to be a sacrament but not a contract as in the case of other Communities/Religions. Such was the sanctity of Marriage System in Hinduism, marriages used to be settled only by elders in the olden days by the Bride's parents thoroughly enquiring about the family traditions antecedents and culture of the Bridegroom's family as it is an important event in anybody's life and with a view to see that they live and lead a happy and harmonious marital life understanding each other well. Thus arranged marriages generally never used to be a failure in one's life in olden days. Now, as the Society advanced gradually, the individuals themselves i.e, the boys and girls are setting their marriages of their own accord hastily without the intervention or knowledge of their respective parents in the name of love, as a consequence of which, most of such marriages are becoming failures in view of lack of understanding each other properly and lack of harmony and thus leading to Divorces.

In olden days, child marriages were very much prevalent in our society as it was considered as a sin to marry a girl after attaining puberty and it was treated by the Society as an evil. As years rolled on, Reformers tried to put a stop to such practice of child marriages by introducing a Bill in the legislature in 1929, viz., Sarada Act prohibiting child marriages.

Subsequently, it was decided by the legislature that it is better to fix the ages for the girls and boys to perform the marriage and prescribed the ages as 15 years and 18 years for the girls and boys, before which, marriages should not be performed as per the .... 1954. Later on, it was considered better to change the ages as 18 years and 21 years for the Girls and Boys respectively as per the Hindu Marriage Act 1955 according to which marriages should not be performed before the aforesaid ages prescribed, failing which, they are liable to be punished and thus the ages of eligibility to get married have been legalized. The object behind prescribing/stipulating the said ages for the Girls and Boys is obviously due to the fact that their (Girls and Boys) understanding capacities and mental faculties would be sufficiently developed due to attaining maturity of mind and one can understand the pros and cons of the issues before them.

In human life, Polygamy used to be an important institution. M. Letournean in his renowned work "Evolution of Marriage" says that the most civilized nations must have begun with Polygamy, which, was practised by the Prophets and other Reformers in different stages of history.

By passing the Matrimonial Proceedings (Polygamous Marriages) Act 1972,[1] the Courts are empowered to grant Matrimonial relief to parties of Marriage, whose legal system permits Polygamy, irrespective of the fact whether the Marriage is factually Polygamous or merely potentially Polygamous.

As per Hindu Law, Monogamy was the rule and Polygamy was en exception and to meet the religious and social requirements, Polygamy was permitted under extra ordinary circumstances. In early Societies, Male offspring in particular was desirable due to two reasons:

1. Section 4 now Section 11(d) Matrimonial Causes Act, 1973 deals with Polygamous Marriage.

1. Continuance of the family, and
2. for the performance of funeral rites and offerings.

The Exception was explained by Apastamba saying that if a wife who is willing and capable of performing the religious duties and who bears sons, in such a case, the Man shall not have a second wife.[2]

It was stated by Manu[3] that having thus, at the time of funeral having given the sacred fires to his wife who dies earlier to him he may marry again and again kindle the fires. It was stated by Manu[4] that a women who is addicted to taking liquor, who is characterless, rebellious, suffering from diseases, mischievous or wasteful may at any time be superceded by another wife.

A wife who is barren may be superceded in the eighth year and whose children die in the tenth and who bears only daughters in the eleventh and who is quarrelsome, without delay. From the aforesaid it is to be construed that Bigamy was an exception although permitted under the said circumstances.

Statutory, the law of Monogamy was recognized totally removing the exception under Section 5(1) of the Hindu Marriage Act. Also violation of Section 5(1) renders the marriage void under Section 11 and punishable under Section 17 read with Sections 494 and 495 of the Indian Penal Code.

During the Vedic period and subsequently in the Dharma Sastras or the Smritis much was spoken regarding the ages of the Bride and the Bridegroom. Such requirement was considered at the relevant time about mentioning the age which was amended in 1978 stating that the Bride should be of 18 years and the Bridegroom should be of 21 years of age for marriage.

Even though few reference were there in the Rigveda about Polygamy, the word "Dampati" occurs very frequently in the Rigveda which means there were Monogamous marriages also. From this, it may be construed that Polygamy was

---

2. Apastamba 11-5, 11, 12-13.
3. Manu, V. 168.
4. *Ibid.*, IX, 80-81, See also Yaj 1-73.

common amongst the very rich people but not amongst the common masses.[5]

In Atharva Veda we find the word "Mahishi" which means the chief of the Queens thus indicating that the king had more than one wife. It was stated that "Mahishi" should be given preference amongst the co-wives.

References to Polygamy were there even during the period of Brahmanas. According to Aitareya Brahmana (Ait. Bra, 12-11) one man may have many wives whereas a woman cannot have many husbands—which was later on quoted many times by Smritis favouring Polygamy. A person who had, no son married many wives with a view to get a son. In the later Vedic period this tendency started infiltrating amongst the common people also for the sake of male children as opined by Usha M.Apte.

According to Apastamba Dharmasutra (Apa. Ds. 11.5; 11-12) a man shall not take a second wife in case his first wife is willing and capable of performing the religious rituals or duties, who bears a son.

Manu Dharma Sastra also refers to Polygamy stating that among all (twice born men) the wife of the same caste but not the wife of a different caste shall personally attend her husband and assist him in his daily sacred religious rites. If, among all the wives of one husband one has a son, Manu declares them all to be the mothers of Male children through that son.

As per Manu one can go in for bigamy in extraordinary circumstances, viz., she[6] who is habituated to liquor, is of bad conduct/character, rebellious, diseased, mischievous or wasteful and who is a barren wife.[7]

From the Vedic period of Smritis, Polygamy was in vogue but it was basically confined to the very upper high strata of the Society but not as a regular and common practice. However, the first wedded wife was only the wife in the fullest and the strictest sense, which indicates Monogamy and other

5. Refer USHA M. Apte, 'The Sacrament of Marriage in Hindu Society 1978, p. 13.
6. Manu IX 80.
7. *Ibid.*, IX 81.

wives may be there due to other necessities as spoken about such extraordinary situation.

Monogamy was introduced in Section 5(i) and reinforced by Sections 11 and 17 read with Sections 494 and 495 of IPC and Divorce was introduced as an escape route to nullify Section 5(i). Thus, if a spouse wishes to marry again he or she should get a Judicial Divorce, which gives them the right to have realignment of alliance. Marriage is considered to be valid only when solemnization of Marriage with proper ceremonies/ rituals in due form as per the prevailing Shastras was performed. In case Marriage is not celebrated properly as stated above, it may not be treated as a valid marriage, in which case, the case of second marriage shall not be treated as bigamy.

Monogamy is now-a days favoured by many, considering the present economic condition and hence Polygamy is not warranted. As per the general trend, people are not favouring Polygamy except under some circumstances and Monogamy is still the rule. As a result of bringing in the provision of Monogamy, floodgates were opened for divorce on the plea of cruelty and criminal law was not amended accordingly. Sections 494 of IPC and 198 of Cr.PC should have been more stringent and strict—had the framers of law been really concerned. Due to the opening the escape route of divorce, naturally, people started resorting to it. It is felt that Section 5(i) gave a legal inspiration to resort to divorce and thus created a social evil instead of eradicating it.

Hindu Marriage being a sacrament union and a concept that a tie once tied cannot be untied and the same concept still holds good.

However, a woman may abandon her husband[8] under five specified cases as mentioned by Narada and Parasara. Vasishta stated that a Damsel betrothed to one devoid of character and good family or afflicted by impotency, blindness and the like, an outcaste or an epileptic or an infidel or incurably diseased—should be separated from him and married to another. A woman may abandon her husband under some situations as per Koutilya. Although, different opinions are there, the

8. Narada XII. 81, Parasara, X 26-35.

general tendency of opinion is in favour of non-dissolution of marriage which is considered as a sacrament in Hindu Law.[9]

According to the Sastric law, the qualities of the Bride and the Bridegroom were significantly mentioned. The main consideration for any father, while selecting a partner, was to ensure that the selected spouse does not suffer from any disease and has no deformity.[10]

The Dharma Sutras and Manu Smriti indicated the list of Qualities to be considered in a Bride while selecting. Manu in III.8[11] stated that one should not marry a sickly girl but should marry a girl free from any bodily defects. Asva GS (I.V.3) stated that the girl should be healthy free from any disease. The qualities of an acceptable bride as well as the bridegroom were spelt out in almost all Sutras stressing on various points/ aspects but all are of unanimous opinion saying that he or should be beautiful from physical and mental aspect. Most of the Griha Sutras stress that the Maiden should have such characteristics (including physical and mental beauty) and that she would be a successful wife in ensuring the happiness of her husband and all his family members. The qualities which should be possessed by a bridegroom were mentioned in Apa GS (1-3-20) viz., he should possess brothers and purity of character, learning and free from any disease and healthy.

Man GS (1.7.6-7) speaks about "Vivaha Karakami" which accomplish five traits i.e. wealth, handsomeness, knowledge, intelligence and relatives. Handsomeness and Intelligence should be construed as physical and mental state of the Bride and the Bridegroom. A father gives away his daughter for the attainment of religion, progeny and wealth which means Dharma, Kama and Artha.

Husband and wife should lead their married life with mutual cooperation and understanding. R.V.X-85 on the Vivaha-Suthra is regarded as the foundation of the Hindu Marriage sacrament and it is said that the husband and wife should lead their household with complete spirit of cooperation and in perfect coordination just as the Sun and the

9. Dr. Paras Diwan, Modern Hindu Law, p. 65.
10. K.M. Kapadia; Marriage and Family in India, 3rd end. p. 136.
11. See also Yaj, I.53.

Moon run the show of the world.... RV.1.115.2 Says that the young people eligible for marriage used to follow the young maiden. R.V.X 27.12 says that the marriageable girl finds her own partner from the men. As such the word 'Samana' was used in the sense of union, meeting, collection, going together as occurs in various verses of the Rigveda which means as indication of the maturity of the girl physically as well as mentally. Though Roth and Rischel interpreted "Samana" as a sort of festivity, the evidence from Rigveda indicates that "Samana" was a festivity where, young and mature maidens tried to find their husbands. Various words were used for a Maiden such as Kanya, Duchita, Yosa and Yuvathi and subsequently the word "Nari" also indicated the maiden of marriageable age.

In Atharvaveda XX.126.10 refers to lady who went to Samana where young people gathered to choose their partners for marriage. Various verses in Atharvaveda indicate that when a maiden is married she was grown up and that she knew the implications of lovemaking. Thus the Vedic Bride was grown up, mature and young maiden fully prepared to handle the affairs of a big household—which also indicates that she attained maturity sexually and is capable of bearing children. The Bridegroom has to shoulder the responsibility of a household and should be capable of protecting his wife from diseases and enemies as well as give her a decent and comfortable living. Regarding the maturity of the Bridegroom his spending about 12 years with the teacher and then marrying suggests his age of marrying at about 22 years.[12]

In Sutra texts various ceremonies were mentioned regarding the solemnization of marriage and one of such ceremonies is called "Chaturdhi Karma" which marks the end of the marriage ceremony. The fourth night from the marriage was the night of consummation of marriage. In the Sankhayana Grihya-Sutra (San GS, 1-18-19) this ceremony is called as "Garbhadana" also which is only treated as continuation of the rite to be performed on the fourth night. After the

12. Usha M. Apte, The Sacrament of Marriage in Hindu Society, 1978, pp. 52-3.

consummation of the marriage on the fourth night it was construed that the maiden had attained puberty and the Groom had attained maturity before the marriage. Any negligence on the part of a father to perform his daughter's marriage as asoon as she attained puberty was considered as sin as indicated in the Gautama Dharma Sutra, XVIII. 20-3.

As regards the fixation of age for the Bride and the Bridegroom, majority opinion says that the girl should be married after attaining puberty. In case, however the girls are married at an early age in accordance with the social scenario or custom, they were not sent along with the husband till attained majority or puberty and such practice was continued till 1955. Thus attainment of puberty was considered as the basis of Chaturdhi Karma—and a father always considers daughter's marriage as discharge of religious and spiritual duty.

As per the Hindu Marriage Act, 1955, the ages of the Bride and the Bridegroom were fixed as 15 years and 18 years respectively and the said ages were raised to 18 years and 21 years in the year 1978.[13]

A Hindu Marriage may be celebrated in accordance with the customary rites and ceremonies of either party to the marriage, wherever such customary rites and ceremonies include the Saptapadi viz., taking of seven steps by the Bridegroom and the Bride together before the sacred fire—the marriage is treated as completed and binding as soon as the seventh step is taken as per section 7 of the Hindu Marriage Act – which gives statutory recognition to the marriage under Hindu law as a sacrament. The statutory emphasis is firstly on the customary rites and ceremonies and secondly if those customary rites and ceremonies include Suptapadi, then the performance of Saptapadi is made mandatory. By the expression "customary rites and ceremonies" does not mean that Sastric ceremonies can be ignored. Such an expression includes and means all such Sastric ceremonies which the caste or community follows as per their customs prevailing. Solemnization of marriage means to celebrate or perform the

13. As amended by the Child Marriage Restraint (Amendment) Act, 1978.

marriage with proper ceremonies intending that the parties should be treated as married. Mere performance of certain ceremonies to treat the parties, as married would not make ceremonies prescribed by law or approved by any custom established.

Mere admission of marriage by the accused is not an evidence of marriage for purpose of section 17 of the Hindu Marriage Act 1955 as pronounced by the Supreme Court in Kanwal Ram *v.* H.P. Administration.[14] It must be proved that the Marriage has been solemnized with proper customary rites and ceremonies failing which, no difference would be there between a wife and a concubine.

Various expressions used in Section 7 of the Hindu Marriage Act viz., "Solemnized", "Rites", "Ceremony", "complete", "Binding", all these point out the sacramental character of the Hindu Marriage.

As cited in Smritichandrika (Samskara Kanda 185-5; Mysore edn.) and the Parasar Madhaviyam, a woman becomes one with her husband in Pinda, Gotra and Sutaka and after marriage she loses her father's Gotra on completion of the Seventh Step.[15]

The basic difference between a Marriage and any other contract is that a marriage confers the status of a husband and wife on the parties to it and also confers legitimacy on the children born out of marriage, while any other contract does not confer any status as such. By a marriage, both the Husband and Wife have only obligations but not rights while in contract; the parties to the marriage have both rights and duties. In a marriage rights have no place.

Manu in Chapter IX verses 1 to 103 stated about the duties of husband and wife and the concept of right does not appear in the Matrimonial Law during the Sastric period.

According to Manu, a sick wife who is kind to her husband and virtuous in her conduct may be superceded but only with her own consent but she should never be disagreed. As per the Hindu culture, sex (Kama) is considered to be most supreme along with Artha and Dharma.

---

14. As amended by the Child Marriage Restrain (Amendment) Act 1978.
15. See also Samskara Mayukha, Gharpuse's edn. 52.

People opt for Sastric Marriage even now. Social legislation is required in accordance with the changing social scenario in as much as law is dynamic always and Hindu Law believed in it. Social legislation should be in such a way that its main theme is not confined to Juristic Science but extends to the various social aspects of the community. Then only it discharges its responsibility completely and maintains equilibrium between the Individual and Community in general. In the modern Indian Society social life has not been properly adjusted to suit the forces of the present age and hence conflicts are arising. As such, it is absolutely necessary that changes in law should be preconditioned by the laws of social evolution i.e., changes in law should only be in those directions which, generally, people in the society aspire. It is now established that marriage and family are as old as society. Efforts are being made socially and legally about "saving the family and preserving the home." Family comes into existence out of marriage and all laws pertaining to the family are intended to ensure the happiness of the new home.

In view of the social evils created due to disregarding women the concept of divorce came into existence. The protagonists and supporters of divorce plead that the women had been and are being treated shabbily by the Hindu male dominated society and hence divorce was considered as a remedy to save the woman from cruelty by the male chauvinism or ego.

It is stated in Manu Smriti that an aged woman also should not do anything independently even in her own house. A female in her childhood[16] must be subject to her father, in the youth to her husband and after his death to her son; thus a woman must never be independent. It is further elaborated that her father protects her in the childhood, husband protects her in the youth, and her sons protect her in the old age and thus a woman was treated as not deserving any independence in her life. It is further stated by Manu that though a husband is devoid of good qualities, characterless and without any virtues[17] he must be worshipped as a God by a faithful wife. A

16. *Ibid.*, V. 148 (See also Vis. XXVI. 12-13, Yaj, 185-6.
17. *Ibid.*, V. 154.

faithful wife who desires to live (after death) with her husband should never do anything that may displease him, who married her, whether he is alive or dead.[18]

In Hinduism a woman is given a very exalted status in the society. She is referred to in the Vedas as the Queen and the Mistress of the household, holding full sway over her husband's family.[19]

In Atharva Veda[20] she was called as bliss bringer, furthering her household's welfare, beloved, gladdening husband and his father, enter the husband's house and be gentle to her husband's mother, sweet to her husband and her in-laws.

Many references are there in Bramanas and Upanishads regarding the high status given to the women. In Aitreya Brahmana[21] wife is called as a friend and Jaya[22] as the husband is born again in her. She is called the half of one's own self.[23]

As per Hindu legal philosophy it would be a misconception to say that women were neglected or downgraded by the men folk—as in no other social or legal system women were so much highly treated as in the Hindu Social and Legal System.

According to Manu's statement that a woman never deserves independence it was misinterpreted that a women was in slavery or serfdom—whereas, factually a woman is supposed to be always under protection of Father, Husband or Sons in her three stages of life i.e. childhood, in youth after marriage and in the old age respectively. As a woman is considered to be a precious social unit she has to be guarded and protected with care during all the stages of her life.

According to Manu, where women are honoured[24] the Gods are pleased there while in case they are not honoured any sacred rite will not yield any reward.

---

18. *Ibid.*, V. 156.
19. RV, 10/85.26 See AV 14.2.15.
20. AV. 14.2.27.
21. Ait Bra 33.
22. *Ibid.*, 33.1.
23. Sat Bia V. 1.6, 10.
24. Manu, III. 56.

Women are always held in high esteem. If any enactment is brought out to safeguard their interests to give a legislative support and protection it was never objected in as much as a woman is considered as the Mother of Civilization as well as the foundation of the Society and such foundation must naturally be strong.

When either of the spouses are not at all able to lead or live a happy and harmonious marital life at any cost, there is no alternative except getting separated by seeking divorce from the other partner through Court to get legal sanctity so as to enable them to get a right to remarry, if they so desire at a later date, since the marriage is dissolved by divorce.

Divorce as per the dictionary means:

1. legal dissolution either wholly or partly of the relation arising out of marriage usually by a Court or other body having competent authority.
2. An absolute dissolution of a valid marriage made by a decree of the Court for a lawful cause arising after the marriage.
3. A formal separation of a man and his wife by the act of one party or by mutual consent according to the established custom.

Divorce is a judicial act, by which, the marriage relation is dissolved once for all. In order to channelise the unhappy unions, unsuitable closeness, bad tempers, verifying tastes, some regulations must have come into existence, which gave a form for cancellation as to how this union of one man and wife should come to an end amicably and consequently some restrictions/limitations were imposed according to the nature of the then society and such a development both constructive as well as destructive in nature continued with the evolution of Society.

Historically, we can find the concept of divorce from the time of Romans. Among the Romans, the word "Divorce" had two significances viz., (a) complete abrogation of the marital tie, by which, each party is liberated from the other and obtains perfect right to remarry and (2) the incomplete severance or separation, by which, the man and wife are separated but not so as to enable either to remarry and the Romans called this as Divorce.

Hindu law is the law from time immemorial till the present day punctuated by custom and dominated by the continuously changing social scenario.

Hindu law thus divided into three categories viz. :

1. Divorce and Sastric law,
2. Divorce and customary law, and
3. Divorce and Hindu Marriage Act 1955.

Hindu law is the ancient law of the Hindus having roots or basis in the Vedas and spelt out in the Smritis. Hindu law has the most ancient pedigree of any known system of Jurisprudence.[25]

It is very much clear that the rules of Vyavahara or Civil law relating to Marriage in the Smritis were drawn from the actual usages prevailing during that period and they were modified or supplemented by the opinions of Hindu Jurists.[26]

In various Hindu Scriptures three expressions uttered by the divine Sages and learned Scholars can be found and they are "abandonment", "Supersession" and remarriage. We find in Arthasastra of Kautilya some observations bearing on Divorce. However, we can find unanimity amongst the lawgivers and commentators that Divorce was not known to ancient Hindu law.

The cumulative inference we can draw from the Manu Smriti is that a man who has not married has not fully perfected himself; his personality socially as well as religiously is incomplete and imperfect. In Satpatha Brahmana it is said that the wife is just half of the husband. In the Taithiriya Samhita also it is said that wife is half of the husband. Derret stated very clearly that the intention of the sacrament is to make the husband and wife one physically and psychically for secular and spiritual purposes for this life and after lives.[27]

---

25. Mayne, Hindu Law.
26. Anirudh Jagdeorao *v.* Babu Rao Iralji 1983 HLR 446 Bom.
27. JDM Derett, Death of Marriage Law.

P.K. Virdi opined that there was no evidence regarding the practice of divorce during the Vedic and post Vedic periods. It was considered as a holy union of mind, body and the soul of the spouses and believed that death did not put an end to it as the wife remained linked with her husband even after death in the next world. P.K. Vindi further stated that non-existence of nuptial ceremonies for a second marriage and prohibition of remarriage of women are evidence against the recognition of divorce in the matrimonial system known to Sastra.[28]

Apastamba stated that the sanctity of the marriage vow should not be violated and in case it is violated both husband and wife would certainly go to hell.[29] Regarding abandonment of wife it was stated by Apastamba that a wife should not be abandoned unjustly and any violation of that rule deserves severe punishment.

Sage Vasishta admitted the remarriage of women and gave legal recognition to their sons. He gave two definitions of the term "Re-marriage".

She is called re-married (Punarbhu) who leaves the husband of her youth and having lived with others, reenters his family. She is called re-married having an impotent, outcaste or mad husband or after the death of her husband takes another lord.[30]

Parasara stated that when the husband of a woman has disappeared, is dead, or turned a recluse, is impotent or is ex-communicated, under these five calamities, another husband is permitted to women.[31]

Parasara mentioned that Divorce is allowed on easy terms under certain circumstances under five calamities as mentioned above.

According to Kautilya's Arthasastra, a woman who hates her husband cannot dissolve her marriage against his will. Similarly a man cannot also dissolve his marriage with his wife against her will. But from mutual enmity, divorce may be

28. P.K. Vindi, The Grounds for Divorce in Hindu Law and English Law.
29. Apas DS II.10, 276.
30. Vas DS, XVII, 19-20.
31. Pars, Acarakandam, Prayaschitra Kandan IV, 30, Narada XII 37.

obtained. If a man doubting danger from his wife desires divorce, he shall return to her whatever he was given on the occasion of the marriage. Similarly if a woman doubts of danger from her husband, desires divorce, she should give up her claim to the property.

As regards divorce, nothing is mentioned either in the Vedic texts or in the Post-Vedic literature.[32]

According to Shakuntala Rao Shastri, divorce is permissible by mutual consent under Buddhist Law. When either of the spouse contracts an incurable disease, such as leprosy, divorce is immediately granted. When Buddhism was a prevalent religion in India, it influenced the Hindu culture and legal literature to a considerable extent. Koutilya admitted divorce by mutual consent as done by the Buddhists.[33]

Narada, Parasara, Vasishta and Kautilya authorized a woman to have another husband in five cases as already enumerated.[34]

Even Nandana and Devala of later period were of the opinion that a woman can have another husband and by doing so there would be no sin.[35]

Vasishta, Parasara and Narada authorized a woman to have another husband in certain circumstances, viz. :

1. Virility—After undergoing an examination about his virility and when it is proved that he is not virile, he can obtain the maiden but not otherwise.[36] Narada XII.8.
2. If a man is impotent with his own wife but potent with another woman, his wife can take another husband as per the law promulgated by the creator of the world. Narada, XII. 18.
3. Women having been created for the same of propagation. Wife being the field and the husband being giver of the seed the field must be given to him

32. P.V. Kane, History of Dharma Sastr p. 619.
33. Shakuntala Rao Shastri, Women in the Sacred laws p. 9.
34. Narada, XIII. 97, Parasara, IV. 30, Vasishta XVII. 75.7.
35. R.C. Das, Women in Manu and his Seven Commentators.
36. Sacred Books of the East, Vol. XXXIII, Chap XII, tr. By Jolly.

who has seed. He who has no seed is unworthy to possess the field. *Ibid.*, XII. 19.

4. When the husband is lost or dead, when he became an ascetic, when he is impotent, when he is expelled from caste, in such five cases of legal necessity, a woman may be justified in taking another husband. *Ibid.*, XII. 97.

Even under the worst situations, the wife has been deprived of her worldly/spiritual rights to perform certain duties and also subjected to penance and that is the end. Divorce under Sastric law cannot be contemplated.

According to Narada, Parasara, Vasishta, Goutama, Manu and Yajnavalkya referred to only abandonment or supersession but not to divorce as propounded by Kautilya. Hindu Marriage being a sacrament and the object of marriage being continuity of progeny and performance of religious duties, the provision to have another wife is contemplated positively under certain situations but not divorce as envisaged in the Modern Law.

According to many views, the divorce is not known to the general Hindu law because from the Hindu point of view marriage creates an indissoluble tie between the husband and wife.

Customary divorce was prevalent and recognized. A custom may be described and defined as a continuing course of conduct which by an expressed approval although not in a statutory form of the community observing it has ultimately come to be regarded as fixing a rule or norm of conduct for the members of the community. Custom grows by conduct, from practices followed or observed for the convenience of Society and the Individual. What prevails among a set of people as the result of their consensus of opinion and approval is custom.[37] It is said that what law is to the State, is custom to the Society. A custom is a particular rule which existed either actually or presumptively from time immemorial and obtained the force of law in due course in a particular society/locality even though contrary or inconsistent with the general common law of the realm.[38]

37. P.S. Atchutaen Pillai, Jurisprudence and Legal Theory, pp. 104-5.

38. Halisbury's law of England by Lord Simonds, 3rd end.

"Custom" and "Usage" are two different concepts. They are not synonymous terms though they are often used interchangeably. There is a clear distinction between the two; strictly speaking. "Usage" represents the twilight stage of Custom—Custom begins where "Usage" ends.[39] "Custom" implies practice from time immemorial while "Usage" does not. However, Section 3(a) of the Hindu Marriage Act, 1955, does not maintain this distinction but placed both in the same terms.[40]

A custom, to be binding, must derive its force from the fact that by long usage it has obtained the force of law, but the English Rule that "a custom in order to may be legal and binding, must have been used so long that the memory of man runneth not to the contrary" should be strictly applied to Indian conditions. All that is necessary to prove is that the usage has been in practice for such a long time and with such invariability as to show that, by common consent, it has been submitted to as the established rule of a particular Community.

A variety of decisions of the Privy Council, High Courts and Supreme Court recognized the legal supremacy of custom when it attained the force of law as revealed in the Sastric law and as per the modern Hindu law as amended and codified. The sacred books on Hindu Law spoke about custom and insist repeatedly that custom must be enforced and that it may be either override or supplement the Smriti rules and modern law did not lag behind in this aspect.

Section 29 (2) of the Hindu Marriage Act, 1955 postulates:

> Nothing contained in this Act shall be deemed to affect any right recognized by custom or conferred by any special enactment to obtain the dissolution of Hindu Marriage, whether solemnized before or after the commencement of this Act.

This Section should be read with Section 3(a) of the said Act.

---

39. Mayne's Hindu Law and Usage, 13th edn, p. 457.
40. Jagdeo Rao *v.* Irahji 1983 HLR 446 (FB).

The expressions "Custom" and "Usage" signify any rule which having been continuously and uniformly observed for a long time has obtained the force of law among Hindus in any local area, tribe, community, group of family—provided that the rule is certain and not unreasonable or opposed to Public Policy and also that in the case of rule applicable only to a family it has not been discontinued by the family.

These stipulations are to be further read with Article 13(3)(a) of the Indian Constitution:

> "Law" includes any ordinance, order, bye law, rule, regulation, notification, custom or usage having the force of law in the Indian Territory.

These Statutory provisions were incorporated with due regard to the Sastric Law and the various decisions of the higher Courts which laid down rules earlier for recognition of custom pleaded and proved.

Custom is not confined within a particular locality but is prevalent throughout the country having the force of law.

It was stated by Brihaspathi that when a decision is passed in accordance with the local custom, logic or the opinion of the traders living in that town, the issue of the case is overruled by it. Brihaspati II.26.

Further, Brihaspathi stated that the time honoured institutions of each country, caste and family should be preserved intact, otherwise the people would rise in rebellion, the subject would become disaffected towards their Ruler and the Army and treasure would be destroyed.[41]—*Ibid.*, II. 28

Legal importance of custom is supreme since the whole legal concept flows from Dharma, which is a force that supports or holds together.

Manu says that the Vedas, the Smritis, Sadachara—that is the righteous conduct established by custom and public opinion and if these three provide no guidance, then conduct according to one's own conscience—these are the four attributes of Dharma—Manu, II-12.

41. These virses (tr. By Julius Jolly) have been taken from SBE, Vol. XXXIII.

In Indian Jurisprudence, the concept of Dharma is not sastric and the law derives its sanction and its sanctity from the needs of social life and hence if the social conditions change, our law needs change inevitably.

According to Dr. Jagannath Jha, custom should be regarded as of equal authority to the Sruti itself and later on custom was regarded as more authoritative than anything else and it was declared that the custom of a region (Desachara) should be given the first consideration and custom alone should be observed in every region.

Despite custom being supreme, law was based on two-tier system—One for the Intellectuals/cultural elite and the other for the less sensitive or ill informed. Accordingly Hindu law approved the divorce which was applicable to non-caste Hindus viz., the lowest strata of the Society, which was in vast majority. Now, statutory provisions superceded customs.

Section 4 of the Hindu Marriage Act says that any text, rule or interpretation of Hindu law or any custom or usage as part of that law in force immediately before the commencement of this Act shall cease to have effect with respect to any matter for which provision is made in this Act.

After the Britishers came to India as Traders initially, gradually they established their territorial domination and sovereignty and they started expansion and annexation as well as administration of Civil and Revenue cases. Thus various regulations were promulgated especially in the matter of Personal Laws.

Later on, gradually, statutory law in India particularly in regard to Marriage, Divorce and Inheritance etc., took birth and it became almost a movement. Britishers along with their consolidated political supremacy started deforming the devine Personal Laws. In due course of time, Indian States at their own level showed initiative at the instance of the so-called liberals or due to extra-ordinary over zealousness of men in power and brought out legislations bringing in Statutory Divorce. In the Legislative Assembly of British India H.S.Gaur's Bill to introduce divorce was rejected several times between 1928 and 1933.

However, Baroda, a small State with a small Brahmana population compared to its numbers of lower castes who are not governed by so much strict customs, the concept of allowing Judicial Divorce first came to shape in the Indu Lgna Vichecheda Nibandha of 1931 repealed and replaced by Sections 147-54 of the (Baroda) Hindu Nibandha (Hindu Act) 37 of 1937.[42]

By Section 147 of the said Act judicial dissolution of marriage was made available to those who were not covered by the Customary Divorce. Judicially, divorce was on any of the following grounds viz. :

1. Disappearance for seven or more years
2. becoming a recluse
3. changing his/her religion by conversion
4. being guilty of cruelty to cause danger to life, limb, physical or mental health, reasonably apprehending such danger.
5. being guilty of desertion without a valid and reasonable cause for more than three years continuously after commencement of cohabitation.
6. being addicted to intoxicants for more than three years and consequently unable to fulfill marital obligations,
7. committing adultery
8. marrying a second time during the life time of the petitioner.

In addition to the aforesaid eight grounds, the wife had additional grounds viz., 1. Impotency of the husband, 2.Habitually committed an unnatural offence and 3. Disallows the wife to stay with him for more than three years without any reasonable cause.

Similarly, the husband also had additional grounds; in addition to the aforesaid eight grounds, as stated under:

1. If the wife was pregnant at the marriage time by another person and the fact being unknown to him or his guardian in marriage, if he was a minor.

42. J.D.M. Derett, The death of a Marriage Law.

2. Wife's failure to stay with the husband for more than three years without a reasonable cause.

All or most of these grounds caused a statutory relief to the wife against the husband's aberrations—under the social condition.

Although being a pioneer work this enactment attracted the attention of many and particularly Mysore being allured Mysore Act 10 of 1933 was legislated and many other States followed suit subsequently and as a result, the following Acts came into existence.

1. Bombay Hindu Divorce Act 1947.
2. Madras Hindu (Bigamy and Divorce) Act, 1949.
3. Sourashtra Hindu Divorce Act, 1952.
4. Madhya Pradesh Divorce Act 1955.

But all this shall remain incomplete without the Hindu Code Bill, which was passed by the Parliament but could not get the assent of the President and thus lapsed.

Later on, it was felt that the time was up to attempt a codification of Hindu Law and the Govt. of India appointed a Committee for drafting the Hindu Code which was finalized on 21st February 1947. It was ultimately placed before the Parliament for its approval, after final touches were given to the draft Bill.

According to the Hindu Code Bill, two kinds of marriages were mentioned viz., the Sacramental and the Civil. The Civil marriage is in the form of a contract, for which, a certificate of marriage is an essential feature. In sacramental marriage Registration may be done if the parties so desire. As per Section 30 in Chapter II deals with dissolution of marriage on special grounds irrespective of the solemnization of the marriage before or after the commencement of the Code. The following are the grounds on which marriage can be dissolved:

1. Impotency of either party at the time of marriage and after.
2. Either of the spouses becoming concubines to others outside the wedlock.

3. Either of the parties changing his/her religion.
4. Either of the spouse is of unsound mind and under continuous treatment for a period of five years.
5. Either party is suffering a virulent form of Leprosy.

The Hindu Code Bill, though could not become an Act, it was still hailed by many celebrated authorities on Hindu Law such as B.P. Gajendragadkar.[43]

Realizing the irritated thinking of the highly religious Hindus and deep-thinking patriots towards the marriage part of the Code, it was thought better to split the Hindu Code into four parts (instead of nine parts) bringing them one by one. It was thought practicable to reform the Special Marriage Act and thereupon to amend the Hindu Law of Marriage.[44]

So the Special Marriage Act, 43 of 1954 came into statute book. Thus, repealing and replacing the Act of the same name of 1872, the whole range of matrimonial remedies was introduced. So it encouraged the propounders of the reforms in Hinduism or to deform Hinduism and thus paved the way for introduction of the Hindu Marriage Bill in the Parliament in the following year which ultimately became the Hindu Marriage Act 1955.

The object of the Hindu Marriage Act 1955 is to amend and codify the law pertaining to marriage among the Hindus. Section 13 of the said Act deals with Divorce, according to which, any marriage solemnized either before or after the commencement of the Act, may , on a petition submitted either by the husband or wife be dissolved by a decree of Divorce on any of the following grounds: that the other party :

1. is living in adultery; or
2. ceased to be a Hindu by converting to other Religion; or
3. is incurably of unsound mind continuously for a period not less than three years immediately preceding the submission of the petition; or

43. B.P. Gajendragodkar, Two lectures delivered by him before the Karnataka University on December 15th 1951.

44. Derett, The Death of Marriage Law, p. 22.

4. has been suffering from venereal disease in a communicable form for a period of not less than three years immediately preceding the presentation of the petition; or
5. has been suffering from a virulent and incurable form of leprosy for a period of not less than three years preceding the presentation of the petition; or
6. has renounced the world by entering any religios order; or
7. has not been heard of as being alive for a period of seven years or more by those persons who would have heard of it naturally, had the individual, been alive; or
8. has not resumed living together for a period of two years or more after passing of a decree for Judicial Separation against the party; or
9. has failed to comply with a decree for restitution of conjugal rights for a period of two years or more after the passing of the decree.

A wife also may present a petition for the dissolution of her marriage by decree of divorce on the ground:

1. In the case of any marriage solemnized before the commencement of this Act, the husband had married again before such commencement or that any other wife of the husband married before such commencement was alive at the time of the solemnization of the marriage of the petitioner.
   Provided that (i) in either case the other wife is alive at the time of presentation of the petition; or
   (ii) that the husband has, since the solemnization of the marriage been guilty of rape, sodomy or bestiality.

In 1964, Section 13(1) was amended by omitting the last two clauses, i.e. clauses 8 and 9 stated above and the said two omitted clauses were brought in a newly created Section 13(1A) and by thus transferring these two clauses it became significant as it indirectly bring the theory of irretrievable breakdown of marriage in as much as two years period was in fact a period for changing the mind to save the marriage.

According to Section 13(1A), either party to a marriage either solemnized before or after the commencement of the Act, may also present a petition for the dissolution of marriage by a decree of divorce on the ground :

(a) has not resumed cohabitation for a period of two years or more after the passing of a decree for Judicial Separation against the party; or
(b) has failed to comply with a decree for Restitution of Conjugal Rights for a period of two years or more after the passing of the decree.

However, the said amendment gave scope for a judicial controversy as to whether the expiry of the specified period of the decree of Judicial Separation or Restitution of Conjugal Rights is enough to grant divorce or it is only a pre-requisite for creation of a ground for applying for divorce and the divorce is to be granted or not depends upon the merits of a case.

The Marriage Laws (Amendment) Act was passed in 1976, according to which, provisions concerning divorce and other allied matters are as mentioned under:

As per Section 13, any marriage solemnized, either before or after the commencement of the Act, may, on a petition presented either by the husband or the wife, be dissolved by a decree of divorce on the ground that the other partner:[45]

(i) has had voluntary sexual intercourse with any other person than his or her spouse, after the solemnization of the marriage; or
(ia) has treated the petitioner with cruelty after the solemnization of marriage; or
(ib) has deserted the petitioner for a continuous period of not less than two years immediately before the presentation of the petition; or

45. Substituted by Act 68 of 1976, Section 7, for the former clause.

(ii) has ceased to be a Hindu by conversion to other religion; or

(iii) has been incurably of unsound mind or has been suffering continuously or intermittently from mental disorder of such a type and to such an extent that the petitioner cannot be reasonably expected to live with respondent.

Divorce may be granted by mutual consent subject to the provisions of this Act, a petition for dissolution of marriage by a decree of divorce may be presented to the District Court by both the parties to a marriage together, whether such marriage was solemnized before or after the commencement of the Marriage Laws (Amendment) Act, 1976, on the ground that they had been living separately for a period of one year or more, that they have not been able to live together and that they have agreed mutually for the dissolution of the marriage.

3. On the motion of both parties made not earlier than six months after the date of presentation of the petition referred to above in Sub-section (1) and not later than eighteen months after the said date, if the petition is not withdrawn in the meantime, the Court shall, on satisfaction, after hearing the parties and after making suitable enquiry as it deems fit, that a marriage was solemnized and that the statements made in the petition are true, then pass a decree of divorce declaring the marriage to be dissolved with effect from the date of the decree.

Section 14 of the Hindu Marriage Act, 1955, was modified by Section 9 of Marriage Laws (Amendment) Act 1976, by which, the period of three years was reduced to one year. As such, wherever "three years" was mentioned in the Section it was substituted by "one year", but under this provision, discretionary power is conferred on the Court to entertain the petition before one year if it finds on the allegations in the affidavit in support of the petition that prima facie there is exceptional hardship to the petitioner or exceptional depravity on the respondents' part. Thus Section 14 has a special bearing on the petition for divorce.

Hindu Marriage Laws (Amendment) Act, 1976 is a step forward making the divorce easier and quicker even though the social thinking did not reach that stage warranting such changes.

Greavson observes as follows:

> For the present, we may, perhaps rejoice in the opportunities for easier divorce as one of the outstanding features of the past century. But we cannot forget that "if the divorce as is no longer a disgrace, it remains a tragedy. Ten percent is a high mortality rate for marriage. The victory of emancipation has its shadow of Greek Tragedy. For emancipation in so far as it connotes easy divorce, carries in its train disintegration of family as a unit of the society and so ultimate of the society itself.[46]

As the concept of divorce in Hindu law is a pure act of imitation and hence we have to look through the global perspective firstly, and then to see as to how we destroyed our own ethics and ethos, of which, we are always proud of and how we have defiled our own Dharma being the foundation of Hindu Society. To support this, Prof. Derret in his Book on "Death of Marriage Law" commented that the Hindu Marriage Act 1955 and its Amendment Act 1976 destroyed the Hindu Law of Marriage (the Dharmic Law)

In ancient days, the concept of Divorce was not there amongst the spouses, as marriages used to be settled/arranged by the elders thoroughly considering the traditions and the family background of the other party and the youngsters were not having independent thoughts and ideas and the couple used to cohabitate with each other during their entire lifetime irrespective of slight misunderstandings between the husband and the wife.

However, now a days, in the present society, the individuals are influenced by the western culture and imitating them and taking it very light to get separated on simple matters also, quarrelling with each other on petty grounds

46. R.R. Greavson, A Century of Family Law, 1957, p. 412. It refers to Matrimonial Laws Act, 1857 (English Law).

without understanding the consequences of obtaining divorce and becoming unpopular in the Society and thereby ladies becoming insecure. Also the children/progeny will be ill treated in the society belittling them for no fault of them.

To say, in conclusion, however, it is not advisable to try to apply for a divorce, in as much as marriage is a sacrament in Hindu law, treating the same as very pious according to the Hindu customs, traditions and the Sastras. However, now a days, parties are trying to get separated by obtaining a Decree of Divorce, even on flimsy/trivial matters due to lack of mutual understanding between the spouses.

CHAPTER

7

Epilogue

Divorce is a Socio-religious and legal problem. Although Gender equality is not at risk, Gender harmony is lacking which should be achieved. Even though Gender harmony flows out of Gender equality—there should be Gender Consciousness which need not necessarily be the roles assigned by the Society conventionally to men and women. The inherent and inbuilt differences keeping the men and women apart which factually make them complimentary to each other and such differences should not be disturbed in the pretext of equality. It is an accepted matter that the bondage of both men and women starts in marriage and ends in a family and the said bondage gives stability to the family and ultimately to the Society.

The analysis of both sastric law of marriage and statutory law of divorce, the Sastric Law of Hindu Marriage ensures stability of marriage and provides security and safety to Hindu wives. However, the sastric injunction that a wife should cling to the husband inspite of his ill-health, cruelty and desertion is undemocratic and discriminative which is not a welcome feature in a highly democratic society like ours. For this reason after independence, the first Parliament of India under the leadership of Pandit Jawaharlal Nehru, Dr. Rajendra Prasad, K.A. Munshi and Dr. B.R. Ambedkar, the sastric law was modified and codified in order to suit modern conditions of democratic society.

Hindu marriage, though consensual in law, in actual practice it continues to be religious in nature since all the necessary ceremonies such as Panigrahana, Kanyadan and Sapthapadi are observed in all most all caste and communities including the Sudras who would prefer religious marriages apart from customary marriages due to the influence of Sanskritization. Further, it is very significant to note that customary divorces are prevalent since ancient times till the modern era. Of late, it is reported that the backward classes practising customary divorce are required to go to Civil Courts for confirmation of customary divorces granted by caste elders. In other words, the incidence of customary divorce is on the decline.

As it is troublesome to come out of the marital bondage for the husband and wife in the outside world as free bird is not desirable and hence stability being a virtue should be clinging to it. Sometimes more stress is given to gender equality in order to suppress gender repression, which, may be replaced by conflict. It is a mistaken impression to say that things would improve where gender equality is assured in a society. Our slogan, efforts and awareness should be focussed and drawn towards gender harmony, which, of course, is a workable solution but divorce cannot be a solution except running away from the problem.

The ills created by the Society cannot be redressed or remedied by the law, the Courts or the dictates of the State. The malady is social in nature and it needs a social treatment only but not the adversary system of our courts working within the ambit or limitations of a statute. Law should not act as a dictate but should be used as an aid and the courts should act as an agency for solving the matter but their decision should not be imposed.

In view of the above observations, the following suggestions are made :

1. A Counselling Cell should be set up in every District

Headquarters in order to find solutions in the conflicts outside the legal proceedings. The Counselling Cell should include Social Workers, Counsellors of reputed Non-Governmental Organisations apart from legal consultants and case such as matrimonial discord; dowry related issues, maintenance and harassment should be taken up by the said Cell which should be called as Pre-Litigation Centre under the care of the District Counsellor. Ultimately if solution could not be found out, the matter may be sent to the regular court for adjudication.

2. After registering the case referred by the District Counsellor, the court may transmit it to the Mahila Lok Adalt. Such Adalats may be conducted in far off places so that quick relief can be provided to the parties to the dispute. The Mahila Lok Adalat should decide the case as early as possible but in any case not later than six months. In case, however, the Mahila Lok Adalat is unable to decide the case, it may be retransmitted to the Court.
3. Mahila Court may be established to deal with the cases relating to matrimonial cases, in which, the Advocate's services need not be permitted so as to see that tricky institutions may be avoided and to see that stories may not be fabricated to fit in the provisions of Divorce. The Judge should only hear the parties directly to enable him to find out the realities of the case. The Judges may work in the correct spirit to implement the essence of the establishment of Family Courts under the stipulated statutory provisions.
4. Technical rules of Evidence are not to be allowed to come in the way in coming to the correct assessment of the case.
5. Courts have to aim at rendering natural justice.
6. Every endeavour has to be made to bring about reconciliation between the parties in dispute before granting any relief under the Act and it must be most religiously and scrupulously followed by the Judge

because granting of one decree of nullity or divorce causes a damage to innocent children of the divorced couples adversely affecting the future development of children: The Act will not prove a doom for the community by following these safeguards.

7. Certain changes in the Divorce Law may be made with the proposed amendments by the Government under Marriage Laws (Amendment) Act 2010. But before the law for irretrievable breakdown can be introduced, the request made by the groups working for separated, deserted and divorced women needs to be considered and the following rights and entitlements must be guaranteed to women and children as separated women suffer a great deal of social discrimination apart from the economic hardship:
   (a) A law must be enacted to give wives equal rights in any property acquired by the couple during the subsistence of the marriage.
   (b) It must be ensured that a provision is made that women with children have a house/place of residence.
   (c) The laws relating to maintenance for women and children must be strengthened to ensure that women/children receive an adequate amount of maintenance, which will be sufficient for them to live in a life-style, which similar to the one they were used to in the matrimonial home.
   (d) Special laws for disclosure of income of the husbands and shifting of onus of proof in these cases will have to be considered.
   (e) Ways and means to lessen the discretionary of the judiciary in the maintenance matter must be thought of as women and children have invariably been awarded very low maintenance amounts by a large number of courts.
   (f) The Govt. has to enact a law to enforce and recover maintenance amounts. Apart from this a fund will have to be created from which

maintenance can be immediately given to the wife and children.

(g) Separate enforcement agencies are to be created to recover maintenance amounts as was done in several countries.

(h) Entitlement from the State should be made essential for deserted/separated/divorced women and children in cases in which there is no property or cases in which no maintenance can be granted because of poverty and/or other reasons.

8. Section 14 should be amended as follows :

The Court must not be competent to entertain any petition directly from the petitioner, notwithstanding anything contained in this Act, but only through the District Counselling Officer for dissolution of marriage by a decree of divorce unless at the date of presentation of the petition two years elapsed from the marriage date.

The above changes are suggested, as the law must ultimately be consistent with the Hindu notions of the duties and obligations of the spouses to each other, as Hindu Marriage is a sacrament and not a contract.

Spiritual values, if lacking, leave the citizens of the Nations weakened in the essential courage and devotion and loyal wish to serve the common weal. Family thinks always in terms of "brought up" and good "brought up" which come from a happy home, a secure and serene and a joyful home. Hence the happiness and security of the home is connected with the heroism of the nation and hence any reform in the field of marriage and divorce must be done by the State always keeping in mind that India without spiritualism will be too poor and heroism springs from the lap and breast of the mother.

As such spiritualism lies in the adoration and respect of the motherhood and her total merger with the husband for the sake of family. It is the society which requires awakening when every individual cherishes spiritual values.

Divorce is having a bearing on the children, who were not there when the marriage was solemnised and they were procreated to continue the generation. As the saying goes, Man begets the child and the mother bears it. Hence, both are collectively responsible to look after the bounty of God so that these buds may not wither away before blossoming into flowers. Children brought up in broken homes deprived of parental love and affection cannot be humane and good citizens. Injury cannot be caused to the third element of the family who is not a party to the mutual assurance given to each other amongst the spouses to discharge their duties honestly and earnestly. Hence, it is suggested that there should be a declaration to the fulfilment of the decree as stipulated under Sections 25, 26 and 27 of the Hindu Marriage Act, 1955, along with the petition for Divorce and the Court should be satisfied in these aspects before granting the decree of divorce, as the aftermath of Divorce would be very cruel to the Society to bear when the women and children, being uncared for would be seeking shelter in the streets.

It is felt that every law is a divine law and the concept of divorce caused a tremor in the society and consequently happiness in the homes will be lost. Hence divorce is not advisable and desirable in any religion—Particularly in Hindu Religion—as the institution of Marriage being an indissoluble tie binding generation after generation to continue even beyond death. Marriage is a Samskara or religious sacrament for purifying the body from the inherited taint. According to Brihaspathi a wife is stated to be the half body of her husband sharing equally the results or a fruit of pure/pious acts. As per Manu, a wife cannot be released from her husband either by sale or desertion.

APPENDIX I

RELEVANT PROVISIONS OF THE DIVORCE UNDER THE HINDU MARRIAGE ACT 1955

Section 14. No petition for divorce to be presented within one year of marriage: (1) Notwithstanding anything contained in this Act, it shall not be competent for any Court to entertain any petition for dissolution of marriage by a decree of a divorce, [unless at the date of the presentation of the petition one year has elapsed] since the date of the marriage:

Provided that the Court may, upon application made to it in accordance with such rules as may be made by the High Court in that behalf, allow a petition to be presented [before one year has elapsed] since the date of the marriage on the ground that the case is one of exceptional hardship to the petitioner or of exceptional depravity on the part of the respondent, but if it appears to the Court at the hearing of the petition that the petitioner obtained leave to present the petition by any misrepresentation or concealment of the nature of the case, the Court may, if it pronounces a decree, do so subject to the condition that the decree shall not have effect until after the [1][expiry of one year] from the date of the marriage or may dismiss the petition without prejudice to any petition which may be brought after the [expiration of the said one year] upon the same or substantially the same facts as those alleged in support of the petition so dismissed.

(2) In disposing of any application under this section for leave to present a petition for divorce before the [expiration of one year] from the date of the marriage, the Court shall have

1. Substituted by Act 68 of 1976, Sec. 9.

regard to the interests of any children to the marriage and to the question whether there is a reasonable probability of a reconciliation between the parties before the expiration of the [2][said one year].

15. Divorced persons when may marry again: When a marriage has been dissolved by a decree of divorce and either there is no right of appeal against the decree or, if there is such right of appeal, the time for appealing has expired without an appeal has been presented but has been dismissed, it shall be lawful for either party to the marriage to marry again.

[3][x x x]

2. Substituted by Act 68 of 1976, Sec. 9.
3. Proviso ommitted by Act 68 of 1976, Sec. 10.

APPENDIX II

RELEVANT PROVISIONS OF THE DIVORCE UNDER THE SPECIAL MARRIAGE ACT 1954

Section 29. Restrictions on petitions for divorce during first three years after marriage—(1) No petition for divorce shall be presented to the District Court [1][unless at the date of the presentation of the petition one year has passed] since the date of entering the certificate of marriage in the Marriage Certificate Book:

Provided that the District Court may, upon application being made to it, allow a petition to be presented [2][before one year has passed] on the ground that the case is one of exceptional hardship suffered by the petitioner or of exceptional depravity on the part of respondent, but if it appears to the District Court at the hearing of the petition that the petitioner obtained leave to present the petition by any misrepresentation or concealment of the nature of the case, the District Court may, if it pronounces a decree, do so subject to the condition that the decree shall not have effect until after the [3][expiry of one year] from the date of the marriage or may dismiss the petition, without prejudice to any petition which may be brought after the [4][expiration of the said one year] upon the same or substantially the same, facts as those proved in support of the petition so dismissed.

1. Substituted by Act 68 of 1976, Sec. 30.
2. *Ibid.*
3. *Ibid.*
4. *Ibid.*

(2) In disposing of any application under this section for leave to present a petition for divorce before the [5][expiration of one year] from the date of the marriage, the District Court shall have regard to the interests of any children of the marriage, and to the question whether there is a reasonable probability of a reconciliation between the parties before the expiration of the [6][said one year].

30. Remarriage of divorced persons—Where a marriage has been dissolved by a decree of divorce and either there is no right of appeal against the decree or if there is such a right of appeal, the time for appealing has expired without any appeal having been presented, or an appeal has been presented but has been dismissed [7][*******], either party to the marriage may marry again.

---

5. Substituted by Act 68 of 1976, Sec. 30.
6. *Ibid.*
7. Omitted by Act 68 of 1976, Sec. 31.

List of Cases

A. *v.* G., 1985 (1) HLR 313 (Del)
Anjali Devi *v.* Krushna Chadra AIR 1954 Orissa 117
Arun Kumar *v.* Anita AIR 1993 P&H 33
A.C. Poswal *v.* Parkashwati, 1980 HLR 189 (P&H).
A.P. Mary *v.* K.G. Raghwan, AIR 1979 MP 40
A. *v.* G., (1995) 1 LW 113 (Mad)
Adhyatma Bhattar Alwar *v.* Ahyatma Bhattar Sri Devi AIR 2002 SC 88
Akkamma *v.* Jagannadham, AIR 1981 AP 269
Alka Sharma *v.* Abinesh Chandra Sharma, AIR 1991 MP 205
Aloda Dey *v.* Mrinal Kanti Dey, AIR 1973 Cal 393
Alwar *v.* Sri Devi, AIR 2002 SC 88
Amarendranath *v.* Krishna, 1993 (1) HLR 606 (Cal.-DB)
Amarjit *v.* Chainsingh, 1984 HLR 352 (P&H)
Amarjit *v.* Govind, 1986 (1) HLR 259 (P&H)
Amarjitpal Singh *v.* Kiran Bala, AIR 1985 P&H, 356
Amit Kumar *v.* Sefali, 1998 (1) HLR 196 (Cal-DB).
Ammim *v.* Union of India, AIR 1995 Ker.252
Ananth Nath *v.* Lajjabati AIR 1959 Cal 778
Angrez Kaur *v.* Baldeo, 1979 HLR 561 (P&H)
Anil Jayanti Vyas *v.* Sudhaben, AIR 1978 Guj.74
Anil *v.* Aruna, 1994 (1) HLR 362 (Cal.-DB)
Anil *v.* Indira, 1986 (1) HLR 584 (MP).

Anil *v.* Sudha Ben, AIR 1978, Guj. 74
Anirudh Jagdeorao *v.* Babu Rao Iralji 1983 HLR 446 Bom.
Anita *v.* Babloo, 1999 (2) HLR 555 (MP)
Annamilia *v.* Perumayee Ammal AIR 1965 Mad 139
Annapurna Devi *v.* Nara Kishore, AIR 1965 Ori.72
Annapurnamma *v.* Appa Rao, AIR 1963 AP 312
Anthony *v.* Mery, ILR 62 Cal, 1080
Archna *v.* Ajay, 1999 (1) HLR 229 (MP).
Armugam *v.* Raj Gopal, AIR 1976 SC 939
Asari *v.* Piara, 1978 HLR 754 (P&H).
Ash *v.* Ash [1972] Fam 135
Asha Handa *v.* Baldev Raj Handa, AIR 1985, Del. 76
Asha *v.* Gurchain, 1986 (1) HLR 462 (P&H).
Ashim *v.* Anusree, 1991 (1) HLR 611 (Cal-DB)
Ashis *v.* Namita, 1986 (1) HLR 672 (Cal-DB).
Ashwani *v.* Anita, 1999 (1) HLR 28 (All-DB).
Ashwini Kumar Sehgal *v.* Smt. Swantantar Sehgal, 1979 Mat LR 26 (P&H)
Atmaram *v.* Jaibala, 1985 (1) HLR 440 (Bom.)
Avinash *v.* Tarunbala, 1984 HLR 360 (Del)
Barker *v.* Barker, (1949) 1 All ER 247
B.Iylaiah *v.* B.Devamma, AIR 1981 AP 74
Baby Ammal *v.* Varadarajulu, (1969) 82 L.W. 18.
Bajinder *v.* Shashi, 1983 HLR 160 (P&H).
Baker *v.* Baker, (1955) 3 All E.R. 193.
Balasubramanian *v.* Vijayalakshmi 1999 (2) HLR 411 (SC)
Balbir Kaur *v.* Dhir Dass, AIR 1979 (P&H) 162
Balbir Kaur *v.* Maghar Singh AIR 1984 P&H 417
Baldeo Parshad *v.* Arya Pratinidhi Subha, AIR 1930 All 643
Baldev *v.* Bimla, 1998 (1) HLR 354 (P&H-DB).
Baldev *v.* Karamjit, 1996 (1) HLR 53 (P&H)
Balmani *v.* Jayantilal, AIR 1979, Guj.209 (DB)
Balram Singh *v.* Sukhvant Kaur, 1988 [1] HLR 307 (P&H)
Bani Devi *v.* A.K.Benerjee, AIR 1972 Del.50
Banik *v.* Banik [1973] All ER 45

Charlton *v.* Charlton [1952] 1 All ER 611, 612.
Chetan Dass *v.* Kamla Devi, AIR 2001 SC 1709
Chhagan Lal *v.* Sakha Devi AIR 1975 Raj. 8
Chinmoy *v.* Bharati, 1990 (2) HLR 128 (Cal.-DB).
Chinnaperumar *v.* Mariyayee. 1976, AIR Mad. 179.
Clarkson *v.* Clarkson (1930) 46 TLR 626
Coleman *v.* Coleman [1955] All ER 617
Collector of Madura *v.* Mootoo Ramalinga, 1868 12 MIA 397.
Collins *v.* Collins, (1963) 2 All ER 966
Cooper *v.* Cooper [1950] WN 200 (HL
Crawford *v.* Crawford, [1955] 3 All ER 592
Dalbara Singh *v.* Mohinder Kaur, 1978 HLR 647 (P&H)
Daljit Kaur *v.* Balwant singh, 1983 HLR 98 (Raj).
Darsabai *v.* Ganga Prasad, 1988 (2) HLR 294 (MP).
Dassi *v.* Dhani Ram, AIR 1969 P&H 25 (DB)
Davender *v.* Lavleen, 1982 HLR 135 (P&H)
Daya *v.* Krishna Lal, 1992 (1) HLR 273 (MP)
Debabarata Bhaumik *v.* Smt. Soumistha San, 1996 Gau.4 FLC
Debo *v.* Jagir Singh, 1985 (1) HLR 582 (P&H)
Deepak *v.* Manisha, 2001 (2) HLR 398 (P&H).
Devi Singh *v.* Sushila Devi, AIR 1980, Raj.48
Devyani *v.* Kauntilal, 1963 Bom. 98
Dhanjit Vadra *v.* Beena Vadra, AIR 1990 Del 146
Dharmendra *v.* Usha, AIR 1977 SC 2218
Dr. G.G. Pamarao *v.* Swarajyalakshmi, AIR 1970 AP 300
Dr. Loudhe *v.* Loudhe AIR 1984 Bom 413 FB
Dr. N.G. Dastane *v.* Mrs. S. Dastana, 1975 S.C. 1534
Dr. N.G. Dastane *v.* Mrs. S. Dastane AIR 1975 SC 1534
Dr. Narayan Ganesh *v.* Mrs. Sucheta, I.L.R. (1969) Bom, 1024
Dr. Srikant Rangacharya Adya *v.* Smt Anuradha AIR 1980 Kant.8
Edwards *v.* Edwards [1948] P 268, Perry *v.* Perry [1952] P 203.
Evans *v.* Evans (1965)2 All. ER 789
Evans *v.* Evans [1950] 2 All ER 398
Evans *v.* Evans 1 Hagg Cons. 35.

Forbes *v.* Forbes [1955] 2 All; ER 311
Frows *v.* Frows [1904] P. 177, 179
Fuller *v.* Fuller [1972] Fam 1247
G. *v.* R., 1986 (1) HLR 5 (MP
G. *v.* G. [1930] P 72.
Gajana Devi *v.* Purushotham Giri, AIR 1977 Del.178
Gajendra *v.* Madhu Mati, AIR 2001 MP 299.
Ganesh *v.* Maya Sundari (1970) 1 Ker.517
Ganpat *v.* Presiding Officer, AIR 1975 SC 420
Gaya Parshad *v.* Bhaguat, AIR 1966 MP 212
Gayatri *v.* Pramod Kumar, 2000 (1) HLR438 (Ori-DB)
Geeta *v.* Mohan 1992 (1) HLR 367 (Ker-DB)
Geethalaxmi *v.* G.V.R. Sarveshuar Rao, AIR 1983 AP 111
Gerald *v.* Esid [1956] 2 MLJ 289
Gitabai *v.* Fattoo AIR 1966 MP 130
Glenister *v.* Glenister [1945] P 30
Gobradhana *v.* Jasadamoni, 1891, 18. Mad. 252.
Gokulchand *v.* Parvin Kumar, AIR 1952 SC 231
Gollens *v.* Gollens [1963] 2 All ER 966
Gomukh Singh *v.* Balvinder Kaur, 1985 [1] HLR 116 [P&H
Goodrich *v.* Goodrich, [1971] 2 All ER 1340
Gopal Chandra *v.* Hira, 1988 (1) HLR 498 (Gau).
Gopal *v.* Neelam, 1982 HLR 545 (P&H)
Gopala *v.* Pushpaveni, 1983 HLR 4 (Ker-DB)
Gopallal *v.* Gayetri Devi, 1989 [2] HLR 149 [Raj.- DB]
Gopilal *v.* Pushpa, 1983 HLR 315 (MP)
Govil *v.* Govil, 1985 (1) HLR 224 (Del).
Govindarajulu Naicker (1886) 1 Weir 382
Graves *v.* Graves [1864] 3 SW & Tr 350, 353
Green *v.* Green LR 3 Prob. 121
Greenwood *v.* Greenwood AIR 1964 Mad 65.
Gulab Rao Nathuji Marthi *v.* Nagorao Vishnagi Marthe, AIR 1952 Nag.102
Guldev Raj *v.* Mohan Kaur, 1985(1) HLR 250 P&H
Gurcharan Kaur *v.* Prithipai Singh, 1977 HLR 523 (P&H)

Kalpana Shripati Rao *v.* Shripatdi Rao [1983] 1 DMC 483
Kalpana *v.* Ranjit, 1980 HLR 787(Pat-DB).
Kamal *v.* Kalyani, 1988 (2) HLR 25 (Cal-DB).
Kamaladevi *v.* Atmaram, 1980 HLR 398
Kamaladevi *v.* Balbir Singh, 1979 J & K.4; Cf.
Kamalijit *v.* Nimrat Preet, 1991 (1) HLR 231 (HP-DB)
Kameshra Rao *v.* Jabilli, AIR 2002 SC 576
Kamla *v.* Suresh Kumar, 2000 (1) HLR 605 (Raj-DB).
Kamlesh Kumari *v.* Balvir Singh Bedi, 1973 P. & H. 152.
Kanai Lal *v.* Rama, 1988 (1) HLR 118 (Cal-DB).
Kanchan *v.* Premananda, 1999 (1) HLR 187 (Ori-DB).
Kankana Rani *v.* Samir Kumar, 1996 (1) HLR 550 (Cal-DB)
Kanta *v.* Suresh, 1993 (2) HLR 434 (P&H)
Kantal Row *v.* Swamula varu, AIR 1918 Mad.794
Karnail Singh *v.* Balbir Kaur, 1980 HLR 24 (P&H).
Kartar *v.* Rattanjit, 1984 HLR 179 (P&H)
Karthikeyan *v.* Sarojini, 1998 (2) HLR 536 (Ker-DB)
Kasiram Kriparam *v.* Umbaram Hurreechanel. 1. Borrodaile. 387.
Kateeram Dokaneeu *v.* Musamut Gendhence, 1975 WR 178
Kaushalya Rani *v.* Vijay Singh, 1973 Raj. 269.
Kaushalya *v.* Daggulal, 2000 (2) HLR 611 (MP)
Keshav Hargovan *v.* Bai Gandi, AIR 1916 Bom.97
Kewal Rani *v.* Jiji Bai, 1984 HLR 609 MP
Khemkar *v.* Umiashankar [1873] 10 BHC 381
Khemkor *v.* Umiashankar, 1873 BHCR 381
King *v.* King, 1952 (2) All ER 584
Kiran Bala *v.* Bhairo Prasad AIR 1982 All 242
Kiran Kapoor *v.* Surinder Kumar, 1982 HLR 379 (Del).
Kiran *v.* Mohini 1989 (1) HLR 565 (P&H-DB)
Kiran *v.* Surinder, 1983 HLR 195 (Del.)
Kishanlal *v.* Mst. Prabhu, AIR 1963 Raj. 95
Kishore Ghose *v.* Krishna Ghosh AIR 1989 Cal.327
Knott *v.* Knott (1955) 2 All E.R. 305.
Kodu and Another *v.* Lola and Another, AIR 1948 Nag.141

Mahabir *v.* Nirmala, 1998 [1] HLR 292 [P&H]
Mahadev *v.* Yadabai, 1995 (2) HLR 29 (AP-DB).
Mahalingam Pillai *v.* Amsavalli (1956) 2 MLJ 289
Major *v.* Gurdev, 1994 (2) HLR 591 (P&H-DB).
Mallappa *v.* Neelawwa, AIR 1970 Mys 59
Mallika *v.* Rajendran, AIR 1995 Mad 100
Mam Kaur *v.* Ram Sarup, 2001 (1) HLR 596 (P&H).
Manga *v.* Venkata Ramana, 2000 (2) HLR 178 (AP-DB).
Mangila *v.* Kalabai, 1983 HLR 324 (MP)
Mani *v.* Zaboo 1926 AIR. Nag. 488
Manisankar *v.* Radhadevi, AIR 1992 Raj.33
Manisha Jah *v.* Koonal Kanti, 1998 [1] HLR 518 [Cal.-DB]
Manjit Kaur *v.* Avtar Singh 2001 [1] HLR 614 [P&H).
Manjulabai v.Ramachandra, 1975 M.P.L.J. 692
Manorama *v.* Karan, 1983 HLR 172 (P&H)
Manorama *v.* Ramesh, 1986 (1) HLR 208 (MP).
Mary *v.* Raghavan, 1979 HLR 771 (MP-DB)
Mayachatherji *v.* Shiv Chandra Chatterji, 1984 HLR 160 All.
McEwan *v.* McEwan [1964] 108 Sol.JO 198 (CA)
Mecra Asthana Vs. Rajendra Nath AIR 1994 MP
Meena Rani *v.* Madan Lal, 1995 [2] HLR 97 [P&H]
Meenskshi *v.* Nammalwar, AIR 1970 Mad.402
Mohana *v.* Thankamani, 1995 (2) HLR 174 (Ker-DB)
Mohinder Kaur Vs. Bikar Singh AIR 1979 HIR 751
Mohinder Singh *v.* Smt. Murti, 1977 GKR 420 P & H
Mohinder *v.* Chanda, 1978 HLR 562 (P&H)
Mohinder *v.* Surinder 1985 (1) HLR 584 (P&H)
Moina Khosla *v.* Amardeep Khosla, AIR 1986 Del.399
Monika *v.* Samaran, 2001 [2] HLR 136 [Gau.]
Mookkakone *v.* Ammakuttiammal, AIR 1928 Mad.299 (FB)
Moti Singh *v.* Charanjit Kaur, 1995 (1) HLR 339 (P&H)
Mt.Savitridevi *v.* Naukhi ram, AIR 1958 HP 15
Mulji Thakersey *v.* Gomti, 1887, 11. Bom. 112
Munda *v.* Timmaju Hensu 1. Mad. 380
Munishwas Datt *v.* Indra Kumar, AIR 1963 Punj. 449

N.G. Parshad *v.* B.C. Vanamala AIR 1988 Karn 162
N.R. Radha Krishnan *v.* N.Dhanalakshmi, AIR 1975 Mad.331
N. Sreepadachar *v.* Vasanthbai, AIR 1970 Mys.32
N. *v.* V., 1979 HLR 37 (Del).
N. Varalalaxmi *v.* N.V.Hanumantha Rao, AIR 1978 AP 6
Nachhator Singh *v.* Harcharn Kaur, AIR 1986 P&H 201
Nagamma *v.* Lachmi Bai, AIR 1963 AP 82
Nallathangal *v.* Nainan Ambalam, AIR 1960 Mad.179
Namai Kumar *v.* Mita, 1986 (2) HLR 71 (Cal.-DB)
Nanak Ram *v.* Santoshibai, 2000 (1) HLR 211 (MP-DB).
Nand Kishore *v.* Munni Bai AIR 1979 MP 45
Narain Dutt *v.* Santosh, 1986 [1] HLR 573 [Del.]
Narain *v.* Trilok, 1907. 29. All. 4.
Narayan Bharthi *v.* Laving Bharthi. ILR. 2. Bom. 140.
Narayanan *v.* Parukutty, 1973 Ker, L.T. 80
Narayanan *v.* Sreedevi, 1989 b(2) HLR 29 (Ker-DB).
Narinder *v.* Khushpal, 1980 HLR 620 P&H-DB).
Nathu Lal *v.* Nathi Bai, 1998 (1) HLR 264 (Raj.-DB)
Naurang Singh *v.* Sapla Devi, AIR 1968 All.412
Navin *v.* Veena Rani, 1995 (2) HLR 532 (P&H-DB)
Navodita *v.* Dinesh Singh, 1993 (1) HLR 16 (P&H)
Neelaveni *v.* Venkateswara Rao, 1989 (1) HLR 410 (AP)
Neelkistodeb *v.* Beerchunder, [1868] 12 MIA 523, 542
Neera *v.* Kishan Swarup, 1975 All. 337.
Nighawan *v.* Nighawan, 1973 Delhi 200.
Nirmal *v.* Brij Mohan, 1981 HLR 106 [P&H]
Nirmala Mohar Jagesha *v.* Mandohar Shivram Jagesha, AIR 1991 Bom.259
Nirmala *v.* Prem Nath, 1985 (1) HLR 785 (P&H).
Nirmoo *v.* Nikkaram AIR 1968 Del 260
Nitu *v.* Krishan Lal, 1990 (1) HLR 571 (Del-DB).
Nityalaha *v.* Soondaree Dossee, 1968 WR 475
Om Prakash *v.* Rajni, 1987 (1) HLR 316 (Del.)
Om Prakash *v.* Sareshta, 1993 (2) HLR 72 (HP-DB).
Omwati *v.* Kishanchand, AIR 1985 Del.43

P (D) *v.* P (J), (1965) 2 All ER 456
P *v.* P & R, AIR 1982 Bom.498
Padma Rao *v.* Swarajya Lakshmi, AIR 1970 AP 300 (DB), affirmed.
Padmalatha *v.* Sudershan Rao, 2000 (2) HLR 70 (AP-DB).
Padmini *v.* Sivananda, 2000 (2) HLR 99 (AP-D
Paramjit *v.* Rajinder, 1986 (2) HLR 312 (P&H).
Parbti *v.* Fakkar, 1991 (2) HLR 233 (P&H)
Pardy *v.* Pardy [1939] P 288. Lane *v.* Lane [1951] P284
Parimi Mehar *v.* Parimi Nageswara, 1993 (2) HLR 222 (AP-DB)
Parmeshwar *v.* Vimala, 1987 (1) HLR 455 (Raj).
Parshotam *v.* Sushila, 1980 HLR 149 (P&H).
Parvati *v.* Shiva Ram AIR 1989 HP 29
Pattayee Ammal *v.* Manickam AIR 1967 Mad 254
Pawan Kumar *v.* Chanchal Kumari, 1996 (1) HLR 213 (P&H).
Perumal Naicker *v.* Sithalaxmi, AIR 1956 Mad. 415
Phillips *v.* Emperor, 1925 Oudb 508
Prabhakar *v.* Managal, 1991 (2) HLR 317 (Bom).
Prabhati *v.* D.K.Mitra, 1982 HLR 397 (Del.)
Prabhati *v.* Jagadish, 1902, 29 IA 82
Prakash *v.* Radha, 1986 (2) HLR 282 (MP).
Pramatha Kumar Nath *v.* Ashina Maiti, AIR 1991 Cal.123
Pranab Biswas *v.* Mrinmayee Dassi, 1976 Cal. 156
Pratap Lal *v.* Kundana, 1998 (1) HLR 153 (Raj-DB).
Pratibha *v.* Prabhakar, 1985 (1) HLR 361 (Bom).
Praveen *v.* Surindar, 2001 (1) HLR 353 (Del.)
Praveenben *v.* Sureshbai, AIR 1975 Guj. 69
Prem Bai *v.* Chanoolal Punao, AIR 1963 MP 57
Prem Chand *v.* Savitri, 1998 (2) HLR 666 (All-DB).
Prem Masth *v.* Kumudani Bai, 1974 M.P. 89
Prem Pati *v.* Ranbir Singh , 1987 (1) HLR 160 (P&H).
Preston Jones *v.* Preston Jones, 1951 (1) All ER 124
Priyamvaba *v.* Sharad, 2000 (1) HLR 473 (Bom-DB)
Pujam Liklai Singh Bhabando Singh *v.* Moramthem Maipak Singh and Another, AIR 1956 Man.18

Pulford *v.* Pulford [1923] P 18, 22
Pullikkottial Chera *v.* Mary Zechariah AIR 1981 MP 112.
Purabi *v.* Basudeb Mukherjee AIR 1969 Cal 293
Purna Chandra *v.* Ranu, 1988 (2) HLR 99 (Cal-DB).
Pushpa Devi *v.* Radheshyam, 1972 Raj, 260
Rahunath *v.* Urmila 1973 AIR All 203
Rajaram *v.* Urmila, 1986 (2) HLR 124 (MP)
Reg. *v.* Karsan Goja, 2 Bom 117
R. *v.* Jacrson, [1891] IQB 671
R. *v.* R., 1987 (1) HLR 476 (AP-DB).
R.v. Ecclesfield (Inhabitants) [1818] IB & Ald 348
R.v.K., 1985 (1) HLR 707 (Del)
Rabindra Prashad *v.* Sita Devi, 1985 (2) HLR 69 Pat.
Radha *v.* Harinarayan, 1986 (1) HLR 340 (MP).
Rafinder Kaur *v.* Man Mohan Singh AIR 1972 P & H 142
Raghuan *v.* Satyabhama Jaya Kumar, AIR 1985 Ker.193
Raghubir *v.* Surjit, 1995 (2) HLR 637 (P&H)
Raibahadur *v.* Bishandayal [1882] 4 All 39
Raj Kishore Prasad *v.* Rajkumari Devi, AIR 1986 Pat.362
Raj Kumar *v.* Ram Dulari, 1997 (1) HLR 32 (P&H)
Raj Rani *v.* Hardish, 1985 (1) HLR 704 (P&H).
Raj Rani *v.* Sukh Raj, 1982 HLR 475 (Del.)
Raja Ram *v.* Deepa Bai AIR 1974 MP 52
Rajagopalan *v.* Usha, 1997 (2) HLR 170 (Mad).
Rajan *v.* Shobha, 1995 (2) HLR 656 (Bom – DB).
Rajani Prabhakar Lokur *v.* Prabhakar Ragvendra Lokur AIR 1958 Bom 264
Rajani *v.* Subramanian, 1990 (1) HLR 635 (Ker-DB)
Rajendra Kumar *v.* Padam Prakash, AIR 1985 P&H, 232
Rajendra Singh *v.* Tharavathi, 1980 HLR, 534 [Del.]
Rajesh *v.* Rukmani, 2000 (2) HLR 104 (MP-DB).
Rajeswara *v.* Revathi, 2000 (1) HLR 361 (AP-DB)
Rajinder Singh *v.* Balbir Kaur, 1993 (2) HLR 85 (P&H).
Rajinder *v.* Kanta, 1979 HLR 443 (P&H).
Rajinder *v.* Rama, 1980 HLR 122 (P&H).

Rajpal Malhotra *v.* Tripata Malhotra, 1981 HLR 168 Del.
Rakesh *v.* Surbhi, AIR 2002 Raj 138 (DB)
Ram Chander *v.* Adarsh, 1986 (2) HLR 167 (Del).
Ram Dayal *v.* Uma, 1991 (1) HLR 41 (P&H-DB).
Ram Kali *v.* Gopal, AIR 1968 Bom 332
Ram Khelawan *v.* Seeta, 2001 (1) HLR 667 (MP).
Ram Murti *v.* Sohan Lal, 1980 HLR 65 (P&H)
Ram Narayan *v.* Rameshwari, AIR 1988 SC 2260
Ram *v.* Mohini, 1986 (2) HLR 20 (MP).
Rama Devi *v.* Ashok Kumar, 1994 [1] HLR 591 [MP-DB]
Ramdhan Puri *v.* Dalmer Puri [1910] 14 CWN 191
Ramesh Chander *v.* Savitri, 1994 (1) HLR 624 (P&H-DB)
Ramesh Kumar *v.* State of Punjab, 1987 (1) HLR 189 (P&H)
Ramesh *v.* Mokheshwar, 1961 AIR Assam.53
Rameshwari *v.* Ram Narayan, 1987 (1) HLR 345 (All)
Ranbhagwan Kaur *v.* J.C.Bose [1903] 30 IA 249
Rangarao *v.* Vijayalakshmi, 1990 [1] HLR 610 [Mad.]
Rani *v.* Amarnadh, 1997 [1] HLR 707 [P&H]
Rapeti Bulli Tatayya *v.* Rapeti Nookaraju, AIR 1958 AP 611
Rasna *v.* Arun, 1997 (2) HLR 546 (MP)
Ratan *v.* Sheela, 1988 (1) HLR 620 (MP).
Ravinder Prasad *v.* Sita Devi, AIR 1989 Pat 128
Reg *v.* Sambhu Raghu, ILR 1. Bom. 352
Rekha *v.* Narendra Mohan, 1995 [2] HLR 228 [P&H]
Rekha *v.* Nathu Ram, 1984 HLR 355 (P&H)
Renold Rajmani *v.* Union of India, AIR 1982 SC 1261
Richards *v.* Richards [1972] 3 All ER 695
Rita *v.* Bri Kishore, AIR 1987 Del 291
Ritu *v.* Dharampal, 1980 HLR 355 (P&H).
Rohini Kumari *v.* Narendra Singh, AIR 1972 SC 459
Romesh *v.* Savitri, AIR 1995 SC 851
Roop Chand *v.* Uma Bai, 1987 (1) HLR 406 (MP)
Rooper *v.* Rooper [1971] 3 All ER 668
Rukmini *v.* Srinivasa, 1984 HLR 210 (Kar-DB).
Russel *v.* Russel, (1897) AC 395

Sarala Bai *v.* Kamal Singh AIR 1991 MP 358
Smt. Prakash Kaur *v.* Bikramjit Singh AIR 1989 P&H 46
Soosannamma *v.* Varghese Abraham AIR 1957 Trav. Co. 277
Sreepadachar *v.* Vasantha Bai, 1970 Mys. 232
Subbrama Reddiar *v.* Saraswathi AIR 1967 Mad 85
S. *v.* R., (1996) 2 LW 288 (Mad-DB).
S. Venugopal *v.* Chandra, 1988 (2) HLR 310 (Ker-DB).
S.P. Thrivedi *v.* Chandra Kal, 1990 [2] HLR 67 [Bom.]
Sachindra Nath *v.* Kalpana, 1988 (2) HLR 507 (Cal-DB).
Sachindranath *v.* Nilima, AIR 1970 Cal 38 (DB)
Sadhu Amma *v.* Satyanarayana, (1967) An, W.R. 179.
Sanat *v.* Nandini, AIR 1990 SC 594
Sanjeevani *v.* Anil, 1994 (1) HLR 529 (Bom-DB).
Sanjhi Ram *v.* Mohindro, 1999 (1) HLR 569 (P&H -DB)
Sanjukta *v.* Laxminarayan AIR 1991 Ori 39
Sankaralingam *v.* Subba, 1894, ILR 17. Mad. 479
Santos *v.* Santos (1972) 2 All ER 246
Santosh Kumar *v.* Parveen Kumar AIR 1987 P&H 33.
Santosh *v.* Nandan Singh, 1983 HLR 528
Sapsford *v.* Sapsford, (1954) P 394
Sarada *v.* Satyamurthi, 2000 (1) HLR 298 (Mad-DB).
Sarala bai *v.* Kamal Singh AIR 1991 MP 358
Sarbjit *v.* Maninder, 1988 (2) HLR 199 (P&H)
Sarla *v.* Krishan, 1982 HLR 420 (Raj).
Saroj Rani *v.* Sudarshan Kumar, 1984 (4) SCC 90
Sashi Lata *v.* Chetan, 1984 HLR 710 (P&H)
Satinder Lal *v.* Swarna Lata, 1981 HLR 580 (Del)
Satish Kumar *v.* Gayatri, 1981 HLR 309 (P&H).
Satrupa *v.* Basant Kumar, 2000 (2) HLR 580 (MP)
Satya Narain *v.* Mamta, 1997 (1) HLR 732 (Raj-DB).
Satya *v.* Gian, 1995 (2) HLR 307 (P&H)
Satya *v.* Siri Rama, 1983 HLR 177 (P&H)
Savitri Pande *v.* Premchand Pande, AIR 2002 SC 591
Savtri Bai *v.* Sitaram, AIR 1986 MP 218
Sehra Alaraham *v.* Pyli Abraham AIR 1959 Ker 75

Sudeshna *v.* Abhijit, 1995 (2) (Cal-DB).
Sudha Alial Gulabi *v.* Sankappa Raj, AIR 1963 Mys.245
Sudha *v.* Narayan, 1994 (2) hlr 633 (Bom-DB).
Sudhakar *v.* Vrinda, AIR 2001 Kar 1 (DB)
Sukhdev Kaur *v.* Ravindra Singh, 1996 [2] HLR 296 [Cal.-DB]
Sukhwinder *v.* Harnek, 1988 (1) HLR 432 (P&H)
Sukhwinder *v.* Shinjara Singh, 1985 [1] HLR 9 [P&H-DB]
Sulekha *v.* Kamala Kanta AIR 1980 Cal 370.
Sullivan *v.* Sullivan [1958] NZLR 912
Sulochana *v.* Rajagopal, 1997 (2) HLR 183 (Mad-DB).
Sumiran *v.* Menoka, 1992 (2) HLR 574 (Cal.-DB)
Sumiti *v.* Aroon, 1992 (2) HLR 30 (P&H)
Sundari *v.* Ram Lal, 1994 (2) HLR 84 (P&H-DB).
Sunder *v.* Vihala, [1889], 84 PR 1889
Sunil Kumar *v.* Sasibala, [1995] 2 HLR 332 [P&H]
Sunner *v.* Madhulata, 2000 (1) HLR 290 (Ker-DB)
Surbhi *v.* Sanjay, 2000 (2) HLR 52 (MP-DB).
Surender *v.* Laxmi, 1998 (2) HLR 437 (P&H-DB).
Surender *v.* Tejender, 1987 [1] HLR 86 [P&H]
Suresh Bala *v.* Gurmohinder, 1983 HLR 405 (Del).
Sureshta Devi *v.* Om Prakash, AIR 1992 SC 1904
Surinder *v.* Chander Kanta, 1993 (2) HLR 157 (P&H).
Surinder *v.* Kamlesh Rani, 1987 (1) HLR 19 (P&H).
Surjit Kaur *v.* Veerender 1986 [1] HLR 417 [P&H]
Surjit *v.* Amjer, 1981 HLR 148 (P&H)
Surjit *v.* Anita, 1996 (2) HLR 345 (Cal.-DB)
Surjit *v.* Tirath, 1980 HLR 52 (P&H)
Surrinder Kaur *v.* Gudeep Singh, AIR 1973 P & H 134
Suryakantham *v.* Laxmichand, AIR 1968 Bom 332
Sushila *v.* Bharorao, 1984 HLR 638 (MP)
Sushila *v.* Om Parkash, 1992 (1) HLR 517 (P&H)
Swapan Kumar *v.* Smiritikana, AIR 2002 Cal 6 (DB).
Swapna *v.* Viplav, 1999 (1) HLR 433 (MP)
Synge *v.* Synge (1900) P 180.
T.R. Rathnam *v.* K. Vardarajulu AIR 1970 AP 246.

Talbot *v.* Talbot, The Times, Oct 19, 1971
Tamizh *v.* Arumugam, 1990 (2) HLR 605 (Mad.)
Tapan Kumar *v.* Biva, AIR 1988 Cal.223
Teerath *v.* Parvati, 1995 (2) HLR 233 (Raj-DB)
Thangammal *v.* Jengayammal and Others, AIR 1945 Mad.308
Thomas *v.* Thomas [1923] 39 TLR 520, 521
Thompson *v.* Thompson , (1957) 1 All. E.R. 161
Thompson *v.* Thompson [1858] 1 SW.Tr 231, 233
Tirath Kaur *v.* Kirpal Singh, AIR 1964 Punj. 28
Tribhat Singh *v.* Vimla Devi, 1959 J & K 72
Triveni *v.* Tej Singh, 1984 HLR 675 (MP).
Tuhin *v.* Arati, 1996 (1) HLR 569 (Cal.-DB)
Udaya *v.* Satya 1970, 36 CLT (Orissa) 1330
Uma *v.* Anil Kumar, 1983 HLR 319 (Del.)
Uma *v.* Arjan, 1995 (2) HLR 334 (P&H)
Umesh *v.* Shakuntala, 1979 HLR 584 (Del).
Umrin Bai *v.* Chittar AIR. 1966 MP 205
Urmila Devi *v.* Deepak Kumar, 1999 (2) HLR 205 (MP).
Urmila Devi *v.* Devinder Kumar, 1983 HLR 120 (Del.)
Urmila *v.* Ravi Prakash, 1985 [1] HLR 310 [Del.]
Usha *v.* Santosh, 1996 (1) HLR 233 (MP).
V.K.Rampal *v.* Chand, 1980 HLR 65 (P&H)
Valliammal *v.* Singaram (1966) 2 MLJ 425
Varadarajulu *v.* Baby Ammal, 1965 Mad.29
Vardarajalu *v.* Balu AIR 1965 Mad 29.
Vasappan *v.* Sarda 1958 Ker. 39 FB & Nangu Vs. Appi 1966 Ker. 4 FB.
Vedavathi *v.* Ramaswamy, 1964 Mys. 280
Veena *v.* Makhan Lal, 1984 HLR 261 (Del).
Veera Reddi *v.* Kistamma, 1969 Mad.235
Vijay Kumar *v.* Rita Kumari, 1982 HLR 539 (P&H).
Vijayalakshmi *v.* Balasubramanian, 1997 (1) HLR 664 (Mad-DB)
Vijayalakshmi *v.* Bheem Reddy 1988 [2] HLR 688 [AP-DB]
Vinod Kumar *v.* Nutan Sharma, 1986 [1] HLR 625 [Del.]
Vinod *v.* Asha, 1986 (1) HLR 508 (MP).

Bibliography

I. ORIGINAL SOURCES

(a) Vedic and allied Sanskrit texts and translations

Atharva Vedana, Ajmer ed. 1917.

Atharvana Veda Samhita, ed. By S.P. Pandit, 4 Vols., Bombay, 1895-98.

Aitareya Brahmana, ed. By Kashinatha Sastri, Anandasrama Press, Poona, 1896.

Rg Veda, Ajmer ed. 1917.

Rg. Veda Samhita, with Sayanas Commentary ed. By F. Max Muller in 6 Vol., London, 1862-74, Reprint Varanasi 1965.

Satapatha Brahmana, ed. By A.Weber, London, 1849.

Taittiriya Brahmana, with the Commentary of Sayana, ed. By R.L. Mitra, 3 Vols., Calcutta, 1859-70.

Taittiriya Samhita, Laipzig, 1872.

Yajur Veda, Vajasaneyi Samhita, Nirnaya Sagara Press, 1912.

(b) Grhyasutra Texts

Apastamba Grhya Sutra, ed. By M.Winternitz, Vienna, 1887.

Aswalayana Grhya Surta, ed. By Jivananda, Calcutta, 1893.

Baudhayana Grhya Sutra, ed. By R. Sharma Sastri, Printed at Government Branch Press, Mysore, 1920.

Bhardvaja Grhya Sutra, ed. By H.J.W. Salomons, Layden, 1913.

Gobhila Grhya Sutra, with the Commentary of Chandra Kanta Tarkalankar, BI Series, Calcutta, A C 1879.

Manava Grhya Sutra, ed. By F. Knauer, St.Petersburg, 1897.
Parasara Grhya Sutra, Leipzig, 1876.
Varaha Grhya Sutra, Gaekawad's Oriental Series, Boroda, 1921.

(c) Dharma Sutra Texts

Apastamba Dharma Sutra, Bombay Sanskrit Series, ed. Poona, 1892.
Baudhayana Dharma Sutra, tr. By G. Buhler SBE Vol. XIV, Oxford, 1882.
Gautama Dharma Sutra, tr. By G. Buhler in SBE Vol. II, Oxford, 1882.
Gautama Dharma Sutra, tr. By G. Buhler in SBE Vol. II, Oxford, 1882.
Vasistha Dharma Sutra, tr. By G. Buhler in SBE Vol. XIV, Oxford, 1882.
Visnu Dharma Sutra, ed. By Julious Jolly, Calcutta, 1881.

(d) Epics, Puranas and Panchatantra

Agni Puranas, Anandastrama ed. Poona, 1900
Bhavisyat Puranas, Venkateswvara Press, Bombay ed. 1910.
Brahma Purana, Anandasrama Press ed. Poona, 1895.
Mahabarata, tr. By P.C. Roy, Calcutta, 1884-90.
Markandeya Purana, ed. By Rev. K.M.Benerjee, BI Series, Calcutta, 1862.
Matsya Purana, ed. by Jivananda Vidyasagara, Calcutta, 1876
Naradiya Purana, Venkateswara Press, ed. Bombay.
Padma Purana, Anandasrama Press ed. Poona 1893-94.
Panchatantra, ed. By F. Edgerton, Poona, 1930.
Ramayana of Valmiki, ed. By Kashinath Pandurang 2 pts., Bombay 1888.
Vayu Purana, ed. By R.L. Mitra, 2 Vols. BI Series, Calcutta, 1880-88.
Visnu Purana, tr. By H.H. Wilson, 5 Vols., London 1864-70.

(e) Smrti Texts

Brhaspati Smrti, tr. By J. Jolly in SBE, Vol. XXXIII, Oxford Gaekwar Oriental Series, 1889.

Katyayana Smrti, Reconstructed by N.C. Benerjee as "Katyayanamata Samgraha", Calcutta, 1927.
Manu Smrti, with seven commentaries, ed. By Rao Sahiba V.N. Mandik, Bombay, 1886.
Narada Smrti, ed. By Smrititirtha, Narayana Chandra Chabispragana, Calcutta, 1873.
Parasara Smriti ed. By V.S. Islampurkar, Bombay, 1893-1906.
Parasar Smrti, with the Commentary Monahara, Benaras Sanskrit Series, 1907.
Visnu Smrti, tr. By J. Jolly, sbe Vol. VII, ed. By Max Muller, Oxford 1880.
Yajnavalkya Smriti, tr. Into English by Edward Roer & W.A. Montriau, Calcutta, 1859.
Yama Smrti, Anandasrama Press, Poona, 1905.

(f) Buddhist and Jain Works

India as described in the Early Texts of Jainism and Buddhism, B.C.Law, London 1941.

(g) Medieval Digests and Other technical works

Arthasastra of Kautilya, ed. With Commentary by T.Ganapati Sastri, 3 Vols. Trivandrum, 1924-25.
Kamasutra of Vatsyayana, ed. By Goswami Damodar Sastri, Kashi Sanskrit Series, Benares, 1929.
Mitaksara by Vijnaneswara, Bombay 1926.

(h) Acts, Statutes and Legislations Pertaining to Hindu Marriage World

The Caste Disabilities Removal Act XXI of 1850.
The Hindu Widow re-marriage Act XV of 1856.
The Indian Divorce Act IV of 1869.
The Special Marriage Act III of 1872.
The Majority Act IX of 1875.
The Inter-religious Civil Marriage Act of 1928.
The Child Marriage Restraint Act XIX of 1929 as amended Act II of 1978.
The Arya Samaj Marriage Validation Act XIX of 1937.

The Hindu Women's Rights to Property Act XVIII of 1937.
The Hindu marriage Disabilities Removal Act XXVII of 1946.
The Hindu Marriage Women's right to separate residence and maintenance Act XIX of 1946.
The Hindu Marriage validity Act XXI of 1949.
The Saurastra Hindu Divorce Act XXX of 1952.
The Special marriage Act XXXXIII of 1954.
The Hindu marriage Act XXV of 1955, as amended by Act 73 of 1956, Act 44 of 1964, Act 68 of 1976 and Act 2 of 1978, 1999 and 2001.
The Family Courts Act of 1984.

II. SECONDARY SOURCES

Acharya Shuklendra's, Hindu Law, Printed & Published by Modern Law Publications, Allahabad, 2002.
Dr. Hari Dev Kohli's, Hinduism and Divorce, 2 Vols. Published by Decent Books, New Delhi, 2000.
Dr. U.P.D. Kesari's, Modern Hindu Law, ed. 4, Printed by Central Law Publications, Allahabad, 2004.
D.F. Mulla's, Principles of Hindu Law, ed. 12, published by N.M. Tripathi Pvt. Ltd., Bombay, 1960.
Dr. Paras Diwan's, Customary Law, Published by Publication Bureau Panjab University, Chandigarh, 1978.
Jagjit Singh Chawla's, All India Hindu Law Digest (1950-86), 2 Vols. SLR Publications, Chandigarh.
J. Duncan M. Derrett's, The Death of a Marriage Law, published by Vikas Publishing House, New Delhi, 1978.
J.D.M. Derrett's, A Critique of Modern Hindu Law, published by N.M. Tripathi Pvt. Ltd., Bombay, 1970.
J.D.M. Derrett's, Introduction to Modern Hindu Law, published by Oxford University Press, 1963.
Mayne's Hindu Law and Usage, revised by Justice Alladi Kuppuswami, ed. 14 Printed by Bharat Law House, New Delhi, 1996.
N.R. Raghavachariar's, Hindu Law Principles and Precedents, revised and enlarged by Prof. S. Venkataraman, ed. 7, Vols. 2, published by Madras Law Journal Office, Madras, 1980.

Paras Diwan's, Family Law, ed. 4, Published by Allahabad Law Agency, Faridabad, 1998.

Prof. G.C.V. Subba Rao's, Family Law in India, edn. 6, Asia Law House, Hyderabad, 1989.

III. LEGAL ARTICLES

Agrawala Rajkumari, "Hindu Divorce Law—Its History", *Supreme Court Journal*, 1959.

A.K. Nandi, "Evolution of Hindu Marriage System", *Folk Lore*, May 1969.

C.V. Jani, "Hindu Marriage Act and Divorce", *AIR Journal*, 1964.

D.R. Khanna, "Indissolubility of Marriage and Easy Divorce", *AIR Journal*, 1982.

N.R. Madhavamenon, "Burying of Roop Kanvar—Trial by Fire", *Women and Media Committee*, Bombay 1987.

R. Jagan Mohan Rao, "The Law of Marriage and Social change", *Studies in Hindu Marriage and Special Marriage Acts*, Bombay, 1978.

Index